UNDERSTANDING
THE TIMES
LIVING COURAGEOUSLY IN PROPHETIC DAYS

PAUL
CHAPPELL

First published in 2010 by Striving Together Publications, a ministry of Lancaster Baptist Church, Lancaster, CA 93535. Striving Together Publications is committed to providing tried, trusted, and biblically-based books that will further equip local churches to carry out the Great Commission. Your comments and suggestions are valued.

Striving Together Publications
4020 E. Lancaster Blvd.
Lancaster, CA 93535
800.201.7748

Cover design by Andrew Jones
Layout by Craig Parker
Edited by Monica Bass and Cary Schmidt
Special thanks to our review team and proofreaders

The contents of this book are the result of thirty years of spiritual growth in life and ministry. The author and publication team have given every effort to give proper credit to quotes and thoughts that are not original with the author. It is not our intent to claim originality with any quote or thought that could not readily be tied to an original known source.

ISBN 978-1-59894-107-4

Printed in the United States of America

We live in a time where the reporting of sensational events seems to appear in our news headlines every day. We read about great natural disasters such as earthquakes, tsunamis, volcanoes, and record breaking storms. We hear of political upheaval at a pace we have never observed before and see how it is linked to financial issues that even a few years ago were inconceivable. Yet, all of these events are so clearly spoken of and predicted by the Word of God. Understanding the Times *does a brilliant job of bringing to our understanding the message of the prophets in the light of our experience. It is a balanced, accurate, and encouraging look at Bible prophecy.*

Dr. Michael Edwards
Pastor, Heritage Baptist Church
Woodbridge, Virginia

Pastor Chappell did a remarkable job in taking the salient points of prophecy and integrating them with current events. Understanding the Times *reads like a novel revealing to us the prophetic events that have happened, are happening now, and will be happening in the not-too-distant (Lord willing) future. It is written so that the man in the pulpit and the person in the pew will both be challenged and blessed! "Even so come, Lord Jesus!"*

Dr. Bud Calvert
Pastor Emeritus, Fairfax Baptist Temple
Fairfax, Virginia

My consideration of Paul Chappell's book, Understanding the Times, *followed a Sunday night preaching series at Southwest Baptist Church. The series included numerous sermons from Jeremiah, Ezekiel, Daniel, and most of the Minor Prophets. I am of the persuasion that Pastor Chappell's title is very appropriate. God's people need not fear the times; we need only to understand the times. God has revealed clearly that He will fulfill His purposes upon Israel, upon His saints of this age, and upon an unbelieving world.* Understanding the Times is indeed motivation to wholeheartedly serve God. May this book encourage many to intensify all efforts to godliness and the spread of the Gospel of Jesus Christ.

Dr. Sam Davison
Pastor Emeritus, Southwest Baptist Church
President, Heartland Baptist Bible College
Oklahoma City, Oklahoma

Pastor Paul Chappell has diligently examined the Scriptures and has given a clear and concise understanding as to the prophetic events of which the Bible speaks. In this day, when the Bible events are manifesting themselves around the world, this book will be a wonderful challenge and comfort to every Christian. Each believer will find this book to be a magnificent help to see how God foretold and is in control of what is happening in our world. This is a great book!

Dr. David C. Gibbs, Jr.
Christian Law Association
Seminole, Florida

If you like Bible prophecy, you are going to love Understanding the Times *by Dr. Paul Chappell. Countless hours of research have gone into this theological and logical presentation of future events. It is both a tremendous resource for serious prophecy students and yet a simple and inspirational work for the laymen. This book can also be a wonderful evangelistic tool for your family and friends who are interested in prophecy. You will be glad you read* Understanding the Times.

Dr. Tom Farrell
Evangelist, Tom Farrell Evangelistic Ministries
Brevard, North Carolina

Living in a world that is consumed with the immediate, it is refreshing to read Dr. Chappell's newest book presenting God's eternal perspective applied to our twenty-first-century world. The truths addressed in Understanding the Times *are timeless and thus appropriate for every generation. Pastor Chappell has creatively and succinctly simplified, explained, and applied the prophecies of the end times to meet the challenges of today. Having read this highly recommended volume, I find myself focusing on the return of our Saviour with greater intensity and anticipation. This book is a "must read" in my opinion, and I look forward to its wide distribution.*

Dr. Paul Kingsbury
Pastor, North Love Baptist Church
Rockford, Illinois

Prophecy is an important and significant topic. The Scripture tells us of "men that had understanding of the times…" (1 Chronicles 12:32). In his new book, Bro. Chappell demonstrates not only an understanding of the times, but an understanding of how we ought to live in these times. You will be amazed at the breadth of information and depth of research in this book. It will motivate us to "work for the night is coming." It will also encourage our hearts that in spite of the tumult and chaos that surround us we are in God's hand, part of His plan and on the winning side.

Dr. R.B. Ouellette
Pastor, First Baptist Church of Bridgeport
Saginaw, Michigan

With his new book, Understanding the Times, *Dr. Paul Chappell has put his finger to the pulse of the times, and with biblical authority, diagnosed the hour is late, indeed! I am particularly impressed with the vast amount of prophetically relevant, and current information that is documented in this book. It will prove to be a valuable resource that I will want near to hand when preparing sermons, or lessons, on the subject of end-time prophecy. If you are looking for a book that makes prophetic Scripture easy to understand and powerfully relevant to our changing times,* Understanding the Times *delivers.*

Jerry W. Scheidbach
Pastor, Lighthouse Baptist Church
Santa Maria, California

Understanding the Times *by Dr. Paul Chappell has successfully presented biblical prophecy in a way that can be understood by those who have a underlying fear of approaching such books as Ezekiel, Daniel or Revelation while at the same time challenging the minds of those given to these studies! Dr. Chappell has taken a subject of extreme biblical importance and shows the relevance to our world and culture by incredible research that is eye-opening. I heartily recommend this book. With times and events changing daily, I know of very few books that are as up-to-date as* Understanding the Times. *Maranatha!*

Dr. David L. Smith
Fellow Helpers Ministries
Beaumont, California

DEDICATION

To my son, Larry, whose recent battle with cancer has been a testimony
of the grace of God, and has better prepared me to live in the light of
eternity. I am deeply grateful for your courageous testimony.

Table of Contents

ACKNOWLEDGEMENTS _____

I would like to thank my wife, Terrie, for her prayers and support during the seasons of extra labor and intensity required in fulfilling a project such as this.

I greatly appreciate the assistance in chapter development and Scripture study provided to me by Rick Houk, chairman of the Bible Department of West Coast Baptist College.

We are indebted to Pastor Jerry Schiedbach from Santa Maria, California, for his willingness to read through the original notes and provide needful comments or questions along the way.

I'm thankful for the following men who gave their time and biblical insight to review this manuscript: Dr. Bud Calvert, Dr. Sam Davison, Dr. Michael Edwards, Dr. Tom Farrell, Dr. Mike Gass, Dr. David Gibbs,

Jr., Dr. Dave Hardy, Dr. Paul Kingsbury, Dr. R.B. Ouellette, and Dr. David L. Smith.

Monica Bass has been a tremendous blessing throughout this project, both in the editing and overall development of the manuscript.

Finally, I would like to thank Cary Schmidt for the oversight he provided for this book, as well as his final editing work.

God has given us a great team at Striving Together Publications. Thanks again to each and every one who has invested in this project.

Newscasts leave us numb. Politicians polarize us. The financial world frustrates. Ethics leave us exasperated and the lack of morality maddens. Religion has become routine, and the average church is cowering or changing. Sadly, many Christians have become consumed with worry; calloused in will; comfortable in worship; and conformed to this world. God's people everywhere are succumbing to fear, frustration, and fatalism. We have become weary in well doing.

The book you hold in your hand can change your perspective! We often see life from the "playing field" but God's Word shows us life from the "blimp." Rather than looking at things through our earthly vision, we need God to show us an eternal view. Dr. Paul Chappell has done a masterful job of unveiling the timeless truths of the Bible as it relates to the time we live in now and that which is just around the corner in the future. God is always right and He is always right on time.

God's prophetic calendar is one of the most fascinating subjects ever studied. Pastor Chappell points out however that our response to the unfolding of Scripture before our eyes can be threefold: "You could become alarmed and begin searching for a new conspiracy behind every election and every news story. You could become distracted by venturing into a lot of pointless speculation. You should become engaged in living out God's plan in steadfast, sanctified obedience until He comes!"

A careful read of this book will leave you encouraged, edified, and engaged in the work of God. It is not written with a desire to frighten you with the unknown. Rather, it encourages you as you realize that everything is right on schedule—God's schedule. Your heart will thrill as you see prophecy from hundreds of years ago being unveiled in your lifetime. The news accounts are exactly as God predicted. And should we be surprised? *"God is not a man, that he should lie; neither the son of man, that he should repent: hath he said, and shall he not do it? or hath he spoken, and shall he not make it good?"* (Numbers 23:19). *"For all the promises of God in him are yea, and in him Amen"* (2 Corinthians 1:20A).

These chapters will edify your life as you realize how close we may be to Christ's return. Nothing will bring about revival faster than a realization that *"in a moment, in the twinkling of an eye, at the last trump"* we could *"be absent from the body, and...present with the Lord."* The Apostle John reminds us, *"Beloved, now are we the sons of God, and it doth not yet appear what we shall be: but we know that, when he shall appear, we shall be like him; for we shall see him as he is. And every man that hath this hope in him purifieth himself, even as he is pure"* (1 John 3:2–3). The pages of God's prophetic calendar are quickly turning and Peter exhorts us: *"But the day of the Lord will come as a thief in the night; in the which the heavens shall pass away with a great noise, and the elements shall melt with fervent heat, the earth also and the works that are therein shall be burned up. Seeing then that all these things shall be dissolved, what manner of persons ought ye to be in all holy conversation and godliness, Looking for and hasting unto the coming of the day of God, wherein the heavens being on fire shall be dissolved, and the elements shall melt with fervent heat? Nevertheless we, according to his promise, look for new heavens and a new earth, wherein dwelleth righteousness. Wherefore, beloved, seeing that ye look for such things, be diligent that ye may be found of him in peace, without spot, and blameless"* (2 Peter 3:10–14).

You won't put this book down without also sensing your responsibility to become engaged as never before in the work of God. The domination of Satan in this world today and the pollution of sin on every hand prompts us to cry with John *"Even so, come, Lord Jesus."* The Bible predicts that *"evil men and seducers shall wax worse and worse, deceiving, and being deceived."* In the next verse however, Paul passionately pleads: *"But continue thou in the things which thou hast learned and been assured of, knowing of whom thou hast learned them"* (2 Timothy 3:13–14). In Ephesians 5:16, Paul says, *"Redeeming the time, because the days are evil."* The days are evil and they will get worse, but now is the time to re-enlist and engage in fulfilling the Great Commission.

"The night cometh, when no man can work" (John 9:4).

In 1 Chronicles 12:32, the Bible tells us that the children of Issachar, *"were men that had understanding of the times."* Dr. Chappell has diligently studied the prophecy of Scripture and laid that teaching up against the world's events of our day. With the help of the Holy Spirit, he gives us in this book an "understanding of the times." But I'm glad that the children of Issachar were not limited to a mere understanding. The verse goes on to say *"...to know what Israel ought to do."* In this book, Pastor Chappell will not simply provide a knowledge of prophecy and how it relates to current events, but will lead you to a decision of salvation, a desire for sanctification, and a determination to serve the King of kings and Lord of lords.

Dr. John Goetsch
Executive Vice President of West Coast Baptist College
June, 2010

INTRODUCTION _____

Times are changing rapidly—globally, economically, politically, militarily, and technologically. Do you understand what these changes mean? Do you look at the world around you through the lens of a confident, courageous, settled heart; or are you—like the rest of our race—troubled, fearful, and wondering?

If you spend any time watching news, listening to the current political discussions, or tracking the motion of our society at large, you know it is very easy to become deeply concerned—even unsettled. Economic challenges and unparalleled financial crisis have gripped the Americas, Europe, and Asia. World leaders are scrambling for answers and groping for solutions.

People all over the planet are looking for change and hope. Yet for all the talk radio shows, political rallies, cable news pundits, financial bail-outs, and global summits, humanity remains in a state of perpetual unrest and deep, soulful disquiet. Mankind is discontent and empty—searching for answers—for salvation.

Amidst this growing and discouraging state of concern and despair is a group of people whose paradigm is not shaped by cultural trends or current events. Their hope is not found in humanity. They are not looking to politicians, economists, or educators for salvation. They have a completely different understanding of world events, their place among those events, and where the times are truly leading.

As if watching the global stage from a front row seat in a spectator's grandstand, they look on as participants with a larger perspective. Theirs is a grander context that sees current events not as chance or fate, but rather as determined destiny. They see the direction of the world and the progression of humanity through the lens of God's written Word, and they connect the dots that confound the wisdom of world leaders.

These are the people who know the Truth. They know Jesus Christ, and they rest in His sovereign plan for the ages. They know that current events are but a small part of an eternal purpose unfolding by God's timetable. They know peace, because they know the Prince of Peace. They know hope, because of a risen Saviour. They know promise, because they trust the God of exceeding great and precious promises. They know courage, because their confidence does not rest in the political or economic processes of men, but in the powerful hand of an Almighty Father.

Do you know Him—personally? If not, it is my prayer that the pages of this book will compel you to trust Him. You cannot trust media outlets, political processes, financial indicators, or the empty promises of power holders. But you can trust Jesus Christ. You can know Him, you can trust Him, and you can find rest for your soul in His marvelous grace. I encourage you to read on with an open heart. Consider with me the events of our time through the lens of the Bible. Consider what God has already said about the state of our world; then trust fully the God who is Sovereign over all.

If you know Him, are you troubled? Are you anxious? Does the evening news put worry into your heart? Do you find yourself concerned with government structure, financial stability, future job markets, and your children's futures? From a human perspective, there is surely much with which to be concerned. Human perspective offers nothing but scepticism, frustration, and worry.

Together, our pursuit in these pages will be a heavenly perspective! What is God doing? What is on God's heart, and where is His plan ultimately leading? A heavenly perspective is really the only way to live life joyfully and abundantly. Heavenly perspective is truth! It's reliable. It's hopeful. It's unavoidable. And it's good.

I invite you to join me on a journey through the following pages. You have picked up this book because your heart is curious. If there is confidence to be found, you want it. If there is sense to be made of current events, you seek it. If there is something you don't know that can give you stability in the midst of a jittery humanity, you long for it!

All of this and much more can be found in the pages of God's Word. In the coming chapters, we will take the words of Scripture and superimpose them upon present-day events. We will view today through the clarifying principles of eternal, unchanging truth.

Together, we will discover that God is alive, and His hand still governs the affairs of men. We will discover the quiet confidence and the enduring hope that only a child of God can experience, though he be surrounded by unrest. We will discover that understanding the times through the wisdom and promises of God truly does bring courage and hope.

Bible prophecy is not troubling to someone who trusts God—it is comforting. First Thessalonians 4:18 sums it up so beautifully, *"Wherefore comfort one another with these words."*

I heard of an old farmer who was awakened one night by the grandfather clock down the hall. The clock had been in the family for several generations and faithfully marked each passing hour with its chimes. But it wasn't the chiming that brought the farmer to an upright position—he was used to hearing it. It was the count of the chimes.

Something in the clock went haywire, and it counted out fourteen hours. Still groggy and only half awake, he shook his wife. "Wake up, Nellie. It's later now than it has ever been before!"

We don't have a universal grandfather clock, but times do seem to be going haywire. It's later than it has ever been before! Thankfully, Bible prophecy allows us to step back from the stage of global events, set aside our human anxiety, and courageously live each day with a heavenly perspective—a God-given "bird's-eye view" of the ages.

It is my sincere prayer that a heavenly perspective will settle your heart with God's peace and comfort, and that more than ever, you will live purposefully for your Heavenly Father!

Thank you for reading. Let's begin unraveling the events of our time through the understanding of God's Word.

The Basics of Bible Prophecy

Noise. Everywhere you go, everywhere you turn, you will hear noise. Chatter. Talk. Promises. Voices. On the news, in print, on the radio, over the web, and from every corner of the globe voices lend their strength to the desperate attempt of mankind to perpetuate and improve our existence. It's as though with every passing year, we instinctively know that world history is somehow winding down. We are clutching to the belief that we can preserve and sustain ourselves through meticulous care of our planet and careful structuring of global powers. These voices are both persuasive and powerful, and their influence is being experienced worldwide.

Amazingly, the above-mentioned voices reinforce what the Bible predicted thousands of years ago. They may surprise and spellbind the ignorant, but for the Bible believer, their arrival has been expected and their significance is heartening. Briefly listen to these voices with me, and bear in mind, God foretold they would rise. Listen to them for a moment.

THE RISE OF END TIME VOICES

The voices for a New World Order

Daily in the news we hear American politicians from both sides of the aisle and world leaders calling out for a "new world order." The basic objectives proposed for this new world order consist of the very elements Scripture warns will signify the eventual global empire of the Antichrist—a world government, a world economy, and a world religion.

Many of the voices calling for globalization (primarily in Europe, but rising in volume in America as well) suggest plans for the surrender of national sovereignty to a **world government** headquarters and a world court. In some embryonic forms, these suggestions are already becoming a reality. For example, in the Netherlands there is already a European Union court, and in other European countries, there is discussion of entrusting greater powers to the president of the European Commission.

The rampant spread of globalism is fueled by the driving desire for a **world economy.** From 2008–2010, the United States, along with many other nations, experienced an economic downturn of massive proportions. As of this writing, the ongoing recession seems to have accelerated the discussion of centralized control for the world's economy.

In a recent *USA Today* article, Cathy Lynn Grossman reported: "Pope Benedict XVI today called for reforming the United Nations and establishing a 'true world political authority' with 'real teeth' to manage the global economy with God-centered ethics. In his third encyclical, a major teaching, released as the G-8 summit begins in Italy, the pope says such an authority is urgently needed to end the current worldwide financial crisis."[1]

Both China and Russia have recently called for the centralization of economies. While a one-world currency looked like an extreme idea thirty years ago, it is now mainstream in the discussion of world economies.

The final phase of the new world order will most likely be a **world religion**, an increasingly popular topic today. The idea of a new world religion as a means of world peace and cooperation has already been suggested and promoted by many leaders. Several of the popes, as well as the Dalai Lama and leaders of the World Council of Churches, have endorsed the idea of religious unity. We will learn more about this in chapter 7. For now, it is important to note that these moves are motivated by a desire for more than unity. Those who preach religious unity actually want religion without Christ as the head. The new world religion will stand for no biblically-based or specific truth, and thus it will have no real spiritual value.

The voices against Israel

The most significant historical event, prophetically speaking, in the last seventy-five years was the rebirth of the state of Israel. As we will see in chapter 3, Israel stands today as a powerful testimony to the accuracy and timing of Bible prophecy. Yet voices of anti-Israel sentiment are rising in volume.

At a political ceremony, Iranian president Ahmadinejad said, "With God's help, the countdown button for the destruction of the Zionist regime has been pushed by the hands of the children of Lebanon and Palestine…. By God's will, we will witness the destruction of this regime in the near future."[2]

The growth of anti-Semitism actually confirms the God of Israel as the true God and His Word as completely reliable. Many passages of Scripture prophesy a growing hatred toward Israel, and Ezekiel 38 specifically

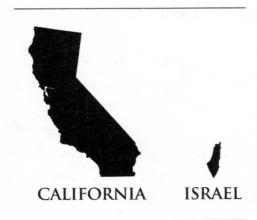

CALIFORNIA   ISRAEL

prophesies that Russia and Iran will come together in a coalition against Israel (more on this in chapter 5). It is no secret today that the political and military powers of many nations are aligned against Israel.

Geographically, Israel is a very small nation. About one-nineteenth the size of California, Israel is approximately the size of the state of New Jersey. It is only 260 miles long, 60 miles at its widest, and approximately 9 miles at its narrowest point. Yet the nation of Israel is a democratic republic surrounded by 22 hostile Arab/Islamic dictatorships that combined are 640 times her size and 60 times her population![3]

When you visit Israel, it is amazing to see the proximity of her enemies. Organized terrorist groups operate just outside important Israeli cities such as Jerusalem and Tel Aviv.

For decades, Israel has been bullied, harassed, cajoled, and pressured by both friends and enemies to give up her land. The Oslo Accords of the early 1990s increased that pressure. Even the liberal Labor Party in Israel supports the radical European-funded Peace Now movement. One author explained, "The organization calls for Israel to withdraw from the entire West Bank, eastern Jerusalem—including the Temple Mount—and the strategic Golan Heights."[4]

An *Associated Press* article on May 14, 2009, ran with the headline "Jordan King: Israel must accept Palestinian state."[5] The article said:

> Jordan's king pressed Israeli Prime Minister Benjamin Netanyahu on Thursday to immediately commit to the

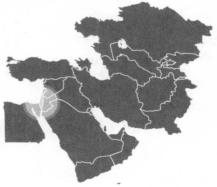

ISRAEL IS
SURROUNDED BY

22 ISLAMIC NATIONS

640 TIMES IN SIZE

60 TIMES IN POPULATION

> establishment of a Palestinian state, as he pursues a sweeping resolution of the Muslim world's conflicts with Israel....
>
> Abdullah said there "is consensus in the international community that there is no alternative to the two-state solution."

In that same article, we are told that the pope is lending his voice to the argument for a twenty-first century solution:

> Pope Benedict XVI, on his first visit to the Holy Land, has also delivered a powerful plea for an independent Palestinian state alongside Israel. He will meet the Israeli leader later Thursday in the biblical town of Nazareth.

Every day, Israel faces yet more pressure to make concessions. While the specific news changes from week to week, the voices against Israel are certainly on the rise. The rhetoric of Armageddon is reflected time and again against Israel throughout the Middle East.

The voices speaking of the last days of history

Not only do we hear calls for a new world order and cries against Israel, but there is also a gradually growing belief that we are living in the final hours of human history. People are enamored with the idea that the world, as we know it, may be coming to an end.

For example, some who have studied the Aztec calendars point to the "fifth epic of history" which supposedly began in 3113 BC. According to their mythology, this epic will end on December 21, 2012. Many people in Central and South America believe that the end of the world is coming soon. Is this a coincidence? Or is this a heathen, twisted response to biblical truth, perhaps understood many centuries ago?

Pagan cultures around the world, many generations removed from exposure to God's truth, have distorted stories of a worldwide flood or the creation of the world woven into their culture. Likewise, the Aztecs integrated a twisted view of what we refer to as the Second Coming of Christ into their calendars.

(Of course, a true biblicist will never put a date on end time events or even suggest when these events will occur. These examples and the dates cited are simply used to illustrate the growing interest in the end of this present world.)

Other religious groups have variant stories and expectancies related to the end of time as we know it.

The Jewish allegorical cult Kabbalah predicts the end of the world in 2012. According to their teaching, they will then enter a time called "Shabat Hagadol," the last Sabbath, which will last one thousand years.

Even some Hindus believe the end of the world is soon coming. They believe the Kalki Avatar will appear and bring a golden age of peace.

The Islamic people are looking for the twelfth Imam. And the Shiite Muslim President of Iran, Ahmadinejad, believes this man is alive today. In an address to the United Nations General Assembly, Ahmadinejad prayed, "O mighty Lord, I pray to you to hasten the emergence of your last repository, the promised one, that perfect and pure human being, the one that will fill this world with justice and peace."[6]

Then, in a speech at Columbia University, Ahmadinejad stood before great intellectuals, many of whom are pushing globalism and are anti-Christ in their spirit, and prayed, "Oh, God, hasten the arrival of Imam al-Mahdi and grant him good health and victory and make us his followers and those to attest to his rightfulness."[7]

It is interesting to note that one billion people, in addition to Bible-believing Christians, are looking for a world ruler to appear. The world is ripening for the coming of the Antichrist. Many believe such a ruler will be a deliverer—a solver of world-problems, ending the world as we know it and ushering in a new age of peace and safety. This expectancy could set a platform for the coming of the Antichrist and the Tribulation. First Thessalonians 5:3 tells us, *"For when they shall say, Peace and safety; then sudden destruction cometh upon them, as travail upon a woman with child; and they shall not escape."*

So we hear many voices today—voices calling for a new world order, for the destruction of Israel, and for a Muslim world leader. Among this myriad of voices is one authoritative voice—the voice of the Bible. What does God disclose about the end times?

Numerous prophetic truths are given in the book of Revelation, the last book of the Bible. Revelation is a source of comfort for today's Christian, giving him hope and the ability to live with courage and confidence in the promises of Almighty God. It reveals that through disaster and turmoil, there is victory in the completion of God's plan for the ages. Notice in the following chart[8] how Revelation shows the consummation of what commenced in Genesis.

Genesis	Revelation
The commencement of Heaven and Earth (1:1)	The consummation of Heaven and Earth (21:1)
The entrance of sin and death (3:1–19)	The end of sin and death (21:4, 27)
The dawn of Satan's activities (3:1–7)	The demise of Satan's power (20:10)
The expulsion from paradise (3:23–24)	The entrance to paradise (21:23–24)
The plan of redemption foretold (3:15)	The plan of redemption fulfilled (20:6)
The Tree of Life relinquished (3:24)	The Tree of Life restored (22:2)
The curse engulfs creation (3:12–13)	The curse eliminated from creation (22:3)
The beginning of sorrows (3:16)	The banishing of sorrows (21:4)
The formation of all nations (10:1–32)	The finality of all nations (19:15; 21:24–27)
The formation of Israel (12:1–4)	The finality of Israel (20:1–6)

The English word for *revelation* comes from two Latin words—*re* and *velum*. It means "unveiling." The Greek word for *revelation* is also from two words—*apo* and *kalypto,* or *apocalypse.* This word means "uncovering." In the book of Revelation, God lifts the curtain of time and reveals the end, especially as it relates to the final triumph of Jesus Christ and the eternal reward of those who received Christ as Saviour. In Revelation, we see the final

A•poc•a•lypse

noun

uncovering or revealing

answer to the Lord's prayer, "*Thy kingdom come. Thy will be done in earth, as it is in heaven*" (Matthew 6:10).

To lay a solid foundation for any discussion of specific aspects of Bible prophecy, we must first consider the foundational principles of Bible prophecy. How do we understand and interpret God's Word? And why do we believe it is authoritative?

THE REVELATION OF BIBLE PROPHECY

We have also a more sure word of prophecy; whereunto ye do well that ye take heed, as unto a light that shineth in a dark place, until the day dawn, and the day star arise in your hearts: Knowing this first, that no prophecy of the scripture is of any private interpretation. For the prophecy came not in old time by the will of man: but holy men of God spake as they were moved by the Holy Ghost.—2 PETER 1:19–21

In times of uncertainty, we can rest assured that we have *"a more sure word of prophecy."* When many voices are heralding the changing philosophies of this world, we can be thankful there is a sure voice of truth in Scripture. Rather than trusting in prophets who came on the scene hundreds of years after Christ rose from the dead or in cults who allegorize the Scriptures into nothingness, we can place our complete confidence in God's written Word. The uniqueness of the Bible is expressed in the supernatural character of Bible prophecy.

Peter, directed by the Holy Spirit of God, penned the book of 2 Peter shortly before his death. He reminded his readers that, although he and the other eyewitnesses of Christ's life, death, and resurrection were passing off the scene, he was leaving behind *"a more sure word"*—a *written* record of God's *spoken* word.

Knowing that shortly I must put off this my tabernacle, even as our Lord Jesus Christ hath shewed me. Moreover I will endeavour that ye may be able after my decease to have these things always in remembrance. For we have not followed cunningly devised fables, when we made known unto you the power and coming of our Lord Jesus Christ, but were eyewitnesses of his majesty.
—2 PETER 1:14–16

This passage is one of many pointing to the preeminence the Word of God must have in our lives. A basic commitment to following the Scriptures in word and practice is essential for every child of God.

Some churches teach that only church leaders can accurately interpret Scripture. But God instructs every believer to *"Study to shew thyself approved unto God, a workman that needeth not to be ashamed, rightly dividing the word of truth"* (2 Timothy 2:15). God gave us His Word, and He desires that we would read it, study it, and learn its truths. The final authority on prophecy does not rest with a man (even if he is a religious leader) or a church. The final authority is the Bible.

Therefore, the question is how do we approach the prophecies of Scripture? What process do we use to understand them accurately and thoroughly?

Interpret literally.

Many will mock the practice of literal interpretation, but in reality their scorn is a reflection of their low opinion of the Bible and high opinion of themselves. "If the literal sense makes good sense, seek no other sense, lest it result in nonsense" is a basic rule of Bible interpretation. In other words, where God has spoken plainly, we must not allegorize away His literal meaning.

We understand, of course, that there are times the Bible uses figurative language. For example, Jesus is called the Lamb of God 28 times in the book of Revelation. This does not mean that He is a literal lamb. The term *lamb*, in reference to Christ, is intended to give us a symbolic picture of Christ as our atoning sacrifice. But the symbolic use of *lamb* does not eliminate the literal truth of Christ as our atoning sacrifice.[9]

Figurative language is not a problem for those who interpret the Bible literally. The literal method of interpretation does not preclude recognition that some terms are used symbolically. Literal means we take words in their usual or commonly accepted sense. However, our interpretation of those words is also controlled by the context in which they are found. Whether a term is to be interpreted symbolically and how it is to be interpreted, are both determined by the context in which it is used.

Understand contextually.

Just as we can take each others' words out of context and produce a completely twisted meaning from the original intent, so do many with their interpretation of the Word of God. Yet, to understand prophecy accurately, we must interpret biblical prophecies in context. Scripture must be understood in the grammatical, doctrinal, and historical context in which it is set.

Understanding Scripture contextually requires that we view each passage in the context of the whole of the Bible—comparing Scripture with Scripture. As many have explained, "The Bible is the best commentary on the Bible." Throughout this book, we will cross-reference Scripture often to insure that we are not lifting a passage out of its context.

Bible prophecy is history written in advance. It is God's forecast for the future, and it is always 100 percent accurate!

> *Remember the former things of old: for I am God, and there is none else; I am God, and there is none like me, Declaring the end from the beginning, and from ancient times the things that are not yet done, saying, My counsel shall stand, and I will do all my pleasure: Calling a ravenous bird from the east, the man that executeth my counsel from a far country: yea, I have spoken it, I will also bring it to pass; I have purposed it, I will also do it.*—Isaiah 46:9–11

As we study, we will focus on God's pinnacle moment of prophecy— the coming of Jesus Christ for His own. *"Looking for that blessed hope, and the glorious appearing of the great God and our Saviour Jesus Christ"* (Titus 2:13).

> Most evangelical Christians hold to the dispensational premillennial view of eschatology, which looks forward to the rapture of believers to Heaven as the next major prophetic event to be fulfilled. This, they believe, will end the church age and prepare the way for the Tribulation and the return of Christ.[10]

An overview of Bible prophecy can be illustrated by the following chart.

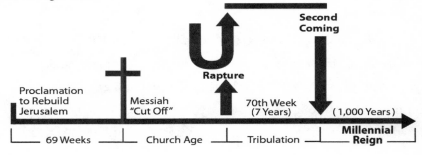

In coming chapters, we'll thoroughly study passages that relate to the events pictured on the chart. For now, it provides a big-picture view of where we are headed.

THE RELIABILITY OF BIBLE PROPHECY

Why do we trust the Bible as being authoritative? How do we know it is reliable?

The Bible has an impeccable track record. It has *never* been wrong—not even slightly off—in its prophetic predictions. Hundreds of Bible prophecies have been fulfilled, down to exact details. Other world religions cannot even come close to making such claims.

For example, Scripture accurately prophesied such events as the fall of Babylon (Daniel 5, Isaiah 13, Jeremiah 51) and Egypt's fall as a world empire to never again rule over the nations (Ezekiel 29:15). The prophet Isaiah named the future king of Persia, Cyrus, and predicted that he would give the decree for the Jews to return to Israel and rebuild the temple (Isaiah 44:28). This prophecy was given before Cyrus was even born and before the Jewish captivity had ever begun; in fact, it was delivered about 175 years before Cyrus made the decree!

Daniel 11 gives an incredibly detailed prophecy of the fate of the Grecian Empire, and it was written before Greece became a world empire. It describes with perfect accuracy the division of the empire upon Alexander the Great's death and the subsequent wars between those divisions.

Scripture provides about 120 already fulfilled prophecies of Christ's first coming, all of which were penned before He was conceived in Mary's womb. The following is a list of only ten of these prophecies.[11]

Prophecy	Subject	Fulfillment
Genesis 3:15 "her seed"	**Seed of woman**	Galatians 4:4 "made of a woman"
Genesis 12:3 "all families of the earth shall be blessed"	**Descendent of Abraham**	Matthew 1:1 "the son of Abraham"
Genesis 49:10 "The sceptre shall not depart from Judah"	**Tribe of Judah**	Luke 3:33 "the son of Juda"
Isaiah 9:7 "upon the throne of David"	**Heir of David**	Luke 1:32 "the throne of his father David"
Micah 5:2 "Bethlehem...shall he come...ruler in Israel"	**Born in Bethlehem**	Luke 2:4–7 "unto the city of David, which is called Bethlehem...she brought forth her firstborn son"
Isaiah 7:14 "a virgin shall conceive"	**Born of a virgin**	Matthew 1:23 "a virgin shall be with child"
Psalm 2:7 "Thou art my Son"	**Declared the Son of God**	Matthew 3:17 "This is my beloved Son"
Isaiah 53:3 "He is despised and rejected of men"	**Rejected by His own**	John 1:11 "his own received him not"
Psalm 41:9 "mine own familiar friend...against me"	**Betrayed by a friend**	Matthew 26:50 "Friend, wherefore art thou come?
Zechariah 12:10 "upon me whom they have pierced"	**Death by crucifixion**	Matthew 27:23 "Let him be crucified"

Because Christ fulfilled these prophecies of His first coming with perfect accuracy, we have confidence that He will also fulfill the three hundred prophecies of His Second Coming.[12] When it comes to future events, God has given His Word, and true to His nature, God will keep His Word. *"The Lord is not slack concerning his promise, as some men count slackness; but is longsuffering to us-ward, not willing that any should perish, but that all should come to repentance"* (2 Peter 3:9).

Consider for a moment the track record of Bible prophecy. For thousands of years it has been 100% accurately fulfilled—its margin of error is *zero*. This gives us every confidence that when we read of future prophecies we can fully believe and trust that world events are running on God's timetable.

THE RESPONSES TO BIBLE PROPHECY

The Bible, in 2 Peter 3, discloses four varying responses toward Bible prophecy.

Some will scoff.

When scoffers hear the prophetic truths of God's Word, that are intended to warn them to avoid coming judgment, they mock them as "old-fashioned" or "irrelevant." It may be of interest to scoffers that predictions of their attitude are included in the very prophecy they scorn: *"Knowing this first, that there shall come in the last days scoffers, walking after their own lusts"* (2 Peter 3:3).

I'm deeply concerned that most Americans have been tainted by the mainstream media's definition of "tolerance." The media in general has attempted to silence Christians. The world demands tolerance of various causes but remains intolerant towards the name of Jesus, the rights of the unborn, and a Christian's freedom of expression just to name a few. Many who scoff at biblical truth wouldn't dare mock Islam's prophecies of the twelfth Imam—that would be "intolerant." Many are careful not to offend world religions while simultaneously finding it easy to mock Christianity and take God's name in vain publicly. And woe be to the Christian who dares to stand in defense of Christianity. If a Christian protests the growing influence of an unbiblical lifestyle, that Christian is labeled as "intolerant." This is at best a twisted, distorted view of tolerance. At worst, it is a deliberate move to undermine and compromise the receptivity of nonbelievers to hearing the truth of the Gospel.

Scripture points out the reason people mock Bible prophecy—that they might continue *"walking after their own lusts"* (2 Peter 3:3). In other words, they would prefer to deny God's authority and His judgment upon their sin rather than repent and receive God's salvation.

Some will seek.

While there will always be some who scoff, many sincere hearts will seek to verify the truth of Bible prophecy.

By studying the past, especially the flood God sent in Noah's day, they will understand that God does indeed judge sin: *"Whereby the world that then was, being overflowed with water, perished: But the heavens and the earth, which are now, by the same word are kept in store, reserved unto fire against the day of judgment and perdition of ungodly men"* (2 Peter 3:6–7).

By studying prophecies of the future, sincere seekers will see that just as God released global judgment through the flood, He will once again judge the entire world—this time by fire: *"But the day of the Lord will come as a thief in the night; in the which the heavens shall pass away with a great noise, and the elements shall melt with fervent heat, the earth also and the works that are therein shall be burned up"* (2 Peter 3:10).

Those who sincerely search the Scripture will find far more than answers concerning the future of the world. They will find the Saviour who freely offers salvation during these unstable times.

Some will find salvation.

"While biblical prophecies and their literal fulfillment may fascinate our curiosity and challenge our minds, they are ultimately intended to bring us to a personal point of decision and faith as well."[13]

If you haven't trusted Christ as your Saviour, Bible prophecy reminds you of your need for salvation. One day this changing world will end, and eternity will continue. The very reason God provided the prophecies of His Word was that we might know the truth and find our salvation in Him alone.

Scoffers point out that the prophecies of Christ's return have been awaiting fulfillment for two thousand years. They interpret this delay as proof that the prophecies are not valid. In 2 Peter 3:9, however, God explains His reason for waiting: *"The Lord is not slack concerning his promise, as some men count slackness; but is longsuffering to us-ward, not willing that any should perish, but that all should come to repentance."* God has a timetable for His return, and He will indeed come, but if you have never trusted Christ as your personal Saviour, God is holding back His judgment for *you!*

A full-service gas station had several dozen cars waiting in line on the first day of a holiday weekend. At the end of the line was the pastor of a local church. Spotting the pastor, the attendant made his way to the last car. "Pastor, I'm sorry for the delay. It seems like folks always wait for the last minute to get ready for the trip they've known they were taking."

The pastor smiled and replied, "I know what you mean. It's the same in my business."

I often talk to people about their eternal destination, and I find many would rather put off even thinking about it. Don't put off the matter of salvation. The Lord may return today! Don't delay in accepting His gift of salvation. In chapter 7 we will examine more closely what it means to place your trust in Christ as your personal Saviour.

Some are strengthened.

Many Christians are concerned about the loss of patriotism, the influx of vain social philosophies, and the secularizing of our nation. But studying biblical prophecy strengthens and encourages us to live more fervently for the Lord in changing times.

Our oldest daughter recently gave birth to our first grandchild. Soon after Peter and Danielle announced to us that they were expecting this little one, things began to change at our house. Right away my wife began stocking a nursery for the new baby. (This is in addition to the preparations Peter and Danielle made at their own house!) Before Camden was even born, we had a full shelf of diapers, clothes, blankets, and our own crib. The expectancy of a new little life coming into our family began to change *us*—our schedule, plans, home, even our budget!

That's the way it should be in the Christian's life. Christ's coming should create an expectancy that changes us. Perhaps it will change our habits, relationships, plans, schedules, or even our budgets. Every area of our lives should be ordered in light of God's prophetic promises.

Biblical prophecy should motivate the child of God to be involved in eternal investments. It should encourage us to focus our attention on purifying ourselves *"even as he is pure"* (1 John 3:3). Second Peter 3:11 admonishes, *"Seeing then that all these things shall be dissolved, what manner of persons ought ye to be in all holy conversation and godliness."*

Since this world will culminate in God's global judgment, shouldn't we live differently than those who do not know Christ? Shouldn't our values change as a result of our study? Shouldn't we put more emphasis on what matters most?

Our material possessions will never make it into eternity. But the people who accept Christ will. You can't take your car to Heaven, but you could bring your neighbor.

Ultimately, Bible prophecy reminds us, as Christians, to fulfill the Great Commission (Matthew 28:19–20) and reach every person we can with the Gospel before it is too late. Christ is coming soon, and it is the responsibility of every Christian to tell the world. Not everyone will respond positively to the warning of future judgment and the offer of salvation by grace alone, but many will. We must be faithful to share the good news of the Gospel. For God *"will have all men to be saved, and to come unto the knowledge of the truth"* (1 Timothy 2:4).

Before we move on to the next chapter, I ask you to resolve what *your* response to Bible prophecy will be. Your response will determine what you receive from this book.

If you *scorn* the message of the Bible, not only will you receive very little, but you will lose very much. The truth that could give you hope for the future and security in times of uncertainty will be lost to you.

If you *sincerely search* the Scriptures, you will find that God's Word is absolutely accurate and you can trust it. You will learn that Jesus is the only way to eternal life, and I pray that you will receive Him as your Saviour.

If you, as a Christian, allow yourself to be *strengthened* in your relationship with the Lord, you will be motivated to shift your values from the temporal to the eternal. When at last you stand before Him, what a joy it will be to present a well-lived life invested in eternal values! *"And, behold, I come quickly; and my reward is with me, to give every man according as his work shall be"* (Revelation 22:12).

CHAPTER TWO
World Empires Old and New

I n twelve centuries of existence, ancient Rome expanded to become
one of the largest empires of world history. Her contributions, many
of which are still reflected in today's society, spanned a far-reaching
gamut: government, law, architecture, language, literature, war, art—
almost every area of life.

Yet even before this magnificent empire was making her influence felt,
Scripture prophesied her rise and decline—and future reviving. Yes, today
ancient Rome is in the process of being revived as a modern empire.

In 604 BC, the then-ruling empire, Babylon, invaded Jerusalem and
the Hebrew nation of Judah. Nebuchadnezzar, co-regent with his father,
led a group of royal and upper class young people back to Babylon to
serve as slaves in the Babylonian government.

Included in this group was Daniel, a young man of purpose and
holiness who was probably in his late teens. Daniel publicly stood for

his God amidst the debauchery that surrounded him in Babylon. God blessed his loyalty, and Daniel was soon standing before the mighty King Nebuchadnezzar himself as a royal advisor.

This young man, gifted by God with supernatural wisdom, relayed to Nebuchadnezzar—and to us—prophecy of the coming modern Roman Empire. God first delivered these prophecies to Nebuchadnezzar in a dream, but He decoded and explained them through Daniel. Daniel 2 records the king's uncommonly troubling dream, his demand of the wise men and magicians to declare both the dream and its interpretation, and Daniel's bold assertion that God would reveal the dream.

When Nebuchadnezzar dreamed a singularly disquieting dream, he demanded of his magicians, astrologers, and sorcerers that they would tell him both the dream and the significance of it. When the men protested this demand, the king decreed their death.

Although Daniel had not been called with the other men to stand before the king, he was included on the roster of "wise men," so his fate was sealed with the group. When the executioner came to Daniel's house and Daniel was made aware of the situation, he made a bold request—for time to seek the Lord and find both the dream and its interpretation.

Soon after, Daniel stood before King Nebuchadnezzar and explained, *"...there is a God in heaven that revealeth secrets, and maketh known to the king Nebuchadnezzar what shall be in the latter days. Thy dream, and the visions of thy head upon thy bed, are these"* (Daniel 2:28).

Daniel pulled back the curtain of time, and from the truths that God revealed to him from Nebuchadnezzar's dream and his own visions, he revealed future world empires, including what some call the revived Roman Empire. He foresaw trends of this forthcoming empire that we are only now experiencing. Let's examine the dream God gave to Nebuchadnezzar and observe how it relates to us today.

THE PROPHECY DELIVERED

Thou, O king, sawest, and behold a great image. This great image, whose brightness was excellent, stood before thee; and the form thereof was terrible. This image's head was of fine gold, his breast and his arms of silver, his belly and his thighs of brass, His legs of iron, his feet part of iron and part of clay. Thou sawest till that a stone was cut out without hands, which smote the image upon his feet that were of iron and clay, and brake them to pieces. Then was the iron, the clay, the brass, the silver, and the gold, broken to pieces together, and became like the chaff of the summer threshingfloors; and the wind carried them away, that no place was found for them: and the stone that smote the image became a great mountain, and filled the whole earth. This is the dream; and we will tell the interpretation thereof before the king.

—DANIEL 2:31–36

Nebuchadnezzar's dream pictured a symbolic image representing coming world empires. From Babylon to the Antichrist's empire, the time frame prophesied in this dream began during Nebuchadnezzar's reign, but it will not end until the return of Christ.

Daniel explained that the image Nebuchadnezzar saw foretold *"what shall be in the latter days"* (Daniel 2:28). *"The latter days"* is a phrase that refers to the extended period of time during which the Gentiles would have control over Jerusalem. Scripture elsewhere calls this period *"the times of the Gentiles"* (Luke 21:24). (The prophecy in Daniel 2 of a giant figure of a man is parallel to the prophecy in Daniel 7 of four beasts. Both prophecies tell of five world empires, each from a different vantage point.)

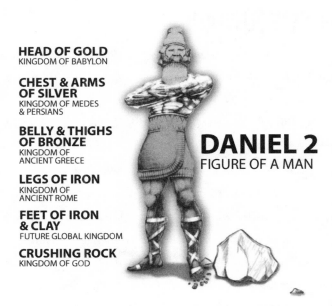

HEAD OF GOLD
KINGDOM OF BABYLON

CHEST & ARMS OF SILVER
KINGDOM OF MEDES & PERSIANS

BELLY & THIGHS OF BRONZE
KINGDOM OF ANCIENT GREECE

LEGS OF IRON
KINGDOM OF ANCIENT ROME

FEET OF IRON & CLAY
FUTURE GLOBAL KINGDOM

CRUSHING ROCK
KINGDOM OF GOD

DANIEL 2
FIGURE OF A MAN

The image Nebuchadnezzar saw in his dream was pieced with various metals arranged with greater *value* on the top but greater *strength* on the bottom. The order of these metals is significant, as it represented the sequential glory and strength of world governments.

The head of gold symbolized the Babylonian kingdom (606–539 BC). The silver arms and chest pictured Babylon's successor, the Media-Persian Empire (539–330 BC). The brass belly and thighs represented the Greek Empire (330–63 BC). And many scholars believe the legs of iron represent the Roman Empire (63 BC–AD 476). The feet of iron mixed with clay prophesied a continuation of the fourth empire that is divided—partly strong (iron) and partly weak (clay) in its structure. This fourth kindgom continues to the end, but it changes over time and will eventually become a shared kingdom among ten kings. This kingdom will be a government unlike anything the world has yet to see. Because many Bible scholars believe the legs to represent the Roman Empire, and because the toes represent a future global government that is connected in some way to the legs, it's not uncommon to hear of this coming kingdom referred to as the

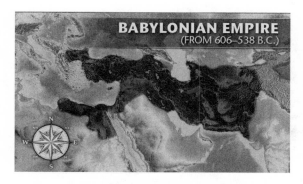

revived Roman Empire. For the sake of discussion, I will use that term in this text. However, it is needful to point out that Daniel's prophecy does not. While the ten toes may include much of the geography of the ancient Roman Empire, Scripture makes it clear the ten toes represent the last phase in the development of the fourth kingdom.

For Nebuchadnezzar, all the kingdoms following his were prophetic. For us, all but one is history. The final kingdom has yet to fully shape into the world power it will become, but events we see unfolding before us today point to this coming kingdom.

The crushing stone that ended Nebuchadnezzar's dream represents Christ's coming kingdom that will end all world empires (covered more thoroughly in chapter 10). Let's take a closer look at what Nebuchadnezzar saw and Daniel interpreted.

THE PROPHECY DEFINED

And the fourth kingdom shall be strong as iron: forasmuch as iron breaketh in pieces and subdueth all things: and as iron that breaketh all these, shall it break in pieces and bruise. And whereas thou sawest the feet and toes, part of potters' clay, and part of iron, the kingdom shall be divided; but there shall be in it of the strength of the iron, forasmuch as thou sawest the iron mixed with miry clay. And as the toes of the feet were part of iron, and part of clay, so the kingdom shall be partly strong, and partly broken. And whereas thou sawest iron mixed with miry clay, they shall mingle themselves with the seed of men: but they shall not cleave one to another, even as iron is not mixed with clay. And in the days of these kings shall the God of heaven set up a kingdom, which shall never be destroyed: and the kingdom shall not be left to other people, but it shall break in pieces and consume all these kingdoms, and it shall stand for ever. Forasmuch as thou sawest that the stone was cut out of the mountain without hands, and that it brake in pieces the iron, the brass, the clay, the silver, and the gold; the great God hath made known to the king what shall come to pass hereafter: and the dream is certain, and the interpretation thereof sure.—DANIEL 2:40–45

Notice the prophetic, and now historic, accuracy of the first four parts of the image.

Babylon was the head of gold. Daniel told Nebuchadnezzar, *"Thou, O king, art a king of kings: for the God of heaven hath given thee a kingdom, power, and strength, and glory"* (Daniel 2:37). Nebuchadnezzar would not have been surprised to see his kingdom represented by gold, for Babylon was gloriously wealthy. The chief god of Babylon, Marduk, was reportedly made of pure gold. Daniel 3 records that Nebuchadnezzar later constructed a colossal golden image that flaunted the wealth of Babylon.

At the time of Daniel's prophecy, during the height of the Babylonian kingdom, it would require faith to see the possibility of a succeeding empire, represented by the chest and arms of silver. Babylon was impregnable. The only entrance through the heavily fortified walls surrounding the city was through the guarded gates or the bed of the Euphrates river.

History and Daniel 5 both record the brilliant military strategy of Cyrus the Persian who, under Darius the Median's administration, redirected the mighty Euphrates river and marched his soldiers under the walls into Babylon during Belshazzar's drunken feast. Not a soldier was there to defend his city, so the golden head of Babylon was quietly set aside and replaced by the **Media-Persian Empire** in 539 BC.

Two hundred years later, Alexander the Great conquered this silver empire and ushered in the third and bronze world empire—**Greece.** Almost three hundred years before Alexander's conquests, Daniel specifically named Greece as a world power (Daniel 8:21), once again displaying the accuracy of Bible prophecy. Daniel 11 further records details of the demise and division of the Greek Empire after Alexander's death.

The fourth kingdom, represented by the legs of iron, was in power during the time of Christ and the early church. Iron was an appropriate representative metal for the **Roman Empire,** as the Romans extensively used iron for weaponry and advancement.

From a historic view, we have already seen four world empires rise and fall, exactly as Daniel prophesied. As we noted earlier, the future development of the fourth kingdom, represented by the feet of iron mixed with clay, has yet to come to full power. This will be the future kingdom of ten kings sharing power—a coming global empire. Again, this empire will have some probable connection with ancient Rome, and may even include Rome as a critical component, yet this future kingdom will be distinct and unlike anything in history.

The basic tenants of this kingdom are appearing with such increasing vividness in current events that it becomes obvious this empire is forming even now. Notice the characteristics of this coming kingdom.

A final days kingdom

Both Daniel and Revelation associate the Antichrist with a confederation of ten European nations that correspond in some way to the old Roman Empire. Daniel 2:31–45 symbolizes this by the ten toes of the great statue in Nebuchadnezzar's dream. Daniel 7:19–28 and Revelation 13:1–9 symbolize this by the ten horns on the beast.[1]

The future world empire is represented by iron mixed with clay, but, as Daniel notes, iron and clay do not mix together (Daniel 2:43). The effort to mix the two speaks of both the diversity and attempted unity that will characterize this empire. As noted in chapter 1, there is already great energy being invested into blending world religions. More than ever before, Western culture seeks to justify moral degradation through "civil rights" measures such as those that protect homosexual unions and promote godlessness. On the political plane, this mixture may speak of the bringing together of various world governments—monarchies, democracies, dictators.

> When you come to the iron and clay, you have our present governments: the iron represents law and justice, the clay represents mankind, and together they make up democracy. What is the strength of democracy? Law. What is its weakness? Human nature. We are seeing today that lawlessness comes when human nature refuses to be bound by God's order and laws.[2]

In this final days kingdom, there will be an attempted unification that will result in an ultimate crumbling as the iron and clay are incapable of holding a permanent union.

A transferring of world power

The ten toes represent ten kings over the final stage of the fourth kingdom, and they indicate that global power is spread throughout the European and Middle Eastern regions. Most scholars struggle to know the exact nature of this final kingdom, but we can be certain that it includes America at the present, since the fourth kingdom continues to the end. As we approach the formation of the final kingdom, the role of America is not specifically mentioned in the Bible. Many agree that our role internationally will diminish. Since there will be ten confederacies or ruling leaders that eventually unite to give their leadership to the Antichrist (see chapter 6), the prominence of any one super-power would naturally be reduced.

This shift in world power is already anticipated by many today. The decline of American patriotism is seen even in government officials. The

New York Times bestseller, *The Post-American World*, has become a popular book of many of our elected officials, including President Barack Obama.[3]

Several years ago, most Americans would have rejected a title that suggested a decrease of America's global influence. But today people are turning their thinking toward a world in which America is no longer the dominant leader.

During a recent trip to Europe, Vice President Biden went so far as to suggested that Brussels is more suited to be called the "capital of the free world" than Washington DC. In a May 25, 2010 article, FOX News reported on Biden's statements:

Biden Says Brussels Could Be 'Capital of the Free World'

It's not unheard of for Vice President Biden to get lost in the moment, but during a speech earlier this month to the European Parliament his flattery of the host may have gone a bit overboard, ceding Washington, D.C.'s role as the world's center of liberty.

The U.S. vice president, opening his address in Belgium, argued that Brussels—considering its rich history and abundance of international institutions—could well be the "capital of the free world."

He suggested that Washington, D.C., his home, is undeserving of that title—notwithstanding its wealth of global organizations and the countless international summits that take place there.

"As you probably know, some American politicians and American journalists refer to Washington, D.C. as the 'capital of the free world,'" Biden said. "But it seems to me that in this great city, which boasts 1,000 years of history and which serves as the capital of Belgium, the home of the European Union, and the headquarters for NATO, this city has its own legitimate claim to that title."[4]

Perhaps this shift in our leaders' thinking is a sign of things to come. Unlike the earlier world empires which were conquered and overthrown by their successors, the revived Roman Empire will transfer global powers by mutual consent, so that each member in the alliance retains its own identity while working together as a total empire. This is seen in the ten individual toes all associated with the same image. Revelation 17:13 explains, *"These have one mind, and shall give their power and strength unto the beast."*

A confederation of ten powers

We cannot predict how the lines will be drawn or who the leaders will be, but we do know that ten powers will confederate under some type of a multi-national rule. Perhaps these will be ten European powers, or they may be global sections.

Many have speculated on the location for the headquarters of this revived Roman Empire. What location will be the ultimate home site of power for a one-world government? It may be in Europe, or it may be ancient Babylon itself (modern Iraq). It is interesting to note that the ancient Roman Empire extended all the way to modern day Iraq, and some believe it went as far as India.

A supreme leader

The final days kingdom of the ten-leader confederation will set the stage for a supreme world ruler—the man the Bible refers to as the Antichrist or the beast: *"And the ten horns which thou sawest are ten kings, which have received no kingdom as yet; but receive power as kings one hour with the beast. These have one mind, and shall give their power and strength unto the beast"* (Revelation 17:12–13).

The parallel passage to Nebuchadnezzar's dream is Daniel 7. This chapter describes how ten world leaders will eventually transfer power to a supreme leader: *"And the ten horns out of this kingdom are ten kings that shall arise: and another shall rise after them; and he shall be diverse from the first, and he shall subdue three kings"* (Daniel 7:24). Through strategic diplomacy, a leader will rise and set aside three of the ten rulers. This will place him in a majority leadership position. The others will acquiesce, and thus one will come to power as the supreme leader of the revived Roman Empire.

But is this really conceivable? Is it possible that ten powers will form and then desire to give their authority to a one-world leader?

From a biblical standpoint, the answer is obviously "yes." But even from a socio-economic and political standpoint, this is becoming more conceivable. As economies continue to crumble and nationalism declines, the apparent solution for peace is global unity. At the rate that people are embracing globalism, it appears that anything can happen.

Consider the following statement made years ago by Paul-Henri Spaak, the first president of the United Nations: "We do not need another committee, we have too many already. What we want is a man of sufficient stature to hold the allegiance of all people, and to lift us out of the economic morass into which we are sinking. Send us such a man and be he god or devil, we will receive him."[5]

There are many who desire not only globalism, but a centralized leadership for the entire planet. As we near the days of the revived Roman Empire, this desire will only increase.

THE PROPHECY DEVELOPING

While the fulfillment of Daniel's prophecy and the revealing of the Antichrist will not take place until the Tribulation, we can already see developments that have brought many people closer to accepting a one-world ruler. This prophecy is ripening as modern globalism gains influence and world powers realign in preparation for the revived Roman Empire.

Note these three ways in which we can observe the prophecy developing:

A lessening of national pride

On my first trip to Europe, I was surprised at the stamp on my passport. Rather than each country stamping my passport with their respective national stamps, they used a stamp with the flag of the European Union. There is a centralized identity, stronger than individual national pride, throughout the twenty-seven-member nations comprising the European Union.

Here in the United States, we see a progressive lack of patriotism. For instance, when was the last time you saw an NBA player put his hand over his heart when the national anthem was played at a game? How about at baseball games? More often than not, the players are distracted, digging in their pockets for sunflower seeds or gum, and many of the fans remain seated with their hats still on while the flag is displayed.

Several years ago former Vice President Dan Quayle visited our church. The American president during his term, George Bush, Sr., often spoke of "the new world order." As I visited with Mr. Quayle after church, I mentioned that the concept of a "new world order" makes many of us uneasy. "You know," he replied, "every time I get around conservative Christians, they say the same thing." The lessening of national pride is of significance to those who believe God's prophecies will be fulfilled literally. It signals the development of the spirit that will lead to the creation of the revived Roman Empire.

Our children are being re-educated to identify themselves as global citizens, which lessens their sense of national identity. The current emphasis in education and media encouraging reverence for the planet is part of this re-education. FOX News reported that children of some elementary schools are reciting the following pledge:

> I pledge my support to Planet Earth
> And to the tapestry of life,
> And to the creation and perpetuation of a healthy, prosperous and
>   peaceful world.
> My planet, in harmony with nature, interwoven, with compassion
>   and love for All.

Thanks to the ACLU, these children are not permitted to pledge to "one nation under God," but they can pledge to planet earth. For decades Americans have pledged allegiance to a nation they publicly recognized as being dependent upon the favor of God. Yet, through various modes across our nation, liberals are implementing training that will desensitize the minds of our young people toward national pride and retrain them toward global allegiance.

A call for the lessening of national pride is not a twenty-first century phenomenon. One early call was sounded by none other than Winston Churchill, a courageous man who tirelessly and selflessly gave of himself during World War II. He suggested that European grouping might be a means to peace.

> In 1946, following the devastation of Europe during the Second World War, Winston Churchill forcefully asserted that "the tragedy of Europe" could only be solved if the issues of ancient nationalism and sovereignty could give way to a sense of European "national grouping." He said that the path to European peace and prosperity on the world stage was clear: "We must build a United States of Europe."[6]

Perhaps unknowingly, Churchill was suggesting the start of what Scripture prophesies will usher in the final world empire.

Increasing interest in centralized world power is decreasing allegiance to national pride and paving the way for a global government.

An increasing of global government

The European Union has three bodies of government: the European Parliament, the Council of the European Union, and the European Commission. The twenty-seven-member countries of the European Union favor global government in their elected representatives. Not only do they elect representatives for their national bodies, they elect an additional set for the European body, thus giving the European Union individualized power and authority.

The European Union is deeply involved in Middle East politics, including sanctions against Israel and policies designed to pressure Israel into giving up part of her land (covered more thoroughly in chapter 3). Presently, the European Union is wooing members into their assembly that include terrorists states—such as Syria, as journaled in the *Jerusalem Post*:

> European Union Commissioner for External Relations
> Benita Ferrero Waldner on Friday said that the European
> Union is close to agreeing [on] an offer to Syria of closer ties,
> Reuters reported.
>
> "Engaging with Syria is absolutely in our interest,"
> Ferrero Waldner reportedly told journalists at a meeting of
> EU foreign ministers in Stockholm.
>
> "I would say that we are coming to an agreement. There
> are still some modalities that have to be found, there are
> some reserves…but I am confident that in the near future
> we will get this agreement really going."[7]

A couple years ago, I had the privilege of preaching in the country of Romania for the organizational service of one of our missionaries' churches. After preaching for this young church, our group took a train into Budapest, Hungary, where we waited overnight for our flight back to the United States.

As we walked into our hotel, I noticed several black limousines with the European Union flag. We purchased our sandwiches, and then my curiosity took over. I found my way up to the second floor and, through glass, saw a large meeting room. Seated around a conference table were forty or fifty people, and I wondered aloud to my wife if perhaps the Antichrist himself were in that meeting.

The next morning, we purchased a newspaper before boarding our plane and learned what had been discussed.

> Former Soviet leader Mikhail Gorbachev last week called for
> the European Union and Russia to put their differences aside
> to create a major European voice that would counteract the
> influence of the U.S. in defining global politics. "If we don't
> get Russia in, Europe won't have a big voice in the world,"
> Gorbachev said at the opening of a two-day meeting on the

future of Europe in Budapest. "The way forward is to search for a formula to remove obstacles to [EU] cooperation with Russia."

"I believe Europe can, and must, take the initiative," he continued. "The hour of Europe is coming in international affairs…if it doesn't we will see a time of global troubles."[8]

Time Magazine reports how President Barack Obama has been vocal in expressing his views on the need for greater global unity in governments and his support for European leadership.

> At a town hall in Strasbourg, France, Obama stood before an audience of mostly French and German youth and admitted that the U.S. should have a greater respect for Europe. "In America, there's a failure to appreciate Europe's leading role in the world," he said before offering other European critical views of his country.[9]

Another major advancement of the power of the European Union was the Lisbon Treaty—signed by all twenty-seven countries in the European Union. This treaty strengthened the European Union, giving them a more unified world voice and created the office of a European Union president. Herman van Rompuy was chosen for this position in a November 20, 2009 election.

An earlier consideration for this post was Tony Blair, former United Kingdom Prime Minister. When I visited Israel in the spring of 2009, I learned that Tony Blair was serving as the Quartet Envoy for Mideast Peace. The Quartet includes the United States, Russia, the European Union, and the United Nations.

Later, we will discuss the interest world powers have in Israel and what the Bible says about her role in the end game of world history. From a biblical prophecy point of view, it is interesting to note that a man who is very involved in Middle East affairs *and* who has great power in the European Union was considered for a unifying leadership position. This demonstrates how easily the increase of global government can tie into affairs in the Middle East.

According to Bible prophecy, Israel stands as the geopolitical center of the world (more on this in chapter 3), and global power will one day rise from the Mediterranean/European region. Even today, we are seeing a shifting of world powers to align to this final days model.

A quest for a global currency

Most people have heard of "the mark of the beast," as well as the number of his name—666. Both of these come from references in Revelation foretelling that the Antichrist will require people to receive a mark of identification of loyalty to him in order to buy or sell.

> And he causeth all, both small and great, rich and poor, free and
> bond, to receive a mark in their right hand, or in their foreheads:
> And that no man might buy or sell, save he that had the mark, or
> the name of the beast, or the number of his name. Here is wisdom.
> Let him that hath understanding count the number of the beast:
> for it is the number of a man; and his number is Six hundred
> threescore and six.—REVELATION 13:16–18

Before such a concept could be integrated, there must first be a worldwide, centralized monetary system. I remember reading an article in the late 1980s in which an economist predicted a future world currency. At the time, people laughed and called him an extremist. Recent events, however, indicate that this extreme is looking more like reality.

The U.S. dollar is declining against the euro regularly. While it is possible that this trend will reverse, many economic experts believe that within five years, the euro may actually replace the dollar as the standard world currency.

Further jeopardizing the stability of the U.S. dollar is Iran's refusal to accept it as payment for oil. Currently, Iran is requiring payment to be made in the euro. Other Arab states are threatening to do the same.

China, too, has voiced a concern for an international currency independent of the U.S. dollar, as the *New York Times* reported in the following article:

> In another indication that China is growing increasingly concerned about holding huge dollar reserves, the head of its central bank has called for the eventual creation of a new international currency reserve to replace the dollar.[10]

Amazingly, the U.S. Treasury Secretary, Tim Geithner, responded with interest to China's statements.

> U.S. Treasury Secretary Tim Geithner shocked global markets by revealing that Washington is "quite open" to Chinese proposals for the gradual development of a global reserve currency run by the International Monetary Fund. The dollar plunged instantly against the euro, yen, and sterling as the comments flashed across trading screens. David Bloom, currency chief at HSBC, said the apparent policy shift amounts to an earthquake in geo-finance. "The mere fact that the U.S. Treasury Secretary is even entertaining thoughts that the dollar may cease being the anchor of the global monetary system has caused consternation," he said.[11]

While the U.S. dollar has been the standard-bearer of world currency for many years, its value and prestige are quickly declining, making way for increased demand for a global currency.

The lessening of national pride, increasing of global government, and quest for global currency are working together to realign world powers in a truly remarkable way. The events that we see unfolding before us on a daily basis herald the coming fulfillment of Daniel's prophecy.

The stage is being set for the grand finale of world history—the return of Jesus Christ. Daniel 2:34 describes the end of all world empires and the beginning of Christ's millennial kingdom: *"Thou sawest till that a stone was cut out without hands, which smote the image upon his feet that were of iron and clay, and brake them to pieces. Then was the iron, the clay, the brass, the silver, and the gold, broken to pieces together, and became like the chaff of the summer threshingfloors; and the wind carried them away, that no place was found for them: and the stone that smote the image became a great mountain, and filled the whole earth"* (Daniel 2:34–35).

Nebuchadnezzar's dream pictured a stone cut without hands crushing the final kingdoms once and for all. Daniel interpreted the significance of this imagery: *"And in the days of these kings shall the God of heaven set up a kingdom, which shall never be destroyed: and the kingdom shall not be left to other people, but it shall break in pieces and consume all these kingdoms, and it shall stand for ever"* (Daniel 2:44).

Some suggest that this prophecy was fulfilled with the fall of ancient Rome. But one sure indicator that this prophecy has yet to reach fulfillment is that when Constantinople fell, there was no eternal kingdom established. Christ's earthly kingdom is yet to come.

Another indicator is that a ten-power kingdom, destroyed with one blow, has never transpired.

> The ten-toe stage is simultaneous, that is, the kingdoms existed side by side and were destroyed by one sudden catastrophic blow. Nothing like this has yet occurred in history.[12]

The final form of the revised Roman Empire will be alive and thriving on Earth when Christ returns to set up His kingdom. *"And I saw heaven opened, and behold a white horse; and he that sat upon him was called Faithful and True, and in righteousness he doth judge and make war. And he hath on his vesture and on his thigh a name written, KING OF KINGS, AND LORD OF LORDS"* (Revelation 19:11, 16).

Even as we see this prophecy developing, the knowledge that Christ will one day return gives hope and expectancy to every Christian who understands Bible prophecy. Paul encouraged those of us who are saved to look for *"that blessed hope, and the glorious appearing of the great God and our Saviour Jesus Christ"* (Titus 2:13). While we may sometimes be discouraged about the lack of patriotism and wonder about the rise of global government, remember that our hope is in the coming of Christ.

Over 250 years ago, Isaac Watts, a non-conformist preacher in London, wrote a song based on Psalm 98 which describes the future glory of Christ's return. It was not until years later that his hymn was categorized and sung as a Christmas carol. Consider these familiar words in reference to Christ's Second Coming:

Joy to the world! The Lord is come;
Let earth receive her King;
Let every heart prepare Him room,
And heav'n and nature sing.

Joy to the earth! the Saviour reigns;
Let men their songs employ;
While fields and floods, rocks, hills, and plains
Repeat the sounding joy.

No more let sins and sorrows grow,
Nor thorns infest the ground;
He comes to make His blessings flow
Far as the curse is found.

He rules the world with truth and grace,
And makes the nations prove
The glories of His righteousness,
And wonders of His love.

Apart from God, human reasoning could conclude that global unity is the only path to world peace. In actuality, it is merely a sign that God's plan for time is coming to a close. As the planet continues to reject God, defy His Son, and resist His truth, we will see mankind try to master his own destiny. But apart from God, mankind is hopelessly lost.

We see in current events that the characteristics that describe the Antichrist's kingdom from Daniel's prophecy seem to be developing before our very eyes. The trends of global economies and politics all point to a coming one-world government, a one-world monetary system, and a one-world ruler. Furthermore, the population of the planet is increasingly more supportive of such ideas.

For the Bible-believer, all of these events draw our hearts toward the heavenly hope of the soon return of our Saviour.

History suggests that the sport of bowling originated in ancient Egypt or Babylon. Reportedly, the pins represented kings, and the ball represented a conquering king who would destroy the pins simultaneously. In a fashion not unlike ten bowling pins prepared for a strike, world powers are aligning themselves for the return of the Lord.

World power may shift to form a mighty revived empire, but even a union ten-global-powers strong will be no match for the "stone cut without hands" that will destroy man's last global government and fill the Earth with truth and mercy.

CHAPTER THREE ___
The Focus on Israel

D oes it seem disproportionate that a country of only 7.2 million people with a land area slightly smaller than the state of New Jersey is the focal point of the modern world? Is it mere coincidence that it is also the focal point of Bible prophecy? People often question why Israel carries so much prophetic significance—and in recent decades, a large portion of global attention. Think about it. Why all the emphasis on Israel?

Israel is a critical component in God's global plan—a key piece in the prophetic puzzle. In many ways, Israel's news marks the dates on God's prophetic calendar.

One of the most significant events of modern history occurred in 1948 when God allowed the Jews to return to Palestine. From that time on, the focus on Israel has been captivating.

Only hours after the rebirth of this modern nation, Israel made the news when she was attacked by the armies of five Arab countries. Now we hear news almost every day from the Middle East.

Two terms in particular are frequently heard in the news: the West Bank and the Palestinian State. Both terms deserve a brief explanation.

The **West Bank**, the region along the western bank of the Jordan River, is home to some wonderfully historic places, including Bethlehem, Jericho, and Hebron.

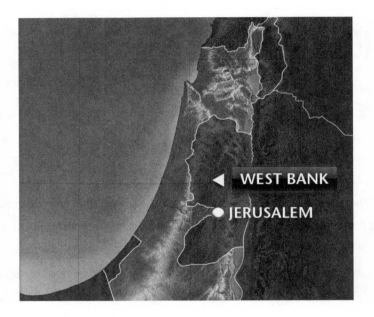

In *The Late Great State of Israel,* Aaron Klein explains the importance of Hebron to Israel.

> Take Hebron. Located in the biblical heartland of Judea on the West Bank, Hebron is the oldest Jewish community in the world. Jews have lived there almost continuously for over thirty-five hundred years. The city is home to the Tomb of the Patriarchs, the second holiest site in Judaism, believed to be the resting place of the biblical patriarchs

and matriarchs Abraham, Isaac, Jacob, Sarah, Rebecca, and Leah. King David, progenitor of the eventual Jewish Messiah, was anointed in Hebron, where he reigned for seven years.

Ten centuries later, during the first Jewish revolt against the Romans, Hebron was the scene of extensive fighting where many Jews were killed. Throughout the Byzantine, Arab, Mameluke, and Ottoman periods, there are accounts of the trials of Hebron's Jewish community. In 1929, after an Arab attack left sixty-seven Jews dead, the entire Jewish community fled the city, with Hebron becoming temporarily devoid of Jews. Jews returned when Israel recaptured the area in the 1967 Six Day War.[1]

This region is significant and special to Israel. The Israeli settlements in the West Bank and East Jerusalem have become the homes of approximately half a million people. Yet the United Nations, as well as many in the United States and the European Union, are pressuring Israel to stop allowing her residents to dwell in these regions. The following excerpt from a TIME *Magazine* article is just one of many news reports with a similar theme.

> The Obama Administration says negotiations between the Palestinians and the Israelis can only proceed if Israel agrees to stop settling occupied land. "The settlements have to be stopped in order for us to move forward," said Barack Obama when he met with Netanyahu in May.[2]

The feelings of the current United States' administration are so strong on this point that new settlements have become a watershed issue. When Vice President Joseph Biden visited Israel in March 2010 to assure her of continued U.S. security support, he quickly changed his attitude after a poorly-timed announcement of new construction.

> Hours after Vice President Joseph R. Biden, Jr. vowed unyielding American support for Israel's security here on Tuesday, Israel's Interior Ministry announced 1,600 new housing units for Jews in East Jerusalem. Mr. Biden condemned the move as "precisely the kind of step that undermines the trust we need right now."
>
> ...Mr. Biden came to Jerusalem largely to assure the Israelis of Washington's commitment to its security and to restart peace talks with the Palestinians.
>
> He began the day on a note of support, asserting the Obama administration's "absolute, total, unvarnished commitment to Israel's security."
>
> But by the end of the day, Mr. Biden's tone had a very different quality. He issued a statement condemning "the substance and timing of the announcement" of the housing, and added, "Unilateral action taken by either party cannot prejudge the outcome of negotiations on permanent status issues."
>
> He said the announcement "runs counter to the constructive discussions that I've had here in Israel."[3]

But while some encourage Israel to stop settling in the West Bank to appease her enemies (particularly Iran), others argue that Israel's enemies cannot be appeased and simply want Israel's destruction. In that case, pulling out of the occupied territory would only increase Israel's vulnerability.

> Speaking at a ceremony on Monday evening in Hebron, Knesset Speaker Reuven Rivlin attacked Prime Minister Binyamin Netanyahu's plans to freeze construction in

the settlements. [Rivlin said,] "He who thinks that in this way we will save ourselves from the pending holocaust is holding out a false hope."[4]

The second oft-employed term in relation to the significance of Israel is the Palestinian State. This, too, is an issue of great controversy. The debate centers around the Arab world's demand for an Israeli-recognized Palestinian State. This is often referred to as the "two-state solution" to the Middle East conflict.

Israel is being pressured by many to enter such an agreement, as the following articles reveal.

> Jordan's king pressed Israeli Prime Minister Benjamin Netanyahu on Thursday to immediately commit to the establishment of a Palestinian state, as he pursues a sweeping resolution of the Muslim world's conflicts with Israel.[5]

> The most serious tensions could arise over Iran. Israel believes that stopping the Iranians from acquiring nuclear-weapons capability is an existential must, and Israeli officials worry that Obama may be too inclined to compromise. Whether that fear is justified or not, **the Obama administration believes that the best way to get international leverage over Iran is to make real efforts to achieve a Palestinian state.** Netanyahu says he wants to negotiate with the Palestinians, but he won't endorse the idea of an independent state.[6] [emphasis added]

CBS *60 Minutes* correspondent Bob Simon explained how the settlements on the West Bank and the issue of the Palestinian State interrelate:

Getting a peace deal in the Middle East is such a priority to President Obama that his first foreign calls on his first day in office were to Arab and Israeli leaders. And on day two, the president made former Senator George Mitchell his special envoy for Middle East peace. Mr. Obama wants to shore up the ceasefire in Gaza, but a lasting peace really depends on the West Bank where Palestinians had hoped to create their state. The problem is, even before Israel invaded Gaza, a growing number of Israelis and Palestinians had concluded that peace between them was no longer possible, that history had passed it by. For peace to have a chance, Israel would have to withdraw from the West Bank, which would then become the Palestinian state.

It's known as the "two-state" solution. But, while negotiations have been going on for 15 years, hundreds of thousands of Jewish settlers have moved in to occupy the West Bank. Palestinians say they can't have a state with Israeli settlers all over it, which the settlers say is precisely the idea.[7]

Whatever the immediate outcome of these issues, one thing is certain: the nation whose people were scattered across the globe for many centuries has in the past several decades become a worldwide focal point. This should not be a surprise to a student of Bible prophecy, for it fits in precisely with end time events foretold in Scripture.

The intense nature of Israeli-Arab peace talks reveals that whoever can broker the peace deal with Israel and her enemies will be a significantly powerful person. In chapter 6 we will see the prophesied magnitude of power this leader will wield as he rises to the position of a one-world ruler. But for now, we simply note that the worldwide focus on Israel, coupled with the conflict in the Middle East, are staging the scene for his arrival.

Of course, much of the conflict in Israel centers around the land itself. Both Israel and nearby Arab nations claim that strategic portions of land rightfully belong to their respective countries. So how does this land dispute relate to Bible prophecy? What is the significance of the land?

It all goes back to a promise God made to Abraham almost 4,000 years ago.

THE PROMISE TO ABRAHAM

Now the LORD had said unto Abram, Get thee out of thy country, and from thy kindred, and from thy father's house, unto a land that I will shew thee: And I will make of thee a great nation, and I will bless thee, and make thy name great; and thou shalt be a blessing: And I will bless them that bless thee, and curse him that curseth thee: and in thee shall all families of the earth be blessed.—GENESIS 12:1–3

Bible students refer to this promise as the *Abrahamic Covenant*. Through it, God made a specific promise to Abraham in three areas: the land, his seed, and a blessing.

God promised to bring Abraham to a land he had never seen and to make of him a great nation. In Deuteronomy 30:1–10 (called the *Palestinian Covenant*), God reconfirmed His promise to give this land to Abraham's seed forever.

In 2 Samuel 7:12–16, God again confirmed this promise through the *Davidic Covenant*. He specifically promised to perpetually bless Abraham's seed through David.

These covenants promise special blessing to Abraham's seed and to other nations who bless Israel. The promised blessing also shows that God chose to bless the entire Gentile world through Abraham and his seed. He promised to bless those who bless Israel and to bless all nations through Israel.

Isaiah 9:6–7 prophesied of One who would fulfill this promise: *"For unto us a child is born, unto us a son is given: and the government shall be upon his shoulder: and his name shall be called Wonderful, Counsellor, The mighty God, The everlasting Father, The Prince of Peace. Of the increase of his government and peace there shall be no end, upon the throne of David, and upon his kingdom, to order it, and to establish it with judgment and with justice from henceforth even for ever. The zeal of the* LORD *of hosts will perform this."*

A parallel passage is Luke 1:31–33: *"And, behold, thou shalt conceive in thy womb, and bring forth a son, and shalt call his name JESUS. He shall be great, and shall be called the Son of the Highest: and the Lord God shall give unto him the throne of his father David: And he shall reign over the house of Jacob for ever; and of his kingdom there shall be no end."*

Jesus, born in Bethlehem's manger, was the child born and the Son given to us. But when Christ first came, the Jews rejected Him. *"He came unto his own, and his own received him not"* (John 1:11). Christ has yet to set up a government upon the throne of David. (We'll see more prophecies about this coming kingdom in chapter 10.)

Some suggest that because the Jews rejected their first opportunity for Christ's kingdom, the promises given to Abraham and David have now been transferred to the church and will be fulfilled symbolically or spiritually. Note, however, some important characteristics of this covenant.

The covenant is unconditional. God's promise to Abraham was not based on Abraham's performance, but on God's faithful immutability. To be sure, there were times that the Israelites were expelled from the land God promised them because of their sin, but ultimately, God has promised the land to Abraham and to his seed.

Even after Abraham committed adultery with Hagar, God repeated His unconditional promise to give Abraham and his seed the land of Palestine (Genesis 17:4–8). And when Israel committed spiritual adultery by worshipping idols, God reassured them of His unconditional covenant (Jeremiah 33:24–26).

The covenant is literal. While some try to attribute only symbolic significance to the Abrahamic Covenant, Abraham clearly understood God's promise to mean exactly what God plainly said.

The literal interpretation of these promises indicates that only when Christ returns to set up the final kingdom will the covenant be fulfilled. Thus, the Jews' rejection of Christ did not dismiss God's unconditional, literal promise. It simply deferred it for a later time.

The covenant is eternal. Psalm 105:8–11 says, *"He hath remembered his covenant for ever, the word which he commanded to a thousand generations. Which covenant he made with Abraham, and his oath unto Isaac; And confirmed the same unto Jacob for a law, and to Israel for an everlasting covenant: Saying, Unto thee will I give the land of Canaan, the lot of your inheritance."* The eternal covenants of God stand unmoved by the rejection of men and unchanged by the passing of time.

God's covenants to Israel are the hinge on which the door of future events swings. To understand these events, one must recognize the covenants as unconditional, literal, and eternal.

THE PROVISION TO ISRAEL

For I will take you from among the heathen, and gather you out of all countries, and will bring you into your own land.
—EZEKIEL 36:24

One of the common points in all future prophecy is the fact that Israel will exist as a nation and will occupy the land that God promised to Abraham years ago. This is significant because, prior to 1948, the Jews had not occupied this land since AD 70.

A mere seventy-five years ago, Christians who studied Bible prophecies involving an organized nation of Israel scratched their heads in confusion; for at that time, there *was* no nation of Israel. The Jews had been long scattered.

The establishment of modern-day Israel was truly a significant event that sets the stage for the ultimate fulfillment of Ezekiel 38. Let's briefly examine the time line leading up to the rebirth of Israel in 1948.

In 64 BC, Rome conquered Israel and assumed military occupancy of her land. In AD 70 the Romans leveled the Hebrew temple and banished the Jews from Palestine. Men, women, and children fled for their lives, and thousands were murdered at the hands of the Roman soldiers. At Masada, the last holdout for the Jews, 960 Jews chose to take their own lives rather than surrender to the Romans.

In the ensuing years, Palestine came under the rule and influence of a succession of many different powers. (See chart.) There was the Byzantine period followed by the early Muslim period. Then the Crusaders began to infiltrate the land.

The Mameluke Empire, a slave-based Muslim militant system, defeated the Crusaders and ruled until they were conquered by the Ottoman Empire. An interesting sidelight of the Ottomans is their attempt to overrule biblical prophecy. Understanding that the Jewish Messiah was expected to come through the Eastern Gate of Jerusalem, they purposefully discouraged the Jews by encasing the Eastern Gate with concrete and defiling the entrance with a graveyard just outside the gate.

For almost 1,900 years, Palestine was occupied by Muslim tribes and Islamic faiths. For God to bring His people back to the land He promised to them, it had to be freed from Muslim control. History shows that World War I accomplished this. At the close of that great war, Palestine was governed by the British under the terms of the British Mandate

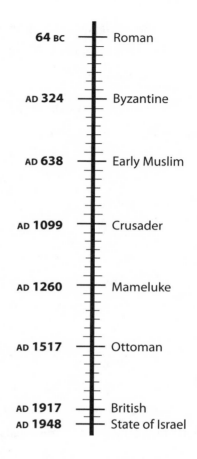

64 BC	Roman
AD 324	Byzantine
AD 638	Early Muslim
AD 1099	Crusader
AD 1260	Mameluke
AD 1517	Ottoman
AD 1917	British
AD 1948	State of Israel

in an effort to provide a home for Jewish people. Following the second World War, the Jews were allowed to organize the modern state of Israel.

This twentieth century miracle bears a powerful testimony to God's faithfulness.

The restoration of the land

Not only did God promise to bring the Jews back to the land of Israel, He also promised to restore the land itself through the efforts of His people. We see this in Ezekiel 36, a unique prophecy directed to the land of Palestine itself.

Also, thou son of man, prophesy unto the mountains of Israel, and say, Ye mountains of Israel, hear the word of the LORD:
—EZEKIEL 36:1

Therefore, ye mountains of Israel, hear the word of the Lord GOD; Thus saith the Lord GOD to the mountains, and to the hills, to the rivers, and to the valleys, to the desolate wastes, and to the cities that are forsaken, which became a prey and derision to the residue of the heathen that are round about;—EZEKIEL 36:4

Prophesy therefore concerning the land of Israel, and say unto the mountains, and to the hills, to the rivers, and to the valleys, Thus saith the Lord GOD; Behold, I have spoken in my jealousy and in my fury, because ye have borne the shame of the heathen:
—EZEKIEL 36:6

God promised Abraham that the land would belong to Abraham's seed. When the Israelites were exiled into Babylonian captivity, God reassured His people of His intent to keep this promise by prophesying that the land would come back to life.

But ye, O mountains of Israel, ye shall shoot forth your branches, and yield your fruit to my people of Israel; for they are at hand to come. For, behold, I am for you, and I will turn unto you, and ye shall be tilled and sown: And I will multiply men upon you, all the house of Israel, even all of it: and the cities shall be inhabited, and the wastes shall be builded: And I will multiply upon you man and beast; and they shall increase and bring fruit: and I will settle you after your old estates, and will do better unto you than at your beginnings: and ye shall know that I am the LORD.
—EZEKIEL 36:8–11

From the first century until 1948, the Jews were scattered across Europe, throughout America, and all around the world. But when the Jews returned to Israel, the land began to blossom. When visiting Israel, you will see fields, vineyards, and orchards flourishing under the hand of diligent cultivation and irrigation. This is just the beginning of God's provision to Israel.

The return of the Jews

The miraculous reunification of thousands of Jews in Israel was prophesied in Ezekiel 36:24: *"For I will take you from among the heathen, and gather you out of all countries, and will bring you into your own land."* In perfect harmony with the events following World War II, God pictures Israel gathering out of other nations and becoming a sovereign state once again.

The saga of how this came to be demonstrates that *history* truly is *His*-story. Six men in particular were instrumental in God's prophecies for the return of the Jews being fulfilled. A brief overview of these men and their role in the Jew's return provides a context for the beginning of this fulfilled prophecy.

Theodor Herzl was a Viennese journalist in the 1880s and 90s who noticed anti-Semitism forming in Europe and felt the solution was to form a Jewish state. In 1897, Herzl formed the First Zionist Congress, an organization birthed to solicit diplomatic support for a Jewish country.

In the early 1900s, Jewish immigrants came into the land. By 1903, ninety thousand acres of land had been purchased, and about ten thousand Jewish settlers had entered Israel. **Edmond James de Rothschild** played a major role in financing this movement.

Lord Balfour, a British foreign secretary, wrote the "Balfour Declaration," a letter to Lord Rothschild that explained the British government's endorsement of the establishment of a Jewish home in Palestine.

Foreign Office
November 2, 1917

Dear Lord Rothschild,

I have much pleasure in conveying to you on behalf of His Majesty's Government, the following declaration of sympathy with Jewish Zionist aspirations which has been submitted to, and approved by, the Cabinet.

His Majesty's Government view with favour the establishment in Palestine of a national home for the Jewish people, and will use their best endeavors to facilitate the achievement of this object, it being clearly understood that nothing shall be done which may prejudice the civil and religious rights of existing non-Jewish communities in Palestine or the rights and political status enjoyed by Jews in any other country.

I should be grateful if you would bring this declaration to the knowledge of the Zionist Federation.

Yours,
Arthur James Balfour[8]

On December 11, 1917, **Sir Edmund Allenby** led the British expeditionary force into Jerusalem and officially ended the control of the Muslim Ottoman Empire.

…His expeditionary force had successfully rolled through Beersheba, Gaza and Jaffa. Now he was about to possess the pearl—Jerusalem. On December 11, 1917 General Allenby, as the official emissary of the British crown strode through

the streets of the Old City in ceremonial gesture marking
the end of Ottoman rule.[9]

In 1945, the world first became aware of the Nazi atrocities performed against the Jews. When people learned that millions of Jews were brutally murdered in a sadist's holocaust, they fervently supported giving the Jews a homeland. America and Great Britain in particular, moved with sympathy for the Jews, pushed for the creation of a Jewish state.

On May 14, 1948, **David Ben-Gurion,** the first prime minister of Israel, rode down Rothschild Boulevard, walked into the Tel Aviv Art Museum, and read the declaration that proclaimed Israel to be a state.

Within minutes of Ben-Gurion's declaration, **Harry Truman,** president of the United States, recognized the state of Israel, and America became Israel's immediate ally. Truman will definitely go down in history as a key player in the establishment of modern-day Israel. According to Clark Clifford in *Counsel to the President,* President Truman's support of Israel was rooted in biblical understanding.

> [Truman] was a student and believer in the Bible from his youth. From his reading of the Old Testament he felt the Jews derived a legitimate historical right to Palestine, and he sometimes cited such biblical lines as Deuteronomy 1:8—"Behold, I have set the land before you: go in and possess the land which the LORD sware unto your fathers, Abraham, Isaac, and Jacob, to give unto them and to their seed after them."[10]

Scripture teaches that God sovereignly oversees the rise and fall of political rulers (Daniel 2:21). Surely it was not an accident that at the precise time in history when a movement to give the Jews their own state had gained momentum, God allowed a man in the White House who was familiar enough with the Old Testament to encourage and support the establishment of a Jewish state.

God used these six men to help shape and lead the effort to restore the land He promised to Abraham's seed. Through their efforts, the Jews once again occupy the Promised Land as a nation.

In Ezekiel 37, God graphically pictures the nation of Israel as dry bones scattered across an open valley. This accurately describes about nineteen centuries of Israel's existence—lifeless, vulnerable, and dispersed. But through a miraculous revitalization, God brought these bones together and gave life to them, raising out of them a great army.

This picture prophesied the return of the Jews to the Promised Land: "...*these bones are the whole house of Israel: behold, they say, Our bones are dried, and our hope is lost: we are cut off for our parts. Therefore prophesy and say unto them, Thus saith the Lord GOD; Behold, O my people, I will open your graves, and cause you to come up out of your graves, and bring you into the land of Israel*" (Ezekiel 37:11–12).

This is exactly what God began in 1948. The land He promised to Abraham is once again His provision for His people.

A PLAN FOR REVIVAL

Behold, the days come, saith the LORD, that I will make a new covenant with the house of Israel, and with the house of Judah: Not according to the covenant that I made with their fathers in the day that I took them by the hand to bring them out of the land of Egypt; which my covenant they brake, although I was an husband unto them, saith the LORD: But this shall be the covenant that I will make with the house of Israel; After those days, saith the LORD, I will put my law in their inward parts, and write it in their hearts; and will be their God, and they shall be my people. And they shall teach no more every man his neighbour, and every man his brother, saying, Know the LORD: for they shall all know me, from the least of them unto the greatest of them, saith the LORD: for I will forgive their iniquity, and I will remember their sin no more.—JEREMIAH 31:31–34

The focus on Israel, from God's perspective, involves far more than the *land* of Palestine; God's primary focus is *people*. The verses above reveal God's heart to bring revival to His people, to see them turn their hearts back toward Him.

Although the land of Israel contains many biblically significant sites, the people of Israel are primarily secular, and many are agnostics or atheists. On my first day in Tel Aviv during a trip in 2009, thousands of Israelis celebrated "gay pride day." How grievous to see this ungodly parade marching down the streets of a city in the Holy Land in defiance of the God who has given them His special blessing!

The orthodox Jews, on the other end of the spectrum, have rejected Christ, their Messiah. Their worship focuses on outer symbolism and conformity to man-made regulations. The secular and the religious Jew alike are in need of repentance and revival.

God has foretold of a coming revival, often referred to in Scripture as the *New Covenant*. This New Covenant will bring complete fulfillment to the Abrahamic and Davidic covenants. It revolves around the coming of Christ, the shedding of His blood, and ultimately, Israel acknowledging Him as their Messiah.

One author wrote, "The return of the people to their land depicted here [the prophecy of Ezekiel 37] is followed by a spiritual transformation of the nation."[11] Indeed, this is the revival God is looking for—not just a return to the land, but a revival of the heart!

When God showed Ezekiel the valley of dry bones, a picture of the condition of Israel, God brought the bones together, but He didn't stop there. He also gave them life (Ezekiel 37:7–9).

As we've seen in this chapter, God has already begun the process of gathering Israel together. But God's complete plan is to restore spiritual life to His people.

Two thousand years ago, Jesus declared to the unbelieving Jews, *"...I am come that they might have life, and that they might have it more abundantly"* (John 10:10). The Jews rejected that life and were soon scattered by the Romans. In the final days of history, however, the Jews will be gathered again to the land of Israel (as is already taking place), and God will bring the revival of the New Covenant.

The timing of the revival

Scripture specifically notes two "calendar points" in reference to the New Covenant revival. First, it had to take place after the sacrifice of Christ. Hebrews 8:12–13 says, *"For I will be merciful to their unrighteousness, and their sins and their iniquities will I remember no more. In that he saith, A new covenant, he hath made the first old. Now that which decayeth and waxeth old is ready to vanish away."* Christ had to come and shed His blood to make the New Covenant possible.

Second, this revival will come at the conclusion of the *"times of the Gentiles"* (Luke 21:24). When Israel rejected Christ, God turned His attention to the Gentiles, urging them to salvation through Christ. But one day, when *"the fulness of the Gentiles be come in"* (Romans 11:25), God will fulfill the New Covenant with His people.

The beginning of the Great Tribulation (see chapter 8) will mark the end of the *"times of the Gentiles."* Scripture indicates that God will use the Tribulation to soften the hearts of His people for this revival (Jeremiah 30:4–9).

Author Tim LaHaye explains, "This time of suffering will finish the transgression of Israel, which is the rejection of her Messiah. During the Tribulation, the people of Israel will turn to Christ in great revival and will become witnesses who will go forth and preach the Gospel around the world…Actually, the Tribulation Period will help cause a great revival in Israel."[12]

As we look at current events, including the return of the Jews to Israel, there is no doubt that God has made the initial preparations to bring about His plan for revival.

The result of revival

Israel is financially and technologically prosperous. But God desires to give them *spiritual* prosperity. Through the New Covenant, God will give Israel a new heart: *"A new heart also will I give you, and a new spirit will I put within you: and I will take away the stony heart out of your flesh, and I will give you an heart of flesh"* (Ezekiel 36:26).

Additionally, God desires to give Israel a renewed relationship. Since God's original promise to Abraham, He has graciously set apart Israel as His own people. Through Israel, God brought Christ into the world and thus used His people to bless all people (Genesis 12:3).

Yet, through the centuries, Israel has spurned God's favor toward her. As God led His people through the wilderness by Moses, they complained and doubted Him. Even after He brought them into the Promised Land, they continually turned their worship to idols and refused to heed God's warnings of judgment. When Christ came, they rejected Him and crucified their promised Saviour. Yet God still desires to renew His relationship with Israel and to claim her once again as His people.

> *…After those days, saith the* LORD, *I will put my law in their inward parts, and write it in their hearts;* ***and will be their God,***

and they shall be my people. *And they shall teach no more every man his neighbour, and every man his brother, saying, Know the* LORD: *for they shall all know me, from the least of them unto the greatest of them, saith the* LORD: *for I will forgive their iniquity, and I will remember their sin no more.*
—JEREMIAH 31:31–34 [emphasis added]

Though Israel has rejected Christ, she is still God's focus. According to biblical prophecy, she will eventually have not only the land of Palestine, but she will have a heart for God as well.

The current global focus on Israel is a reflection of God's focus on His people. He has a plan for Israel, and the changing times around us are being used by God to bring fruition to His purpose.

Meanwhile, all across the Gentile world, people are trusting Christ as their Saviour and establishing an unconditional, literal, and eternal relationship with God through Christ. Our opportunity—and responsibility—during the "times of the Gentiles" is to bring the Gospel to every corner of the globe (Mark 16:15).

Before the Tribulation and the revival in Israel, there is one more event on God's prophetic calendar—the Rapture of His people. Let's learn of this sudden disappearance in the next chapter.

A Sudden Disappearance

The world's largest library is the three-building United States Library of Congress. Inscribed on the wall of the reading room in the Thomas Jefferson Building are the following words: "ONE GOD, ONE LAW, ONE ELEMENT, AND ONE FAR-OFF DIVINE EVENT, TO WHICH THE WHOLE CREATION MOVES."[1]

Millions of Christians through the ages have looked for a "divine event to which the whole creation moves"—the return of Christ. Today, our world is characterized by the very indicators Scripture prophesies will be present in the end times:

- Wars and rumors of wars (Matthew 24:6–7)
- Israel's return to the land (Ezekiel 36–37)
- False prophets (Matthew 24:11)
- Increased transportation and technology (Daniel 12:4)

- Rise in occult practice (1 Timothy 4:1–2)
- Diseases and earthquakes (Luke 21:11)

We know from Scripture that the last days will culminate with a seven-year period of tribulation. While the handwriting on the wall inscribed by the events listed above should be clear to all, many still scoff at such truths. Political strategist and author Kevin Phillips labeled Americans who believe in Bible prophecy as "overimaginative" at best and "radical" at worst. In his book *American Theocracy,* he went so far as to assert that "the Rapture, end-times, and Armageddon hucksters in the United States rank with any Shiite ayatollahs."[2]

How a person interprets current events, however, is determined by the lens through which he views them. Author Joel Rosenberg explained how viewing our world through any lens other than Scripture limits our vision:

> While it is fashionable in our times to analyze world events merely by looking through the lenses of politics and economics, it is also a serious mistake, for it prevents one from being able to see in three dimensions. To truly understand the significance of global events and trends, one must analyze them through a third lens as well—the lens of Scripture. Only then can the full picture become clearer.[3]

For Christians who view these changing times through the lens of Scripture, the unfolding prophecies, as concerning as they may be politically or economically, are actually encouraging rather than discouraging. The development of end times prophecies points our focus upward, *"Looking for that blessed hope, and the glorious appearing of the great God and our Saviour Jesus Christ"* (Titus 2:13).

The hopeful moment to which we look is referred to in Scripture as a catching away—a sudden disappearance. One day all who are saved will be caught away to meet our Lord Jesus Christ and spend eternity with Him. We often call this event "the Rapture."

THE PROMISE OF THE RAPTURE

If the *"blessed hope"* of which Titus 2:13 speaks were based on the promise of a vote-seeking politician, we would have reason to fear. But as it is based on the solid promises of God's written Word, we have a blessed hope indeed.

Let's study the promise of the Rapture as it is given in Scripture.

A frequent promise

The promise of the Rapture is not a vain hope that a few Christians dug out of an obscure portion of Scripture. It is repeated throughout the Bible as a frequent reminder to the child of God.

> More than a fourth of the Bible is predictive prophecy....
> Both the Old and New Testaments are full of promises
> about the return of Jesus Christ. Over 1,800 references
> appear in the Old Testament, and seventeen Old Testament
> books give prominence to this theme. Of the 260 chapters
> in the New Testament, there are more than 300 references to
> the Lord's return—one out of every thirty verses. Twenty-
> three of the twenty-seven New Testament books refer to
> this great event....For every prophecy on the first coming
> of Christ, there are eight on Christ's Second Coming.[4]

The Rapture and the Second Coming (see chapter 9) are topics thoroughly covered in Scripture. The frequency of the promise of Christ's return should tell us that Christ wants us to think of it often and to live in the light of His imminent return.

A sure promise

The Rapture is not simply a prophetic *possibility*; it is an imminent *certainty*. Notice the confident language of the following verses:

> Looking for that blessed hope, and the glorious appearing of the great God and our Saviour Jesus Christ;—TITUS 2:13

> For our conversation is in heaven; from whence also we look for the Saviour, the Lord Jesus Christ:—PHILIPPIANS 3:20

> So Christ was once offered to bear the sins of many; and unto them that look for him shall he appear the second time without sin unto salvation.—HEBREWS 9:28

> And when the chief Shepherd shall appear, ye shall receive a crown of glory that fadeth not away.—1 PETER 5:4

God would not encourage us to look for an event that will not take place. There is not a more sure promise in the Bible than the promise that Jesus Christ will come again for His own.

A securing promise

Having the sure hope of the Rapture gives us security and stability in the midst of change and uncertainty. Jesus' oft-quoted words of comfort to His disciples before His crucifixion includes this securing promise:

> Let not your heart be troubled: ye believe in God, believe also in me. In my Father's house are many mansions: if it were not so, I would have told you. I go to prepare a place for you. And if I go and prepare a place for you, **I will come again,** and receive you unto myself; that where I am, there ye may be also.
> —JOHN 14:1–3 [emphasis added]

With the institution of the Lord's Table, Christ gave the local church an ordinance that would serve as a frequent reminder of His promise to return. Every time we partake of the Lord's Table we *"do shew the Lord's death till he come"* (1 Corinthians 11:26, emphasis added). Thus, the Lord's Table helps us remember both the Lord's death *and* His return. Partaking of the Lord's Table should promote regular spiritual examination for every Christian—it is a reminder to be ready for His return.

A factual promise

In one of the clearest passages on the Rapture, God gives us several facts about this coming event:

> But I would not have you to be ignorant, brethren, concerning them which are asleep, that ye sorrow not, even as others which have no hope. For if we believe that Jesus died and rose again, even so them also which sleep in Jesus will God bring with him. For this we say unto you by the word of the Lord, that we which are alive and remain unto the coming of the Lord shall not prevent them which are asleep. For the Lord himself shall descend from heaven with a shout, with the voice of the archangel, and with the trump of God: and the dead in Christ shall rise first: Then we which are alive and remain shall be caught up together with them in the clouds, to meet the Lord in the air: and so shall we ever be with the Lord. Wherefore comfort one another with these words.—1 THESSALONIANS 4:13–18

This powerful passage shares with us six important facts about the rapture of believers:

1. The Lord will return. As Jesus closed His earthly ministry, He gathered His disciples on the Mount of Olives and in their sight ascended to Heaven. Shortly after Jesus' ascension, an angel promised the disciples

He would one day return: "...*Ye men of Galilee, why stand ye gazing up into heaven? this same Jesus, which is taken up from you into heaven, shall so come in like manner as ye have seen him go into heaven*" (Acts 1:11).

If Jesus will return in like manner as He departed, He will return as 1 Thessalonians 4:16 implies—literally and bodily.

2. We will hear the voice of the archangel and the trump of God. Often on Sunday mornings I hear the brass section of our church orchestra warming up for the service. At those moments I visualize what a glorious day it will be when the trumpet we hear is the trump of God calling His children Home!

3. The dead in Christ will rise. When a Christian dies, his spirit is immediately taken to Heaven. Second Corinthians 5:8 declares "*to be absent from the body, and to be present with the Lord.*" In the Rapture, the soul and spirit of those who have gone before us will be united with their new and glorified bodies.

First Corinthians 15:52 sheds additional light on this part of the Rapture: "*In a moment, in the twinkling of an eye, at the last trump: for the trumpet shall sound, and the dead shall be raised incorruptible, and we shall be changed.*"

4. Christians will be "caught up." Those who are still living on Earth at the time of the Rapture will then join those who rose first. The Latin word for "caught up" is *rapturo,* from which we derive the word *rapture.*

5. We will meet the Lord in the air. This key statement clearly delineates 1 Thessalonians 4 from passages describing the Second Coming. At the Second Coming, the Lord will return to Earth (and we will be with Him). But in this passage describing the Rapture, Paul specifically states that we will meet the Lord "*in the air.*" Jesus is not coming to Earth at the Rapture; He is bringing us up, out of the world.

6. We will ever be with the Lord. We will be instantly in the presence of Jesus, and what an eternity we'll share with Christ!

Some mock the Rapture; some ignore it; others misunderstand it. But those who know the faithfulness of God are listening for His trumpet. They treasure His promise of the Rapture as their blessed hope.

THE HOPE OF THE RAPTURE

In the turmoil of a chaotic world, lasting hope cannot be found in the temporal advancements of economic prosperity or empty promises of political change. This is why Paul, after explaining the details of the Rapture, encourages believers, *"Wherefore comfort one another with these words"* (1 Thessalonians 4:18). For the Christian, the Rapture is a source of comfort and an anchor of hope.

When the trump of God calls believers to meet the Lord in the air, we will leave behind every sorrow, pain, and loss. We will be reunited with our saved loved ones who have gone before us to Heaven, and best of all, we will see Christ face to face.

Additionally, as we near the end times and the Tribulation, the hope of the Rapture is found in its timing, for the Rapture delivers believers from the agonies of the Tribulation.

To better understand the timing of the Rapture, let's revisit the chart we saw in chapter 1.

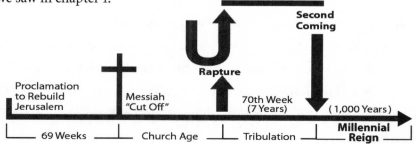

The cross on the left of the chart marks the first coming of Christ: He was conceived in Mary's womb, born in Bethlehem, laid in the manger, crucified on the rugged Cross, and raised triumphant over sin and death.

While Christ was on Earth, He established the church (Matthew 16:18), and we are currently living in the period designated on the chart as the "church age." We do not know how long this period will last, but until Christ returns, we are responsible to give the Gospel of Christ to every person (Mark 16:15).

Christians in the first century actually hoped that Christ would return in their lifetimes and were looking for His coming. When Christ did not immediately return, some suggested (as some do today) that maybe He wouldn't return at all. Peter, however, explained the reason for His delay: *"The Lord is not slack concerning his promise, as some men count slackness; but is longsuffering to us-ward, not willing that any should perish, but that all should come to repentance"* (2 Peter 3:9). In God's graciousness, He is giving men greater opportunity to hear and believe the Gospel before He returns.

At the end of the church age, the chart shifts into two levels—representing the simultaneously occurring events of both Heaven and Earth.

The arrow that represents the Rapture leads us to the upper level of the chart. This is when the trump of God sounds, and all who have trusted Christ as Saviour will meet the Lord in the air. We will then spend at least the next seven years in Heaven with the Lord.

Moving back down to the portion of the chart depicting events on the Earth, following the Rapture, the world enters the seven-year Tribulation. Our study of the horrors of the Tribulation in chapter 8 will show more fully why the knowledge that Christians will not be part of the Tribulation makes the Rapture a blessed hope.

The Tribulation will end with the Second Coming of Christ. We will return with Christ to the Earth, and He will reign as King for the Millennium.

Imminent hope

The Rapture could occur at any moment—literally. It is possible that many of the prophecies that relate to the reign of the Antichrist during the Tribulation (such as the forming of a one-world government and the use of a global currency) could be set in motion prior to the Rapture. But the prophetic calendar given in Scripture does not necessitate any further event to take place before the Rapture. We should be looking for Christ to come for us at any moment.

Following are five reasons I believe Scripture teaches that the Rapture is an imminent hope.

BECAUSE THE CHURCH IS NOT APPOINTED TO WRATH

The Tribulation will be a time of God pouring His wrath on the wickedness of this world, but God promises that He will shield us from that wrath. *"For God hath not appointed us to wrath, but to obtain salvation by our Lord Jesus Christ"* (1 Thessalonians 5:9). *"And to wait for his Son from heaven, whom he raised from the dead, even Jesus, which delivered us from the wrath to come"* (1 Thessalonians 1:10).

BECAUSE THE CHURCH IS ABSENT IN REVELATION 4–18

The first three chapters of Revelation are directed to the Apostle John and the seven churches in Asia Minor. At the beginning of Revelation 4, John hears a trumpet and is called up into Heaven.

Revelation 4–18 focuses on the judgments on Earth during the Tribulation. The church is not mentioned in these chapters except where she is seen in the few brief glimpses in Heaven.

BECAUSE IT IS PROMISED

Before beginning the description of the Tribulation in Revelation, Christ promised the church in Philadelphia, *"Because thou hast kept the word of my patience, I also will keep thee from the hour of temptation, which shall come upon all the world, to try them that dwell upon the earth. Behold, I come quickly..."* (Revelation 3:10–11).

This verse is not saying that the Lord will keep them *during* the "hour of temptation" (the Tribulation), but *from* the temptation. Thus, Revelation 3:10 promises that the saints will be delivered from the Tribulation, pointing to a pre-tribulation Rapture.

The promise, *"Behold I come quickly,"* affirms the imminence of the Rapture.

BECAUSE OF THE ORDER OF SCRIPTURE

After Paul describes the Rapture in 1 Thessalonians 4, he deals with the "day of the Lord," the Tribulation, in the following chapter. This again indicates the Rapture coming before the Tribulation.

BECAUSE OLD TESTAMENT PROPHECY DOES NOT INCLUDE EVENTS RELATED TO THE CHURCH—IT WAS NOT SEEN BY THE PROPHETS

Old Testament prophets heralded future events with precise detail. As we have already seen in previous chapters, they prophesied the rise and fall of world empires, the birth of Christ, and many end-time events. Daniel described the Tribulation in Daniel 9 as the last week of the seventy-week prophecy. In future chapters, we'll see Old Testament prophecies of the Second Coming of Christ and the final kingdom.

Old Testament prophets, however, were silent concerning the church, because this part of God's plan was not revealed until the time of Christ. These prophets were silent also concerning the Rapture, indicating that the Rapture relates to the church. It is God's deliverance to spare her from the Tribulation, which will be used by God to turn the hearts of the Jewish people toward Christ—their Messiah.

(Here is another way of looking at the Old Testament silence regarding the church: Have you ever approached a mountain range from a great distance? From far off, it may appear that you are looking at one peak, and it isn't until you get closer that you realize there is more than one mountain peak. And upon arriving at one peak, you see that further peaks are separated by valleys. As the Old Testament prophets looked to the coming of Messiah and the establishment of His kingdom, they saw them as one future event closely connected. But with the unfolding of God's plan, journeying through time and looking back, we now see them as separate peaks with the church age in between.)

The imminency of the Rapture makes this a hopeful event for those who love their Lord and are watching for His coming.

Inspirational hope

There is nothing like the hope of the Rapture to encourage the heart of the believer. Songs about the Rapture have cheered thousands of hearts to look for this blessed event. "When We See Christ," "What a Day that Will Be," "When the Roll Is Called up Yonder," "We Shall Behold Him," "The Midnight Cry," and "Coming Again" are just a few of these songs of celebration.

One reason for this inspiration is that not every believer will face death. The Christians who are alive when Christ returns will never have to walk through the valley of the shadow of death; they will be caught up to meet the Lord in the air. First Corinthians 15:51 teaches, *"Behold, I shew you a mystery; We shall not all sleep, but we shall all be changed."* Not everyone will die before the Rapture, but all Christians will be changed.

First Corinthians 15:52–53 promises that at the time of the Rapture we will receive glorified bodies: *"In a moment, in the twinkling of an eye, at the last trump: for the trumpet shall sound, and the dead shall be raised incorruptible, and we shall be changed. For this corruptible must put on incorruption, and this mortal must put on immortality."*

Although we are living in corruptible bodies today, when we see Jesus we will receive bodies that will never grow weary, feeble, ill, or old—glorified bodies. Those of us who are feeling our bodies age find this an especially inspirational hope!

But, most significantly, the Rapture is inspirational because we will see Christ. The greatest joy of eternity will be spending it in the presence of Jesus Christ. When we see Christ face to face, we will be completely changed into His image. First John 3:2 says, *"Beloved, now are we the sons of God, and it doth not yet appear what we shall be: but we know that, when he shall appear, we shall be like him; for we shall see him as he is."*

What could be a more blessed hope for the child of God than Christ's imminent coming for His own? Scripture is replete with promises of this glorious event.

THE PREPARATION FOR THE RAPTURE

The certain promise of the Rapture should cause Christians to prepare for this event. Even as a traveler's time, en route *and* at his destination, is made more enjoyable by thorough preparation, the Rapture—a quick trip, taking place in the twinkling of an eye—deserves preparation.

Obviously, the starting point in preparation is to trust Christ as your Saviour. The Rapture only becomes a blessed hope when you believe the Gospel and are certain that you will be part of this quick trip to Heaven. (This matter is covered thoroughly in chapter 7.)

The trump of God will call those who belong to Christ; all others will be left behind to face the Tribulation. Those individuals left behind who have had opportunity to receive Christ but have chosen to reject Him will be under a strong delusion, and many will never choose to trust Him (2 Thessalonians 2:10–12). This is one reason why Scripture admonishes, "...*behold, now is the day of salvation*" (2 Corinthians 6:2).

If we were to hold a magnet over objects of different materials—say glass, clay, and metal—the magnet would only draw to itself the objects that are made of the same material. In the same way, when Christ returns, He will only call up those who are like Him—those who have the Holy Spirit within them.

For those who have already trusted Christ, preparation for the Rapture involves purification—living in such a way that we will be pleased to meet Christ.

In our dormitories at West Coast Baptist College, we conduct periodic "white glove inspections." The ladies' dorms may not be too affected by this inspection, but for the men, major transformation takes place in preparation. They wash the socks that have been leaning against the wall for the past week and throw away the moldy five-day-old food they saved.

When the dean of students inspects the dorms, the men who have prepared for his arrival are glad to see him, but those who have ignored the warnings of his coming wish they had prepared.

When Christ returns to call us Home, no Christian will want his life cluttered with the "dirty socks" of disobedience or disgraced with the "moldy leftovers" of worldliness. Speaking of the Rapture, John wrote, "*And every man that hath this hope in him purifieth himself, even as he is pure*" (1 John 3:3). Prepare for the Rapture by cleansing your life for Christ.

In chapter 11, we'll dig deeper into these preparations as we examine practical applications of all we have learned concerning biblical prophecy.

For now, however, determine that you will not be ashamed when Christ returns; prepare for His coming.

Any day now, the Lord will return. We do not know the date, but we do know that the God who cannot lie will keep His promise (Titus 1:2; 2 Peter 3:8–10). This sudden disappearance of those who belong to Christ is the blessed hope of all who will have a part in it.

Meanwhile, world events continue to set the stage for Christ's Second Coming. In the next chapter, we'll see how the hot-button word of our day—*terrorism*—relates to Israel and the end times.

CHAPTER FIVE

A World in Terror

September 11, 2001, is a pivotal point in the United States' perception of terrorism. Horrendous scenes of carnage and suffering flashed across millions of television and computer screens and burned indelible pictures in the minds and hearts of Americans as hijacked planes crashed into the Twin Towers of the World Trade Center. The sinister word (terrorism) that had previously been used to describe turmoil in parts of the world far removed from home, instantly became personal to Americans.

The military retribution and heightened homeland security directly following the terrorist attacks of 9/11 became a continual reminder to Americans of this formidable and persistent enemy.

Terrorism is a daily reality in the Middle East. The citizens of Israel live under the constant threat of terror and war, and the news from Israel contains regular reports of terrorist concerns and occurrences.

The peaking development of anti-Semitic sentiment from nations such as Russia, Iran, and Libya is especially noteworthy to our study on Bible prophecy, as these nations are among those that Ezekiel prophesied about twenty-six hundred years ago. Ezekiel 38–39 foretells how these countries will align against Israel in the last days.

As we saw in chapter 3, much of the Arab-Israeli controversy concerns the land of Palestine, particularly the West Bank and Gaza Strip. Considering the strong hatred between Arabs and Israelis, asking Israel to give up land in exchange for peace seems unrealistic and naïve. Author Joel Rosenberg points out this difficulty.

> What's more, I should note here that while I strongly support giving the Palestinians autonomy to govern themselves without interference from Israel in return for true peace and stability in the lands run by the Palestinians, I personally oppose the notion of the State of Israel giving away the ancient lands of Judea and Samaria in order to create a sovereign Palestinian state that could become a base camp for anti-Israel and anti-Western terrorism and that could form alliances with radical Islamic regimes such as Iran.[1]

While some of the terror in the Middle East stems from the land issue, much of it is simply the nature of Islamic extremism.[2] The hatred that radical Muslims harbor toward Israel and toward the United States is

---

[2] In this book, and particularly in this chapter, where I point out the danger to Israel and other nations through Islamic terrorism, I recognize an important distinction between the religion of Islam (which denies the deity of Jesus Christ and many doctrines of the Christian faith) and a Muslim person (who needs to hear the Gospel of Jesus Christ). Jesus loves and died for all people, and He teaches us to love all people. I rejoice in reports of Muslims trusting Christ here in the United States and in Islamic countries around the world. I look forward to the day when I stand with people out of every "kindred, and tongue, and people, and nation" and together we sing praises to Christ who redeemed us all by His blood (Revelation 5:9).

vocalized in their names for these two countries—"Little Satan" and "Big Satan" respectively. Make no mistake about it, the extremist enemies of Israel don't intend to share land. By their own admission, their intent is to destroy Israel. (It is important to note, as Christians, we are commanded to love Muslim people and to do our best to share the Gospel and pray that they will open their hearts to Christ.)

While it is evident that the majority of Muslims are peaceful, terrorists are nonetheless recruiting for their cause. Studies indicate that between 10 to 15 percent of Muslim people approve of terrorism. Approximately forty million Muslim young people attend madrasahs—Islamic schools, many of which promote hatred for the Jews.[3] A Muslim cleric in Gaza gave us a glimpse into the Islamic mindset when he said in the mosque, "Israel is a cancer, the Jews are a virus resembling AIDS."[4]

We hear daily about Islamic extremists terror groups. Hamas, in particular, is active in its attempts to further its agenda. Formed in 1987 as an offshoot of the Egyptian Muslim Brotherhood, Hamas desires not only an Islamic state in Egypt, but in other areas as well—including Palestine.

In *The Late Great State of Israel*, Aaron Klein reported on a study published just after Israel retreated from Gaza: "It explained that Hamas would next focus on controlling the West Bank, from which, it stated, Hamas would then fire rockets into Israel and carry out guerrilla operations against nearby Jewish towns."[5]

Much of the terror of Hamas, as well as other groups, is sponsored by Iran. The Iranian president, Ahmadinejad, is a radical Muslim who hates the Jews and desires to see Israel destroyed. His radical mindset is so twisted and bent against Israel that he publicly questioned the historic validity of the Holocaust.

> As recently as last Friday, Ahmadinejad questioned whether
> the Holocaust was "a real event" and said it was used by

Jews to trick the West into backing the creation of Israel. In a speech in Tehran, he said the Jewish state was created out of "a lie and a mythical claim."[6]

It took Hitler years to slaughter millions of Jews. Ahmadinejad would like to do the same in minutes with nuclear warfare. Perhaps this is why Senator John McCain warned, "There's only one thing worse than using the option of military action, and that is the Iranians acquiring nuclear weapons. If Iran gets the bomb, I think we could have Armageddon."[7]

We will see later in this chapter that God's Word prophesies that Iran will be part of the mounting forces against Israel in the last days.

President Ronald Reagan's biographer, Edmund Morris, tells us that Ezekiel was President Reagan's favorite book of the Bible. According to Mr. Morris, the president sometimes quoted from Ezekiel in cabinet meetings as he discussed foreign policy.[8]

Ezekiel 38–39 points ahead to where today's hatred and terrorism will escalate and climax as Israel's foes declare war.

THE DECLARATION OF A BATTLE

And the word of the LORD came unto me, saying, Son of man, set thy face against Gog, the land of Magog, the chief prince of Meshech and Tubal, and prophesy against him, And say, Thus saith the Lord GOD; Behold, I am against thee, O Gog, the chief prince of Meshech and Tubal: And I will turn thee back, and put hooks into thy jaws, and I will bring thee forth, and all thine army, horses and horsemen, all of them clothed with all sorts of armour, even a great company with bucklers and shields, all of them handling swords: Persia, Ethiopia, and Libya with them; all of them with shield and helmet:—EZEKIEL 38:1–5

In this passage, God instructs Ezekiel to prophesy of a future battle—a battle that current events and political relationships suggest is perhaps drawing near.

The timing of the battle

Ezekiel indicates two necessary factors for this battle to take place.

The sequence of the chapters in Ezekiel indicates that **Israel will be in her own land.** In Ezekiel 36, just two chapters before the prophecy of this battle, God promised, *"And I will multiply men upon you, all the house of Israel, even all of it: and the cities shall be inhabited, and the wastes shall be builded...For I will take you from among the heathen, and gather you out of all countries, and will bring you into your own land"* (Ezekiel 36:10, 24).

Ezekiel's war is described as occurring relatively soon after the rebirth of Israel, after the ingathering of the Jewish people from around the world. As we saw in chapter 3, the first part of this prophecy began to be fulfilled in 1948 when Israel was established as a modern state.

Notice that at the time of this battle, **Israel will be assuming peace.** In contrast to the necessarily tense, ever-ready, and thoroughly prepared posture of Israel today, she will be caught off guard by this battle.

In Ezekiel 38, God prophesies to Israel's enemy nations of their sudden attack during Israel's perceived safety: *"...thou shalt come into the land that is brought back from the sword, and is gathered out of many people, against the mountains of Israel, which have been always waste: but it is brought forth out of the nations, and they shall dwell safely all of them. Thou shalt ascend and come like a storm..."* (Ezekiel 38:8–9).

In Bible days, Israel's cities were walled as a measure of protection from outside attacks. But when this battle takes place, the enemy nations will *"go up to the land of unwalled villages...to them that are at rest, that dwell safely, all of them dwelling without walls, and having neither bars nor gates, To take a spoil, and to take a prey..."* (Ezekiel 38:11–12). Twenty-six hundred years ago, God prophesied that modern Israel would not rely on walls for her protection. The text further depicts an Israel who is at rest, dwelling safely; this is not a picture of Israel today.

For purposes of self-protection and self-preservation, Israel today is in a constant state of alert. The hatred of surrounding Arab nations and the nuclear efforts of Iran, in particular, demand her military preparedness, as the following article describes:

> Dan Gillerman, former Israeli ambassador to the United Nations, told FOX News Friday that Israel is prepared to take military action if sanctions don't work—and suggested that it was prepared to act alone.
>
> "Israel is always close to a strike, because Israel cannot afford to be asleep," Gillerman said. "Taking words from your president, yes we can. And if absolutely necessary, and if all other options are exhausted, yes we will. Israel cannot live with a nuclear Iran."[9]

Considering the current state of military tension, the question arises: what will cause Israel to feel secure and not be at a state of heightened alert?

Perhaps Israel's enemies will launch this surprise attack just after the first half of the Tribulation, which Daniel 9 describes as a time of diplomatic peace, created by the Antichrist: *"And he shall confirm the covenant with many for one week: and in the midst of the week he shall cause the sacrifice and the oblation to cease, and for the overspreading of abominations he shall make it desolate, even until the consummation, and that determined shall be poured upon the desolate"* (Daniel 9:27).

The "week" referred to in this verse is the last of seventy "weeks" in Daniel's prophecy. Just as *dozen* means "a set of twelve," *week* means "a set of seven." In common vernacular, *week* refers to a set of seven *days*, but in prophetic language, *week* refers to a set of seven *years*.[10]

As described in Daniel 9:27, at the beginning of this final seven-year period (the Tribulation), the Antichrist will *"confirm the covenant with many for one week."* This covenant is understood as a peace treaty with Israel. Most scholars think this confirmation of the covenant will, at least temporarily, resolve the Middle East issue and begin a period of peace, allowing the Jews to build their temple and appeasing their neighbors.

Assured of global peace, Israel will celebrate by relaxing her security.

Then, in the middle of the Tribulation, *"in the midst of the week,"* the Antichrist will unleash his anti-Semitism in a vicious attack on Israel. He will pollute and halt the revived sacrificial system of Israel and desolate her land. Jesus spoke of this devastation in Matthew 24, *"When ye therefore shall see the abomination of desolation, spoken of by Daniel the prophet, stand in the holy place, (whoso readeth, let him understand:)… For then* [during the last half of the Tribulation] *shall be great tribulation, such as was not since the beginning of the world to this time, no, nor ever shall be"* (Matthew 24:15, 21).

The preliminary blueprints for this battle are already in place— Israel is in her own land. The scene of the battle, however, will not be staged until the yet-evasive peace treaty between Israel and her enemies has been signed. Only after Israel is enjoying a season of peace can her enemies successfully maneuver this brutal attack, at the mid-point of the Tribulation.

The instigators of the battle

Ezekiel's prophecy begins with a list of names, detailing which countries will align themselves against Israel. In the first six verses, he mentions Gog, Magog, Meshech, Tubal, Togarmah, Persia, Ethiopia, and Libya.

Some of these ancient names are unfamiliar to us today. To what regions do these names refer?

RUSSIA

A well-known prophecy teacher John F. Walvoord identifies the land of Magog as the nations that comprised the former Soviet Union.

> Magog is best identified with the Scythians....The ancient historian Josephus makes that identification and we have no reason to question it. The Scythians apparently lived immediately to the north of...Israel, then some of them emigrated north, going all the way to the Asiatic Circle. Interestingly, Herodotus records that these Scythians were of Indo-Aryan heritage and spoke an Iranian language related to Persian. Using these clues, we can identify Magog today as being made up of nations that were formerly parts of the Soviet Union: Kazakhstan, Kyrgyzstan, Uzbekistan, Turkmenistan, Tajikistan, Azerbaijan, Georgia, and possibly Afghanistan.[11]

Neighboring these countries is the ancient country of Rosh—modern Russia. From the text, it appears that Gog was a prince over the area of Magog, currently Russia and the former Soviet Union.

But what of Meshech and Tubal? Genesis 10:2 lists Tubal and Meshech as Japheth's fifth and sixth sons. (Japheth was Noah's son, from whom descended the Caucasian people groups, including those from the nations named previously.) The Russian cities of Moscow and Tobolsk may actually derive their names from Meshech and Tubal. (Some people believe that these names instead refer to modern day Turkey. This is possible as well.)

Continuing the description of this great federation of countries to the north, verse 6 names "...*the house of Togarmah of the north quarters, and all his bands....*" Togarmah was the grandson of Japheth (Genesis 10:3). Modern research has traced Togarmah to the region of

Armenia and Turkey. The *Imperial Dictionary* identifies Togarmah with the Turkomans who have historically joined the Turks (i.e., Gog).[12]

The *"north quarters"* of this anti-Israel federation would be the regions north of Israel, including Syria, Armenia, Turkey, Greece, and Russia. When these countries see Israel's relaxed posture following the Antichrist's peace treaty, they will form a league of nations and join Russia in an attack against Israel.

Therefore, son of man, prophesy and say unto Gog, Thus saith the Lord GOD; In that day when my people of Israel dwelleth safely, shalt thou not know it? And thou shalt come from thy place out of the north parts, thou, and many people with thee, all of them riding upon horses, a great company, and a mighty army:
—EZEKIEL 38:14–15

In previous years, Russia rose and then fell as a world power. Recently, however, she has re-emerged onto the world stage. Current news reports reveal that Russia is strengthening her military muscles and resurfacing as a world power.

But Russia is not strengthening herself alone. She is providing military aid to other countries, such as Venezuela, Syria, and Iran. It appears that Russia is already building the international relationships that will aid her end-times attack on Israel.

According to informed security sources, Syria struck a deal with Russia that allows Moscow to station submarines and warships off Tartus and Latakia. In exchange, Russia agreed to supply Syria with weaponry at bargain prices, including an advanced missile defense system as well as aircraft and anti-tank and anti-aircraft missiles.[13]

In particular, Russia's support of Iran's nuclear development suggests that she is a staunch ally of Iran. Russia's prime minister, Vladimir Putin, a former high-ranking official with the KGB before the collapse of the Soviet Union, defended Iran's nuclear program as "purely peaceful."

Putin: Russia Will Not Support Force, Sanctions on Iran

Vladimir Putin's spokesman says the Russian prime minister has warned against the use of force or new sanctions against Iran over its nuclear program.

Peskov quoted Putin as saying, Russia has no reason to doubt that Iran's nuclear program is purely peaceful.[14]

Recently Vladimir Putin said in a letter to Ahmadinejad released by the Kremlin, adding that the development of Russian-Iranian nuclear ties "contributes to global peace and stability."[15]

In September 2009, Israel's prime minister, Benjamin Netanyahu, made a mysterious visit to Moscow to discuss negotiations that were of great concern to Israel. The *Jerusalem Post* reported speculations concerning this visit.

Netanyahu Mystery Trip Sets off Flap in Israel

JERUSALEM—Benjamin Netanyahu dropped out of sight for most of a day this week, a mysterious absence that has set off feverish speculation about what the Israeli leader was up to—and accusations he lied to cover up a clandestine trip to Moscow.

After initially issuing a vague statement about visiting a top-secret Mossad installation inside Israel, Netanyahu kept silent Thursday as reports emerged that he flew to Moscow aboard a private jet for urgent talks on Iran.

According to various accounts, the Israeli prime minister was either pushing the Russians to halt arms sales to Iran, or warning of an impending strike against Iranian nuclear facilities or discussing the recent disappearance of a Russian-crewed freighter.

Israel considers Iran its greatest threat, citing Tehran's support for Arab militants, President Mahmoud Ahmadinejad's threatening language about the Jewish state and Iran's nuclear program. Israel, like the U.S. and much of the international community, believes Iran's program is aimed at developing a nuclear bomb. Iran denies this.

Russia, which wields veto power in the U.N. Security Council and has close ties with Iran, could play a crucial role in the debate later this month over imposing additional sanctions on Iran.

The Haaretz daily said **Netanyahu discussed Russian arms deals with Iran and Syria, and that Israel presented evidence that Russian arms were making their way to Iranian-backed Hezbollah guerrillas in Lebanon.** In another report, the paper said the talks were also focused on sophisticated anti-aircraft missiles that Russia has agreed to sell to Iran. The delivery of the S-300 missiles would make it much more difficult for Israel to carry out an attack on Iran.[16] [emphasis added]

Russia is lusting for power and dominance in the world once again. Many of her allies are countries who hate Israel and the United States.

It's not surprising, then, to learn the modern identity of another country Ezekiel names in this prophecy.

IRAN AND ALLIES

The Old Testament speaks of Persia no less than twenty-five times, including Ezekiel 38. In 1932, Persia changed her name to Iran.

Iran today is an Islamic republic under the rule of supreme religious ruler Ayatollah Ali Khamenei with Mahmoud Ahmadinejad as the president. Under the leadership of these men, Iran is a radical Islamic state that wants to see Israel decimated.

> In October 2005, President Ahmadinejad spoke at a Conference called World Without Zionism. He said, "Israel must be wiped off the map."[17]

Contrary to the claims of some, such as Russia, that Iran's nuclear program is peaceful, statements like the one above indicate the opposite is true.

Iran has backed statements such as these with her contributions to terrorism, as the following article reveals.

> The "commander," who withheld his name since he was a target of Israeli forces, told the *Sunday Times* that Hamas had been sending fighters to Iran for training in field tactics and weapons technology. He said some Hamas members travel to Syria for more basic training.[18]

> Military officials said they were surprised by the scale of the Hezbollah bunkers, in which Israeli troops reportedly found war rooms stocked with advanced eavesdropping and surveillance equipment, much of it labeled, "Made in Iran."[19]

Dr. David Jeremiah noted that Iran trains the Hamas terrorists and controls Hezbollah (located in Lebanon, to the north of Israel).

Iran's militant influence extends beyond her own borders. In March 2008, Hezbollah chief Hassan Nasrallah railed, "The presence of Israel is but temporary and cannot go on in the region. We will see you killed in the fields, we will kill you in the cities, we will fight you like you have never seen before."[20]

The terrorist activity Iran supports makes the Iranian nuclear ambitions all the more dangerous. As Aaron Klein wrote in *The Late Great State of Israel,* "Its nuclear program, on the brink of weaponization, is clearly intended for hostile purposes."

The growing relationship between Russia and Iran (ancient Magog and Persia) combined with Iran's hatred for Israel puts her in the perfect position to fulfill Ezekiel's prophecy.

But Iran will not be the only country in alliance with Russia. Ezekiel 38 lists a coalition of additional nations: *"Persia, Ethiopia, and Libya with them; all of them with shield and helmet: Gomer, and all his bands..."* (Ezekiel 38:5–6).

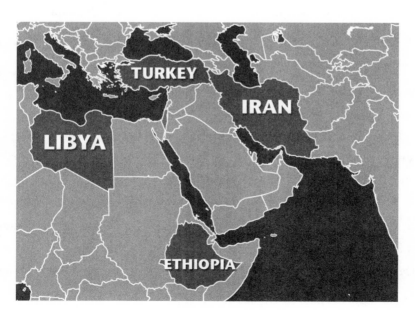

After Persia (Iran), the next country Ezekiel lists is **Ethiopia.** This African nation supported Iraq in the Gulf War and harbors much anti-Semitism.

Libya, an enemy of Israel and the Western world, will also join this alliance. Libya's president, Moammar Gadhafi, already sides with Russia.

> In Libya, President Gadhafi and Putin agreed that the United Nations "needs to be reformed in order to face an 'imbalance of forces' internationally," and especially "the Security Council with which we can work together to resolve problems."[21]

In September 2009, Gadhafi was allotted fifteen minutes to speak to the United Nations world body. In his ninety-five minute speech (during which the United States delegation walked out), he attacked the United States' global role and the Security Council.

> In his first U.N. appearance, Libyan leader Moammar Gadhafi issued a slashing attack on the Security Council and chastised the world body on Wednesday for failing to intervene or prevent some 65 wars since the U.N. was founded in 1945.[22]

It's not difficult to see Libya in the coalition against Israel.

Ezekiel also mentions "Gomer," which many believe to be the modern country of **Germany;** others suggest **Turkey.** Either way, Gomer refers to a northern power that will join forces with those previously mentioned to attack Israel.

Even today, we see the emergence of prophetic alliances. It is not hard to imagine the military aggression that will take place through this coalition. And don't lose sight of the most amazing aspect of what we're studying—God's Word clearly prophesied these alliances thousands of years ago.

Dr. Jeremiah summarized this well when he wrote, "Thus we find that Ezekiel's ancient prophecy, written some twenty-six hundred years ago, informs us as to what is going on in the world today right before our very eyes."[23]

THE MOTIVATION FOR THE BATTLE

And I will turn thee back, and put hooks into thy jaws, and I will bring thee forth, and all thine army, horses and horsemen, all of them clothed with all sorts of armour, even a great company with bucklers and shields, all of them handling swords:
—EZEKIEL 38:4

Much of Bible prophecy relates to God's plan to turn Israel's attention and worship back to Himself. In so doing, His larger purpose is to reveal Himself to the whole world through His dealings with Israel. It is for this ultimate purpose that He chose a people in the first place. He does nothing without purpose, and even the battle of which we read, He will sovereignly use to advance His larger plans for Israel and the world.

In Ezekiel 38, God declares *"I will…put hooks into thy jaws, and I will bring thee forth…."* What are the "hooks in the jaws" that will bring Russia, Iran, and their allies into war with Israel? What, humanly speaking, motivates them to stage this battle?

A lust for power

I heard of a little boy in Sunday school who got confused on the name of the last book of the Bible. He said that the Bible begins with Genesis and ends in *revolution*. He meant *Revelation*, but his statement was right on in describing the end times. There will be intense revolution and war during the Tribulation as world leaders attempt to satisfy their lust for power.

*Thus saith the Lord GOD; It shall also come to pass, that at the
same time shall things come into thy mind, and thou shalt think
an evil thought:*—EZEKIEL 38:10

Ezekiel prophesies that there will be an evil scheme in the heart of
those who come against Israel. They have an agenda behind their actions.

Putin opened a glimpse into his agenda when he said, "We are driving
to create a fairer world based on the principles of equality....Time has
shown our views find support in Arab and other Muslim states."[24]

Russia is finding alliances in the Muslim world to help them balance
the powers against America and give them greater power. This sort
of agenda can only bring a Cold War era mentality back to Russia and
suppress the freedoms of her people.

A *desire for resources*

Aggressive nations know that to the victor belongs the spoils! Ezekiel points
out the desire for personal gain, or spoil, as a motivation for this attack.

*To take a spoil, and to take a prey; to turn thine hand upon the
desolate places that are now inhabited, and upon the people that
are gathered out of the nations, which have gotten cattle and goods,
that dwell in the midst of the land. Sheba, and Dedan, and the
merchants of Tarshish, with all the young lions thereof, shall say
unto thee, Art thou come to take a spoil? hast thou gathered thy
company to take a prey? to carry away silver and gold, to take
away cattle and goods, to take a great spoil?*—EZEKIEL 38:12–13

No doubt some of the desired resources will be the land itself. In
fact, this may be the prime motivation for the Muslim countries involved.
There are many who want that land back. Ever since the secretive Oslo
Accords in 1993, the big message from the West and the European Union
to Israel has been, "Land for peace! Land for peace!"

Former President Jimmy Carter's recent efforts to bring peace in the Middle East carry this tune, as author Aaron Klein describes:

> In the end, Carter's truce boiled down to Israel withdrawing to indefensible borders and accepting millions of Arabs who would destroy Israel from within, all in exchange for a promise by Hamas to refrain from terrorist attacks for a period of ten years.[25]

It seems, however, that Israel struggles with giving land for peace because in the past, every time she has given land, it has not brought peace. These broken promises are easily explained when one considers they are made by terrorists and radical Muslim states.

In reality, Israel's enemies do not want land for peace; they simply want land. Author Joel Rosenberg gives us an insight into the Muslim's quest for the land of Israel.

> If you ever visit Saddam Hussein's main palace in Baghdad, be sure to visit Saddam's throne room and look up, for there you will see a large dome. Painted on this dome are images of the Dome of the Rock on the Temple Mount in Jerusalem. Beside these are paintings of horses attacking Jerusalem. Painted on the walls are Scud missiles pointed at Jerusalem. And at the center of it all is an image of Saddam himself, riding a white horse into the Holy City.[26]

Obviously, Hussein will never lead a triumphant procession into Jerusalem, but the past intentions of this Muslim ruler are revealed through that mural.

The land of Israel also has rich natural resources. One important recently discovered resource is oil.

> An Israeli company has discovered a small amount of oil at a drilling site near the Dead Sea, raising hopes

that Israel could one day join its regional neighbors as a petroleum producer.[27]

More than 200 discoveries [of oil] have been reported so far this year in dozens of countries, including northern Iraq's Kurdish region, Australia, Israel, Iran, Brazil, Norway, Ghana and Russia.[28]

At this point, the size and supply of Israel's oil can only be speculative, but with or without oil, Israel is a producer. Her gross domestic product is currently double that of any other Middle Eastern country, and her agriculture and technological sector are developing and expanding rapidly.

Truly, Israel has "spoil" to envy. The hooks of hatred, power, and greed will easily draw her enemies to a battle she isn't expecting—and a result that will surprise them as well.

THE EXALTATION OF THE LORD

God will be glorified through this battle—even though Israel will be greatly outnumbered. The mounting anti-Semitism of today will escalate in a battle providing a platform for a real time display of God's glory.

Consider the odds stacked against Israel. This relatively small nation will be forced into battle against the world powers of the Tribulation period.

We've seen that Russia and Iran will form an alliance against Israel. Already the European Union is pressuring Israel, and they have stated that if Israel is not willing to concede land for a two-state solution, their attitude will be even less friendly. An *Associated Press* article in the *Jerusalem Post* reported, "The way the EU will relate to an Israeli government that is not for a two state solution will be very different."[29]

United States diplomats and policy makers are also adjusting the previous stance of the U.S. toward Israel. Chief of Staff Rahm Emanuel's mission is to achieve a Palestinian state. *Newsweek* magazine reported the disappointment Israel feels toward negotiations with Emanuel.

> Rahm has such a nuanced understanding of Israeli politics.... The Hebrew-speaking Emanuel, as much as anyone on the American side, will know if the Israeli prime minister is bluffing about his "red line" on Iran, or what he can really do about halting settlements in the West Bank.
>
> ...But some in the Jewish community have been disappointed. Even his own rabbi, Asher Lopatin, has doubts about his absent congregant. "There is a lot of disappointment," says Lopatin, who presides over the Modern Orthodox Anshe Sholom B'nai Israel Congregation in Chicago. "In some ways there was a heightened expectation because Rahm is so connected to Israel and the Jewish community. Instead what we've seen is more of the tough Rahm Emanuel. Not the warm Rahm."
>
> ...Emanuel begins his meetings with Jewish leaders with a warning: if anything leaks, he says, according to several participants in such gatherings, neither he nor anyone else in the White House will ever speak to the leaders again.[30]

Secretary of State Hillary Clinton also supports the creation of a Palestinian State.

> Morton Klein, president of the Zionist Organization of America is just one of many supporters of Israel who say that Hillary Clinton, an outspoken supporter of a Palestinian state, has made an anti-Israel switch of late."[31]

In March 2010, after an announcement from Israel of further settlement building in East Jerusalem, Clinton reacted with "an angry phone call to the prime minister."[32]

> The State Department said Clinton spoke to Netanyahu by phone for 43 minutes to vent U.S. frustration with Tuesday's announcement that cast a pall over a visit to Israel by Vice President Joe Biden and endangered indirect peace talks with the Palestinians that the Obama administration had announced just a day earlier.
>
> The length and unusually blunt tone of Clinton's call underscored the administration's concern about prospects for the negotiations it has been trying to organize for more than a year and its anger over Israel's refusal to heed U.S. appeals not to make provocative gestures.
>
> ...Clinton called "to make clear that the United States considered the announcement to be a deeply negative signal about Israel's approach to the bilateral relationship and counter to the spirit of the vice president's trip," State Department spokesman P.J. Crowley told reporters.[33]

From his early days in office, President Obama has pushed Israel for concessions. In his September 2009 speech to the United Nations, he insisted on "peace without preconditions" and the cessation of continued Israeli settlements.

> In declaring that it was time for Middle East peace "without preconditions," President Obama used his speech to the U.N. General Assembly Wednesday to fire a warning at Israel that "America does not accept the legitimacy of continued Israeli settlements."
>
> Obama's stark declaration, which drew applause, was coupled with a call for Palestinians to end their "incitement of Israel."
>
> But it was the use of the U.N. forum to carry the settlement message to Israel that drew the most enthusiastic

response on the floor and incredulous reaction outside its walls.

Obama just put Israel "on the chopping block," said former U.S. Ambassador to the U.N. John Bolton.[34]

Further indications of the dwindling support for Israel with our current administration was evidenced when dinner plans at the White House suddenly changed while hosting Israel.

For a head of government to visit the White House and not pose for photographers is rare. For a key ally to be left to his own devices while the President withdraws to have dinner in private was, until this week, unheard of. Yet that is how Benjamin Netanyahu was treated by President Obama on Tuesday night, according to Israeli reports on a trip viewed in Jerusalem as a humiliation.

After failing to extract a written promise of concessions on settlements, Obama walked out of his meeting with Netanyahu but invited him to stay at the White House, consult with advisers and "let me know if there is anything new," a U.S. congressman, who spoke to the Prime Minister, said.

"It was awful," the congressman said. One Israeli newspaper called the meeting "a hazing in stages," poisoned by such mistrust that the Israeli delegation eventually left rather than risk being eavesdropped on a White House telephone line. Another said that the Prime Minister had received "the treatment reserved for the President of Equatorial Guinea."[35]

A few days after this occurrence, FOX News posted an article that reported former New York Mayor Ed Koch's disappointment regarding this treatment: "I believe that the Obama administration is willing to throw Israel under the bus in order to please Muslim nations."[36]

Incidentally, based on the promise God made to bless those who bless Israel and curse those who curse Israel (Genesis 12:3) that we studied in chapter 3, I sincerely hope that the expressions of pressure from the United States listed above only represent a momentary move and not a complete change in direction.

Even liberal churches have jumped on the bandwagon and encourage pressure on Israel with an economic boycott, as the following article reveals:

> KELOWNA, B.C.—Delegates to the United Church's 40th General Council instead voted to recommend that members spend more time studying the possibility of an "economic boycott" of the Jewish state.
>
> It was proposed earlier that the church sanction Israel for its enduring conflict with Palestinians. Among the measures suggested at the General Council was the promotion of a "comprehensive boycott of Israeli academic and cultural institutions at the national and international levels."[37]

All over the world, momentum is building against Israel. We can expect that momentum to rise between now and the time before Ezekiel's battle when Israel's enemies will be temporarily appeased and Israel senses a false security.

Then, the attack will come, and in the heat of the battle, God will be exalted.

God will bring victory.

God's power is greater than the combined military force and technology of all world powers. In a mighty display of power, God will be glorified in the eyes of the Israelis. Ezekiel 38 and 39 detail His victory.

First, He will **shake the land.** Modern missiles and even nuclear weaponry are no match against God in battle. When it comes to protecting His people, God has a full arsenal of unconventional weapons—including earthquakes.

> *And it shall come to pass at the same time when Gog shall come against the land of Israel, saith the Lord God, that my fury shall come up in my face. For in my jealousy and in the fire of my wrath have I spoken, Surely in that day there shall be a great shaking in the land of Israel; So that the fishes of the sea, and the fowls of the heaven, and the beasts of the field, and all creeping things that creep upon the earth, and all the men that are upon the face of the earth, shall shake at my presence, and the mountains shall be thrown down, and the steep places shall fall, and every wall shall fall to the ground.*—Ezekiel 38:18–20

With the rumblings of the earthquake still being felt, God will **confuse the armies.**

> *And I will call for a sword against him throughout all my mountains, saith the Lord God: every man's sword shall be against his brother.*—Ezekiel 38:21

Apparently, one of the results of the earthquake will be a breakdown of communication among the invading armies. In the resulting fear and panic, confusion will reign as the armies attack each other in their attempts to harm Israel.

With yet another divine weapon, God will **bring sickness** to the attacking armies.

> *And I will plead against him with pestilence and with blood; and I will rain upon him, and upon his bands, and upon the*

many people that are with him, an overflowing rain, and great hailstones, fire, and brimstone.—EZEKIEL 38:22

The best pilot in the world cannot operate his aircraft or weaponry when he is too sick to sit up. The greatest military commander will find the hospital a poor location from which to dispatch nuclear weapons.

Further augmenting the confusion and sickness, God will bring yet more natural and supernatural disasters—flood, hail, fire, and brimstone. Many today mock the fire and brimstone accounts in Scripture, but firsthand experience will remove all traces of laughter from previous scoffers. When God wants to win a victory, He has a limitless supply of undefeatable weaponry.

With a victor's flourish, God declares He will **destroy the armies.** Not only will they be defeated in this battle, but they will be utterly destroyed.

Therefore, thou son of man, prophesy against Gog, and say, Thus saith the Lord GOD; Behold, I am against thee, O Gog, the chief prince of Meshech and Tubal: And I will turn thee back, and leave but the sixth part of thee, and will cause thee to come up from the north parts, and will bring thee upon the mountains of Israel: And I will smite thy bow out of thy left hand, and will cause thine arrows to fall out of thy right hand. Thou shalt fall upon the mountains of Israel, thou, and all thy bands, and the people that is with thee: I will give thee unto the ravenous birds of every sort, and to the beasts of the field to be devoured. Thou shalt fall upon the open field: for I have spoken it, saith the Lord GOD.—EZEKIEL 39:1–5

The resulting carnage and death from this victory will be so great that Israel will be seven months in burying the victims (Ezekiel 39:12).

The odds that were stacked against Israel will tumble like an army of dominoes when God brings the victory for His people.

God will exalt His name.

As we saw in chapter 3, most of the seven million people living in Israel today are secularists, agnostics, or atheists. Even most of those who believe in Jehovah God have rejected Christ as their Messiah. Yet, through the incredible victory God brings in this anti-Israel battle, Israel will once again have an awareness of God in their midst.

> Thus will I magnify myself, and sanctify myself; and I will be known in the eyes of many nations, and they shall know that I am the LORD. And I will set my glory among the heathen, and all the heathen shall see my judgment that I have executed, and my hand that I have laid upon them. So the house of Israel shall know that I am the LORD their God from that day and forward.
> —EZEKIEL 38:23; 39:21–22

Through the work of 144,000 Jewish evangelists during the Tribulation, thousands of Jews will embrace Christ as their Messiah (more on this in chapter 8). It could be through God's miraculous intervention in this battle that the people of Israel will soften their hearts in repentance toward the Lord. When the Lord exalts His name, Israel will be awakened to their need for their God.

And so we see in Scripture and in present day events the rise of terrorism and anti-Israeli sentiment. It really all adds up to anti-God sentiment—mankind's ultimate desire to defy the one true God and His chosen people.

God's Word has continued to prove true time and time again. Perhaps now is a good time to step back from the minutiae of what we've studied, and examine your own heart towards the truth. In the introduction, I asked you if you knew God personally. I asked if you had ever trusted Jesus Christ as your personal Saviour. We will visit this topic again in chapter 7, but consider deeply this God whom we study.

He chose a people. He blessed them. He has dealt miraculously with them for thousands of years. Why? That you might see Him. That you, like King Darius in Daniel 6:26, might know that "...*the God of Daniel... he is the living God, and stedfast forever, and his kingdom that which shall not be destroyed, and his dominion shall be even unto the end.*"

In this chapter, we've focused on the book of Ezekiel. Fifty-seven times in this one book of the Bible, God rehearses these two statements: "...*ye shall know that I am the* LORD;" "...*they shall know that I am the* LORD." Fifty-seven times in just forty-eight chapters God states His motive—to reveal Himself to you, and to the world, through His Word and through current events. He wants you to KNOW that He is God. He wants you to trust Him for salvation.

See it again in Psalm 46:10, "*Be still, and know that I am God: I will be exalted among the heathen, I will be exalted in the earth.*" Isaiah 45:22 says, "*Look unto me, and be ye saved, all the ends of the earth: for I am God, and there is none else.*"

Surely, the Scriptures we have studied and their modern fulfillment should cause us to become followers of the one true God! In Daniel 4 we read of God's dealing with the heart of a pagan king—Nebuchadnezzar—for the single purpose of drawing this king to Himself. God states His desire in verse 32, "...*until thou know that the most High ruleth in the kingdom of men, and giveth it to whomsoever he will.*"

He is the only true, living God. And you can trust Him!

> ...*that all the kingdoms of the earth may know that thou art the* LORD, *even thou only.*—ISAIAH 37:20

CHAPTER SIX

The One-World Ruler

S everal miles outside of Munich, Germany, stands the remains of Dachau—the first permanent Nazi concentration camp. When my wife and I toured this camp in the summer of 2006, I was overwhelmed with the brutality of Hitler's "New Order."

In stark contrast to the beautiful landscape just outside Dachau's iron gates, the walled confines of the camp are populated with buildings that were once dedicated to terror and death. These cold buildings made it easy to envision the torture they had witnessed. Thousands of Jews (as well as others of Hitler's perceived enemies—Slavs, Catholics, political prisoners, etc.) found a premature death within this camp.

We saw where the prisoners were beaten and deprived. We saw pictures of bodies stacked one upon another. We saw the gas chamber where prisoners were told to enter for a shower, only to have their lives taken in massive numbers. We saw the huge ovens that served as incinerators where their bodies were burned. We saw the laboratories where Nazi doctors performed sadistic medical "experiments" on thousands of helpless victims.

More astonishing, however, than these horrific deaths, was the realization that one man—Adolf Hitler—had such demonic power and influence over his country. How could so many people have allowed these atrocities to take place?

This camp was operated just outside the town of Dachau, Germany, where townspeople continued with their daily business as usual while prisoners on the other side of the wall were being starved, tortured, and mutilated. Somehow, through Hitler's reign of terror, people allowed this slaughter to take place at their doorstep while they ignored it all and pursued their daily routines.

Soldiers were so indoctrinated by Hitler's policies and deluded by his self-promoting promises that they were willing to allow themselves to become an extension of his brutality. Somehow they turned the knobs or pulled the levers to bring gas into the chambers; somehow they shot innocent people; somehow they tortured defenseless victims—and passed it off as part of their normal duties.

Thousands of Germans, particularly young people, were swayed by Hitler's speeches and mesmerized by his authority. Somehow they accepted Hitler's message and adapted to his lifestyle.

The rise of Nazi Germany and the atrocities of the Holocaust stand as a gruesome memorial to the ability of a persuasive, but evil, leader to obtain power and sway an entire country. Scripture prophesies of such a leader—the Antichrist. But when the Antichrist rises to power and organizes his "new order"—a new *world* order—Hitler will, in contrast, appear mild and indulgent. This demonically controlled man will eventually prove to be a savage murderer whose life is entirely anti Christ.

Over the years, many have speculated concerning the identity of the Antichrist. During the first century, some Christians guessed that the emperor Nero would become this world ruler. Martin Luther thought the pope was the Antichrist.[1] Many citizens of Allied countries during World War II believed the Antichrist was Hitler himself.

Jesus prophesied that many would speak of the Antichrist and many possible candidates would arise: *"And many false prophets shall rise, and shall deceive many. For there shall arise false Christs, and false prophets, and shall shew great signs and wonders; insomuch that, if it were possible, they shall deceive the very elect"* (Matthew 24:11, 24).

Looking back through the annals of history, there have been many leaders whose lifestyles and policies were anti-Christ. The Apostle John warned of such people in the first century: *"Little children, it is the last time: and as ye have heard that antichrist shall come, even now are there many antichrists; whereby we know that it is the last time"* (1 John 2:18). It seems that today, more than ever before, these antichrists abound. It will be such a man who will one day rise to prominence as a one-world ruler.

There seem to be two common errors among prophecy teachers. The first is setting a date for the return of Christ. Those who slip into this pitfall overlook Jesus' words in Matthew 24:36, *"But of that day and hour knoweth no man, no, not the angels of heaven, but my Father only"* (Matthew 24:36).

The other fallacy common among prophecy teachers is that of attempting to guess the specific identity of the Antichrist. Scripture indicates, however, that the Antichrist will not be revealed until after the Rapture (2 Thessalonians 2:3).

The purpose of this chapter is not to point out an individual as the Antichrist, but to understand the global power structure developing and the role the Antichrist will assume in world leadership during the Tribulation.

The titles Scripture ascribes to this one-world leader are many. The following chart will help you identify prophecies throughout Scripture that relate to this man.

Titles of the One-World Ruler

- Beast (Daniel 7:11; Revelation 13:1)
- Man of sin (2 Thessalonians 2:3)
- Son of perdition (2 Thessalonians 2:3)
- That Wicked (2 Thessalonians 2:8)
- Antichrist (1 John 2:18)
- Little horn (Daniel 7:8)
- Abomination of desolation (Matthew 24:15)
- The prince that shall come (Daniel 9:26)
- A king of fierce countenance (Daniel 8:23)
- The king shall do according to his will (Daniel 11:36)

When, as a young man, I heard teaching on the Antichrist, I could not envision how the entire world could be aware of or see one person at a single time, much less be ruled by and worship that person! How could the entire world be familiar with his policies? And what would bring the world to desire his leadership?

Yet, as time has unfolded technological advancements, such questions are no longer puzzling. Technology has opened the possibilities for the whole world to hear and follow the agenda of a centralized government. Even in remote parts of the world, it is possible via television or live streaming internet, to view the same events the rest of the world is watching.

The astounding rate at which technology is advancing gains increasing momentum with every major discovery. For example, whereas the radio acquired fifty million users in thirty-eight years, the internet accomplished the same feat in just four years.

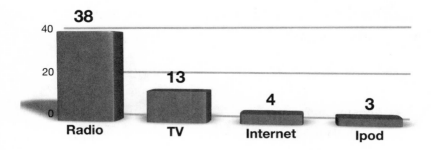

Number of Years to Reach 50 Million Users

Facebook reached the hundred million user mark in just nine months. Hulu, an internet live streaming provider, increased from 63 million to 373 million streams in one year. One can easily see that the world is technologically ripening for the communication necessary for a global government.

Further encouraging the world to desire a one-world ruler is a depressed economy. As we saw in chapter 1, many people are desirous of economic centralization. *USA Today* reported that the pope called for a world economic authority with "real teeth."

> Pope Benedict XVI today called for reforming the United Nations and establishing a "true world political authority" with "real teeth" to manage the global economy with God-centered ethics.
>
> In his third encyclical, a major teaching, released as the G-8 summit begins in Italy, the pope says such an

authority is urgently needed to end the current worldwide financial crisis.[2]

When the leader of a large religious body calls on the United Nations to manage the world economy, it isn't difficult to see how a one-world leader will be accepted by both religious and economic sectors.

The recent replacement of the G-8 by the G-20 further indicates a growing desire for international regulation in a world economy, as the following article reveals:

> An administration official says that the Group of 20 nations will assume the role of a permanent council on global economic cooperation.
>
> The official, who spoke on condition of anonymity before the official announcement, said the Group of Eight major industrial nations would continue to meet on matters of common importance such as national security.
>
> The official said President Obama initiated the move and it will be announced Friday.[3]

The current economic crisis is creating a realignment of international economic power, slowly dissolving national economic boundaries and increasing the pressure for centralized monetary management.

In addition to technology and the world economy, there is another factor advancing the cause of a world government with the Antichrist as ruler. Slowly, yet pervasively, the dark and murky waters of secular humanism have created a strong undercurrent that is moving the hearts of people toward the acceptance of a one-world ruler.

Humanism denies God and denounces accountability to biblical morality. It is an ideal belief system for a demonically-controlled, power-hungry ruler who will dissolve Christian ethics in his global policies.

The basic tenants of humanism are outlined in the Humanist Manifestos. Among the anti-God and anti-Christian beliefs expressed in these documents are pro-globalism ambitions. *Humanist Manifesto II* declares the following:

> We deplore the division of humankind on nationalistic grounds. We have reached a turning point in human history where the best option is to transcend the limits of national sovereignty and to move toward the building of a world community in which all sectors of the human family can participate. Thus we look to the development of a system of world law and a world order based upon transnational federal government.[4]

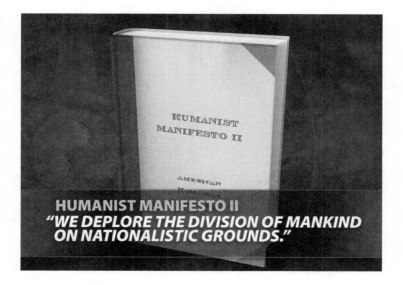

HUMANIST MANIFESTO II
"WE DEPLORE THE DIVISION OF MANKIND ON NATIONALISTIC GROUNDS."

Thus, the humanist would like to remove the nationalistic boundaries, transcend national sovereignty, and create a global government. This philosophy, and the anti-Christian belief structure from which it originates, is doing much to set the stage for the Antichrist.

The unison of increased technology, a world economy, and secular humanism—all present at the same time in history—is creating a unique backdrop for the appearance of the Antichrist.

This world leader, referred to in Revelation 13 and Daniel 7 as "the beast," may already be alive today, perhaps even in a role of leadership. The policies that will characterize his ideals are gaining momentum, and the world is ripening for his control.

The Antichrist is not only against Christ, he is the complete opposite of Christ—in every way. Notice the differences:

CHRIST	ANTICHRIST
Came from above (John 6:38)	Will ascend from the pit (Revelation 11:7)
Came in His Father's name (John 5:43)	Will come in his own name (John 5:43)
Humbled Himself (Philippians 2:8)	Will exalt himself (2 Thessalonians 2:4)
Was despised (Isaiah 53:3; Luke 23:18)	Will be admired (Revelation 13:3–4)
Will be exalted (Philippians 2:9)	Will be cast down to Hell (Revelation 19:20)
Came to do His Father's will (John 6:38)	Will come to do his own will (Daniel 11:36)
Came to save (Luke 19:10)	Will come to destroy (Daniel 8:24)
The "Good Shepherd" (John 10:1–5)	The "idol [evil] shepherd" (Zechariah 11:16–17)
The "true vine" (John 15:1)	The "vine of the earth" (Revelation 14:18)
The "truth" (John 14:6)	The lie (2 Thessalonians 2:11)
The "Holy One" (Mark 1:24)	The wicked one (2 Thessalonians 2:8)
The "man of sorrows" (Isaiah 53:3)	The "man of sin" (2 Thessalonians 2:3)
The "Son of God" (Luke 1:35)	The "son of perdition" (2 Thessalonians 2:3)
"The mystery of godliness; God...manifest in the flesh" (1 Timothy 3:16)	Will be the "mystery of iniquity," Satan manifest in the flesh (2 Thessalonians 2:7)

Truly, "the beast" is an appropriate title for this coming brutal and devouring ruler.

THE DESCRIPTION OF THE BEAST

And I stood upon the sand of the sea, and saw a beast rise up out of the sea, having seven heads and ten horns, and upon his horns ten crowns, and upon his heads the name of blasphemy. And the beast which I saw was like unto a leopard, and his feet were as the feet of a bear, and his mouth as the mouth of a lion: and the dragon gave him his power, and his seat, and great authority. And I saw one of his heads as it were wounded to death; and his deadly wound was healed: and all the world wondered after the beast. And they worshipped the dragon which gave power unto the beast: and they worshipped the beast, saying, Who is like unto the beast? who is able to make war with him?—REVELATION 13:1–4*

The Antichrist's place of origin

As John penned the book of Revelation, he was on the Island of Patmos in the Mediterranean Sea. His description of the beast arising from the sea indicates the Antichrist will come from the European-Mediterranean region.

Because the "sea" in prophetic Scriptures usually represents Gentiles, it is likely that the Antichrist will have a Gentile background. Authors Tim LaHaye and Ed Hindson offer several reasons why the Antichrist will most likely be Gentile.

> Most prophetic scholars believe he will be a Gentile because…
> - He leads the European Union of Gentile nations (Daniel 7:8–24)
> - He will be the leader of the people who destroyed the Temple (i.e., the Romans)
> - His covenant with Israel promises Gentile protection for Israel (Daniel 9:27)[5]

Interestingly, although the beast rises out of the sea, he is a land animal, and he possesses the combined traits of a leopard, bear, and lion. Henry Morris comments on this:

> This beast rises out of that sea as a land animal, and could thus only speak of some powerful personage emerging from the peoples of the Mediterranean lands, with the hybrid characteristics of the beast suggesting that he is somehow a product of them all.[6]

The conglomeration of the beast's traits may refer to interracial origin, inter-religious origin, inter-political connections—or all three! Whatever the case, he will be the renaissance man of all renaissance men. And when he steps on the scene from the Mediterranean region, he will have answers to the world's problems.

In addition to the beast's geographic origin, Scripture speaks of his political origin with the mention of his ten horns. These horns represent the world kingdoms that will give him power, and they correspond to the ten toes in Daniel's vision of the revived Roman Empire (Daniel 2).

Daniel 7 also speaks of the ten horns: *"And the ten horns out of this kingdom are ten kings that shall arise: and another shall rise after them; and he shall be diverse from the first, and he shall subdue three kings"* (Daniel 7:24). The Antichrist will rise to power among the leaders of the world. He will somehow set three of the ten main world powers aside and establish himself as the world authority.

Daniel 7:8 also describes the Antichrist's rise to power: *"I considered the horns, and, behold, there came up among them another little horn, before whom there were three of the first horns plucked up by the roots: and, behold, in this horn were eyes like the eyes of man, and a mouth speaking great things."*

Again, "horns" are a picture of world powers. The "little horn" is the Antichrist, an expert in policy and skilled in diplomacy.

The Antichrist's pivotal moment politically and diplomatically will be the treaty he makes (and later breaks) with Israel. Daniel 9 describes this process:

> *And after threescore and two weeks shall Messiah be cut off, but not for himself: and the people of the prince that shall come shall destroy the city and the sanctuary; and the end thereof shall be with a flood, and unto the end of the war desolations are determined. And he shall confirm the covenant with many for one week: and in the midst of the week he shall cause the sacrifice and the oblation to cease, and for the overspreading of abominations he shall make it desolate, even until the consummation, and that determined shall be poured upon the desolate.*—DANIEL 9:26–27

The first part of this prophecy describes the sacrifice of Christ, the Messiah. As we saw in chapter 5, a prophetic *week* denotes a set of seven years. So, the "threescore and two (sixty-two) weeks" plus the "seven weeks" mentioned in the previous verse make a total of 69 weeks—483 prophetic years. (A prophetic year is 360 days.)

With amazing accuracy, 483 years after Daniel's prophecy, Jesus made His triumphant entry into the city of Jerusalem (John 12:12–15). But the Jews did not receive Him as King; He was "cut off" and crucified just days later.

After the death and resurrection of Christ, there is a divinely appointed gap between His first advent and His Second Coming to establish His kingdom. Presently, we are living in that gap. The final week of years described in this prophecy will occur after the Rapture, which we studied in chapter 4.

Verse 27 of the passage above tells us that this final set of seven years will begin with a covenant with many (perhaps a worldwide peace treaty) that the Antichrist makes concerning Israel. He will *"confirm the covenant with many for one week."*[7]

Negotiations for peace in Israel have been on the table for years. The incredible diplomacy the Antichrist will possess to walk away from peace discussions with a signed treaty will not be overlooked and will perhaps be a major factor in his ascension to worldwide power.

Three-and-a-half years *("in the midst of the week")* after the Antichrist's rise to power, the diplomacy will vanish. With fiendish brutality, the Antichrist will break the treaty and lash out against Israel.

The beast from the Mediterranean will rise to power through maneuvering, bargaining, and feigning peace.

The Antichrist's position in prophecy

The beast pictured in Revelation 13 is a composite of the four beasts of Daniel's vision in Daniel 7 and represents the final realization of a one-world government. As we saw briefly in chapter 2, the beasts of Daniel 7 pictured the same four world empires as the image of Daniel 2—Babylon, Media-Persia, Greece, and Rome.

The Antichrist will possess the appetite for combined conquest of all of these ancient kingdoms. With the power of Nebuchadnezzar, the government structure of Media-Persia, the desire to conquer of Alexander the Great, and the military might of Nero, the Antichrist will arise out of a final global kingdom.

This empire is rapidly being formed today as the European Union expands in power and size. In fact, the EU has nearly *doubled* in size

---

[7] From the context of Daniel 9, we know this treaty is specific to Israel. Verse 24 makes it clear that the entire seventy-week prophecy was a prediction of the future for the Jewish people.

since 2004. As we saw earlier, the Lisbon Treaty, signed in 2009, increased the power of the EU, including creating the office of a president. Not surprisingly, a main factor motivating the ratification of the Lisbon Treaty was the economic recession beginning in 2008, as the following article points out.

> Ireland's recession-hit voters have overwhelmingly approved the European Union's ambitious and long-delayed reform plans, electoral chiefs announced Saturday in a referendum result greeted with wild cheers in Dublin—and nervous sighs of relief in Brussels.
>
> Ireland had been the primary obstacle to ratifying the EU Lisbon Treaty, a mammoth agreement designed to modernize and strengthen the 27-nation bloc's institutions and decision-making powers in line with its near-doubling in size since 2004. The treaty will make it easier to take decisions by majority rather than unanimous votes, and give a bigger say to national parliaments and the European Parliament in shaping EU policies.[8]

Before the recession, Ireland, with her robust economy, had no need to sign the treaty. Now, however, the vast trading agreements and increased monetary liquidity made available through a stronger treaty offset the desire for national sovereignty.

We see again the tremendous role finances play in setting the stage for the Antichrist's world economy. When nations are in dire financial straits, they are more willing to relinquish national control for economic security.

The Antichrist's economic policies will reflect his nature of deceit. Daniel 8:25 says, *"And through his policy also he shall cause craft to prosper in his hand; and he shall magnify himself in his heart, and by peace shall destroy many....*" The word *craft* in this verse refers to crafty deceit and treachery. With suave promises and a cunning agenda, this beastly ruler will actually destroy many by promising a prosperity that is temporary and artificial. Thus assured by a false sense of peace and security, the world will gladly welcome the Antichrist and his policies.

The Antichrist's prominence in the world

The name of the Antichrist will be a household word in every country. His global prominence and power will surpass any leader the world has known before. How can one man have such power?

His prominence will be partially derived from his affiliations. Revelation 13:2 specifically tells us that he will be affiliated with Satan himself, "...*the dragon gave him his power, and his seat, and great authority.*"

A few verses later, Scripture tells us of another power-giving affiliation: "*And I beheld another beast coming up out of the earth; and he had two horns like a lamb, and he spake as a dragon. And he exerciseth all the power of the first beast before him, and causeth the earth and them which dwell therein to worship the first beast, whose deadly wound was healed*" (Revelation 13:11–12). A false prophet will arise who, through spiritual and political means, will promote the Antichrist.

Then there are the ten kings we've noted previously. These ten ruling world powers will give their hearts to this rising ruler. Revelation 17:12–13 tells us, "*And the ten horns which thou sawest are ten kings, which have received no kingdom as yet; but receive power as kings one hour with the beast. These have one mind, and shall give their power and strength unto the beast.*"

The Antichrist will use his satanically inspired affiliations to win worldwide prominence. And world leaders will be only too obliging to aid him in his powerful ascension.

Further boosting the Antichrist's popularity ratings will be his death and resurrection during the Tribulation (Revelation 13:3). Sometime at the middle of the Tribulation, the Antichrist will be fatally wounded. God will allow him to be resurrected, and the world will literally worship him. Dr. Jeremiah wrote, "He will command a cultic worship that will make Joseph Smith and Jim Jones look like boy scout leaders."[9]

The description Scripture provides of the Antichrist paints a picture of a dreadful beast. Although this ruler will portray himself as a peace-loving and peace-giving leader, his satanic backing and demonic affiliations will eventually reveal his true colors—hungry for power and ruthless in conquest.

THE DEFIANCE OF THE BEAST

And there was given unto him a mouth speaking great things and blasphemies; and power was given unto him to continue forty and two months. And he opened his mouth in blasphemy against God, to blaspheme his name, and his tabernacle, and them that dwell in heaven.—REVELATION 13:5–6

The Antichrist will defy all that is holy and godly, and no one will be more proficient in blasphemy than this beast.

The Antichrist will be directly under the influence of Satan—perhaps even indwelt by Satan himself. In Revelation 12, just one chapter before the description of the Antichrist, Satan is cast out of Heaven. Some scholars believe that he will then literally indwell the Antichrist. Thus, Satan, who has always desired the worship that belongs to God alone (Isaiah 14:13–14), will finally have the opportunity to become an object of worship.

Scripture refers to the Antichrist as "*that Wicked*" in 2 Thessalonians 2:8–9: "*And then shall that Wicked be revealed, whom the Lord shall consume with the spirit of his mouth, and shall destroy with the brightness of his coming: Even him, whose coming is after the working of Satan with all power and signs and lying wonders.*"

There are two primary ways in which the Antichrist will express his defiance toward God.

The Antichrist will have a blasphemous mouth.

With ever-swelling pride, the Antichrist will have "*a mouth speaking great things*" (Daniel 7:8).

His importance will be at the expense of the Tribulation saints, however, for "*he shall speak great words against the most High, and shall wear out the saints of the most High, and think to change times and laws: and they shall be given into his hand until a time and times and the dividing of time*" (Daniel 7:25). The persecution leveled at those who become Christians during the Tribulation will be greater than this world has ever known.

The Antichrist will have a blasphemous religion.

This charismatic speaker will lift up religion and spirituality, but he will blaspheme the God of the Bible. He will call for all faiths to come together, but he will persecute the saints of God. He will be the christ of the cults, the Buddha of Buddhism, the Mahdi of Islam, and the seeming Messiah of Israel. Everyone that has ever looked for a coming great teacher or spiritual leader will feel they have found him in the Antichrist.

Full of self-confidence, the Antichrist will ascribe worship to himself. The false prophet will act as the Antichrist's worship leader and use mesmerizing, but satanic, miracles to direct the world's worship to the beast.

And deceiveth them that dwell on the earth by the means of those miracles which he had power to do in the sight of the beast; saying to them that dwell on the earth, that they should make an image to the beast, which had the wound by a sword, and did live. And he had power to give life unto the image of the beast, that the image of the beast should both speak, and cause that as many as would not worship the image of the beast should be killed.
—REVELATION 13:14–15

Then, in an act of complete defiance, the Antichrist will exalt himself in the Jewish temple and demand to be worshipped. Second Thessalonians 2:4 tells of this blasphemous act: *"Who opposeth and exalteth himself above all that is called God, or that is worshipped; so that he as God sitteth in the temple of God, shewing himself that he is God."*

As we saw earlier, three-and-a-half years into the Tribulation the Antichrist will treacherously break his treaty with Israel. He will then desecrate their temple and mandate their worship.

Obviously, for the Antichrist to present himself as an object of worship in the temple, the Jews must first *have* a temple. When the Romans conquered and destroyed Jerusalem in AD 70, they burned the temple, and it hasn't been rebuilt since.

Today, however, Orthodox Jews are building temple furniture in preparation for a new temple.

> The Temple Institute, which has already built many of the vessels for the Holy Temple, such as the ark and the menorah, has now embarked on a project to build the altar. Construction begins Thursday in Mitzpe Yericho (east of Jerusalem) at 5:30 PM.
>
> "Unfortunately, we cannot currently build the altar in its proper place, on the Temple Mount," Temple Institute director Yehudah Glick said. "We are building an altar of the

minimum possible size so that we will be able to transport it to the Temple when it is rebuilt."[10]

While in Israel in the summer of 2009, I visited the Temple Institute and saw some of this very furniture. The solid gold menorah, built at the expense of three million dollars, was particularly impressive.

Who could believe the timing of renewed interest in rebuilding the temple is coincidental? Think of it: at the very same time that the European Union is gaining power and world events are aligning in preparation for the Antichrist's ascension, preparations for a new temple are underway.

The major roadblock for the construction of this temple is the Israeli-Palestinian conflict over the Temple Mount and the city of Jerusalem. The Muslims even deny that a Jewish temple ever existed in Jerusalem.

As late as November 2008, Ahmed Qurei, the chief Palestinian negotiator—meaning the Palestinian Authority official leading all peace talks with the Jewish state—asserted that the Jewish Temples never existed and that Israel has been working to "invent" a Jewish historical connection to Jerusalem. In a press briefing I personally attended, Qurei said, "Israeli occupation authorities are trying to find a so-called Jewish historical connection between Jerusalem and the Temple Mount, but all these attempts will fail. The [Temple Mount] is 100 percent Muslim."[11]

Jews are barred from visiting the Temple mount during most hours of the day, and when they are allowed to ascend, it is under heavy restriction, including a Muslim-mandated total ban on prayer.[12]

While the Jews are building temple furniture, the Muslims are denying Jewish claims to the Temple Mount. How will the temple in which the Antichrist will blasphemously sit ever be erected?

Quite possibly, it will be the Antichrist himself who will span the chasm between the Jews and Muslims. Remember that when he rises to power, he will initially be friendly toward Israel. Perhaps his incredible peace treaty between Israel and the rest of the world will include permission to build on the Temple Mount.

But when the temple is built, the Antichrist will not see it as holy and sacred; instead he will view it as an illustrious place from which to propagate his blasphemous religion and establish himself as an object of worship.

THE DOMINANCE OF THE BEAST

And it was given unto him to make war with the saints, and to overcome them: and power was given him over all kindreds, and tongues, and nations. And all that dwell upon the earth shall worship him, whose names are not written in the book of life of the Lamb slain from the foundation of the world. If any man have an ear, let him hear. He that leadeth into captivity shall go into captivity: he that killeth with the sword must be killed with the sword. Here is the patience and the faith of the saints.
—REVELATION 13:7–10

Just how far will the Antichrist's power extend? In what areas will he exercise his control?

Power to fight the saints

In the name of world peace, the Antichrist will institute a level of anti-Semitism and persecution against Gentile believers that far surpasses anything the world has ever known. Like the Roman emperors of old, he will make the saints of God his particular enemy and single them out for

122 | Understanding the Times

vicious attacks. Revelation 13:7 tells us he will have power to *"make war with the saints, and to overcome them…"* (Revelation 13:7).

For those who will not "coexist" under the Antichrist's plans for a one-world conglomeration of religions, persecution will ensue. This man who will preach tolerance of all faiths will be of all men most intolerant of those who follow Christ.

The saints referred to here are those who trust Christ as Saviour during the Tribulation. All those who were redeemed will have been raptured before the Tribulation (as we saw in chapter 4) and will be in Heaven praising the Lamb of God who redeemed them (Revelation 5:9).

During the Tribulation, God will raise up 144,000 male Jewish evangelists to bring the Gospel of Christ around the globe (Revelation 7). The Tribulation saints will include thousands of Jewish people who finally trust Christ as their Messiah during the Antichrist's reign of terror.

Power to rule the nations

As we have already seen, the world is preparing for a one-world government. When the stage has been sufficiently set for such a government, the Antichrist will quickly enter the spotlight. From the platform built by the revived Roman Empire, he will dominate the globe.

Some view the biblical belief in a coming one-world government as right-winged fanaticism. In an April 2009 "Extremist Report" compiled for the Federal Bureau of Investigation by the Department of Homeland Security under the leadership of Janet Napolitano, investigators reported the following:

> Returning veterans possess combat skills and experience that are attractive to rightwing extremists. DHS/I&A is concerned that rightwing extremists will attempt to recruit and radicalize returning veterans in order to boost their violent capabilities….

The dissolution of Communist countries in Eastern Europe and the end of the Soviet Union in the 1990s led some rightwing extremists to believe that a "New World Order" would bring about a world government that would usurp the sovereignty of the United States and its Constitution, thus infringing upon their liberty.[13]

The insulting statements insinuating that those who believe in a coming new world order are violent, right-wing fanatics, reveal a strong political leaning. The comments were also rejected flatly by patriotic veterans who did not deserve such criticism. In reality, there are people on the far-left who believe in a new world order as well, although not from a biblical perspective. For example, one of President Barack Obama's czars, John Holdren, voiced radically extreme ideas for a world government in his book *Ecoscience: Population, Resources, Environment.*

President Obama's "science czar," John Holdren, once floated the idea of forced abortions, "compulsory sterilization," and the creation of a "Planetary Regime" that would oversee human population levels and control all natural resources as a means of protecting the planet—controversial ideas his critics say should have been brought up in his Senate confirmation hearings.[14]

So, there are people on both sides of the political aisle who are predicting coming global control. This power will be mainstreamed during the regime of the Antichrist.

Crucial to the Antichrist's global control will be his power over the world's financial resources through a one-world currency and monetary system. Twenty or thirty years ago, predictions of a one-world currency were primarily only taken seriously by Bible-believing Christians, and even among them, such a system seemed a long way off. Today, however, a global currency is increasingly suggested as a solution to the world's economic woes.

Revelation 13:16–17 describes the global economy of the Antichrist: *"And he causeth all, both small and great, rich and poor, free and bond, to receive a mark in their right hand, or in their foreheads: And that no man might buy or sell, save he that had the mark, or the name of the beast, or the number of his name"* (Revelation 13:16–17).

Not too long ago, most of us pictured the mark spoken of here as a symbol placed on one's hand or forehead. It seemed impossible to regulate such a mark, as it could wash off or otherwise be tampered with—a puzzlingly impractical system.

Notice, however, that the verse does not say the mark will be received *on* the hand, but *in* the hand. With today's technology, such a system could be effectively managed in multiple ways.

One possibility would be to base the system on an electronic chip, such as are used to track pets, that would be implanted in the hand or forehead of all citizens. The identification technology in these chips could be combined with the financial capabilities of the electronic chips in credit cards.

It would not be that difficult to persuade people of the benefits of such a system; it could solve identity theft and health identification issues, and it would consolidate billfolds full of credit and debit cards into one simple chip.

Whatever system is used, one thing is certain—no legal commerce will take place without it. The choice to receive the mark in one's hand or forehead will clearly identify the individual's loyalty to the Antichrist and thus express rejection of Christ. By the same token, the economic pressure to accept the mark will be so great, that those who refuse will be easily identified as persons committed to Christ.

When the Antichrist has control of global finances, he will be able to rule with all the resources of the world at his disposal.

Power that is worshipped

Instead of the "Heil Hitler" military salutes of a previous generation, followers of the Antichrist will pledge their loyalty through worship: *"...and they worshipped the beast, saying, Who is like unto the beast? ...And all that dwell upon the earth shall worship him, whose names are not written in the book of life of the Lamb slain from the foundation of the world. And he...causeth the earth and them which dwell therein to worship the first beast..."* (Revelation 13:4, 8, 12).

How surprised these worshippers will be when the only one who has ever been or will ever be worthy of worship arrives on the scene! When Christ returns, the kingdom of the Antichrist will crumble like broken clay, and the Antichrist himself will be judged: *"And the beast was taken, and with him the false prophet that wrought miracles before him, with which he deceived them that had received the mark of the beast, and them that worshipped his image. These both were cast alive into a lake of fire burning with brimstone"* (Revelation 19:20).

The dominance of the Antichrist during his seven years of glory can only be temporary, for he will be soundly defeated when Christ returns in triumph. Our next chapter details the provision Christ has made for us to be included in His triumphant return. As you read on, evaluate your personal relationship with the Lord in light of these prophetic truths.

CHAPTER SEVEN

The False Church or the True Saviour?

From the time Jesus first called His twelve disciples from the shores of Galilee, there have been those who have followed Christ in simple faith. In the city of Antioch, these believers were so visibly transformed by their faith in Christ that outsiders noticed and coined a new label—"Christian." Acts 11:26 records, "...*And the disciples were called Christians first in Antioch.*" Ever since that time, those who belong to Christ have been known as Christians.

Yet over the years, many have attempted to pervert the simple Gospel with man-made and man-exalting systems of religion. Through craft and compromise, these have deceitfully employed the title "Christian" to their own advantage. In modern vernacular, not everybody who uses the term "Christian" could be considered such.

Even in the early days of Christianity, it was necessary for the Apostle Jude to warn believers of those who would distort the truth, turning the grace of God into a false system of beliefs:

Beloved, when I gave all diligence to write unto you of the common salvation, it was needful for me to write unto you, and exhort you that ye should earnestly contend for the faith which was once delivered unto the saints. For there are certain men crept in unawares, who were before of old ordained to this condemnation, ungodly men, turning the grace of our God into lasciviousness, and denying the only Lord God, and our Lord Jesus Christ.
—JUDE 3–4

And so, an unseen battle rages between truth and perversion. Revelation 17 gives us a glimpse into the future as it describes how this war of spirituality and religion will culminate during the Tribulation and which side will triumph.

The ultimate perversion of the truth will come in the form of an apostate "church," a global religious system that will be powerful enough to be accepted by and have influence with the Antichrist's government of which we read in the last chapter.

Revelation 17 calls this church a harlot—a title that points to her spiritual fornication in attempting to compromise truth and bring all religions together. *"And upon her forehead was a name written, MYSTERY, BABYLON THE GREAT, THE MOTHER OF HARLOTS AND ABOMINATIONS OF THE EARTH"* (Revelation 17:5).

In similar fashion to a morally impure woman, this church will embrace many religious partners and sell her way into greater world influence. Comprised of a blended version of all world faiths, she will be more concerned with power than with truth. Ultimately, she will give herself over to the Antichrist.

Throughout Revelation 17, the false church is represented by a woman, and the end times government is represented by a beast. The woman is sitting on the beast, picturing the time during the Tribulation when the false church will ride the false government for a season of power.

THE IDENTIFICATION OF THE FALSE CHURCH

While it may seem incredulous that long-established religions will compromise to the point that they will collaborate, I've learned that most religious people don't really know much about their faith. Many are blindly loyal to their church without really understanding its teaching or doctrine. Thus, when their church finds it politically expedient to wed itself to a global religion, those loyal followers will enthusiastically support this new "unity." The promise of peace and global oneness will be more attractive than truth, and many will buy into the lie.

Revelation 17 provides a description of this coming church. Some of her traits are already visible in the world today.

A corrupt church

> *And there came one of the seven angels which had the seven vials, and talked with me, saying unto me, Come hither; I will shew unto thee the judgment of the great whore that sitteth upon many waters: With whom the kings of the earth have committed fornication, and the inhabitants of the earth have been made drunk with the wine of her fornication.*—REVELATION 17:1–2

This false church embraces a philosophy that replaces Christ; the harlotry in which she is engaged is the prostitution of truth. The prophet Isaiah used similar wording to describe the spiritual defection of Jerusalem centuries earlier: *"How is the faithful city become an harlot! it was full of judgment; righteousness lodged in it; but now murderers"* (Isaiah 1:21).

Scripture depicts this corrupt church as sitting *"upon many waters."* This reveals her international prominence known on every continent. She will be well connected both geographically and politically.

Ecumenically, this church will be a composite of all religions, forming a hybrid belief system. Her rally cry will be "tolerance," and she will seek unity at any cost.

> [The great whore]...is a combination of apostate Protestantism, Romanism, and atheism. It is the huge ecumenical church of the last days....and it is being heralded as a step forward toward unity and world peace.[1]

> For as mystery Babylon emerges in her final form she will embrace all of Christendom and all other religions of the world as well.[2]

A compromising church

> *So he carried me away in the spirit into the wilderness: and I saw a woman sit upon a scarlet coloured beast, full of names of blasphemy, having seven heads and ten horns. And the woman was arrayed in purple and scarlet colour, and decked with gold and precious stones and pearls, having a golden cup in her hand full of abominations and filthiness of her fornication:*
> —REVELATION 17:3–4

The worldwide following of this false church will be drawn by her compromise. She will be willing to ride the government, aligning herself with the ten main political powers then in place. As we saw in chapter 2, these ten powers will form the revived Roman Empire, which is already coming to power in the form of the European Union.

As a side note, the currency of the European Union, the euro, holds a unique prophetic intrigue in one of its coins. The 2 euro coin that is minted in Greece has a symbol of a woman riding a beast. While the symbol on this coin does not carry the weight of Bible prophecy, it does illustrate this prophetic truth.

The beast upon which the woman sits in Revelation 17 is *"full of names of blasphemy."* This beast is the Antichrist, and in his arrogant passion for deification (similar to the Roman emperors of old), he will ascribe to himself names that belong to God alone.

The Antichrist and the false prophet (see chapter 6) will work together to advance the worship of the Antichrist, deceitfully leading people astray. Revelation 13:14 describes their approach: *"And deceiveth them that dwell on the earth by the means of those miracles which he had power to do in the sight of the beast; saying to them that dwell on the earth, that they should make an image to the beast, which had the wound by a sword, and did live."* Perhaps like the popular hit "We Are the World," those in the one-world faith will sing and celebrate their global religion.

The wine cup in the hand of the woman reveals that the world will be spiritually intoxicated by the false church. All over the world, people will be enthralled with this gathering of spiritual life and the unification of all faiths.

> From the nature of the ingredients avowedly used, there can be no doubt that they were of an intoxicating nature; and till the aspirants had come under their power, till their understandings had been dimmed, and their passions excited by the medicated draught, they were not duly prepared for what they were either to hear or see.[3]

With elevated passion and dulled reasoning, the world will be mesmerized and will celebrate the integration of the false church as the long-awaited answer to spiritual division.

THE INTEGRATION OF THE FALSE CHURCH

In what ways will the false religions of the world integrate[4] to form this corrupt, compromising church?

Integration of idolatry

Notice the name written on the woman's forehead in Revelation 17:5, *"And upon her forehead was a name written, MYSTERY, BABYLON THE GREAT, THE MOTHER OF HARLOTS AND ABOMINATIONS OF THE EARTH."* Nearly one-eighth of Revelation is devoted to the study of Babylon, so it is not surprising that the idolatrous origins of this coming one-world church trace back through Babylon.

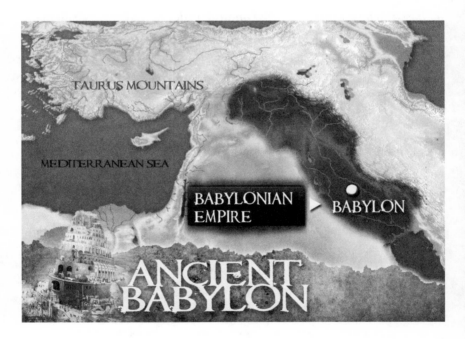

---

[4] The word integration is often used to refer to bringing cultures or races together. In this sense, the true church should be integrated—every person should be welcome in the church. In this chapter, however, integration refers to bringing all faiths together. This cannot be done without compromising Bible truth.

The name *Babylon* comes from the root word *Babel*, simply meaning "to revolt or stand against." The account of the Tower of Babel in Genesis records man's first attempt at a one-world religion:

> *And they said one to another, Go to, let us make brick, and burn them throughly. And they had brick for stone, and slime had they for morter. And they said, Go to, let us build us a city and a tower, whose top may reach unto heaven; and let us make us a name, lest we be scattered abroad upon the face of the whole earth. And the LORD came down to see the city and the tower, which the children of men builded. And the LORD said, Behold, the people is one, and they have all one language; and this they begin to do: and now nothing will be restrained from them, which they have imagined to do. Go to, let us go down, and there confound their language, that they may not understand one another's speech.*
> —GENESIS 11:3–7

Scripture identifies a man by the name of Nimrod as the leader of this movement (Genesis 10:8–10). Dr. Harry Ironside said of Nimrod, "He was the arch apostate of the Patriarchal age….He persuaded his associates and followers to join together in 'building a city and a tower which should reach unto heaven.'…a tower of renown…to be recognized as a temple or rallying centre for those who did not walk in obedience to the word of the Lord."[5]

Nimrod's name means "rebellion" or "the valiant." In complete disregard to God's instructions after the flood, Nimrod gathered all peoples together and formed a world religious system. He then organized a massive effort to construct an idolatrous temple for his rebellious religion.

God judged Nimrod and his followers by confounding what was then a universal language into many languages. The people were scattered across the earth, grouping themselves according to common language.

Although the Tower of Babel was never completed, its builders carried its idolatrous ideology with them, and from that place stem all the false religions of the world.[6] The false church of the Antichrist will bring man-made religion full circle. Once again, man will join together in religious revolt against the one true God.

The ultimate goal of the Antichrist will be to personally receive the worship of the false church. Second Thessalonians 2:3–4 reveals that he will make *himself* the object of the false church's idolatrous worship: *"Let no man deceive you by any means: for that day shall not come, except there come a falling away first, and that man of sin be revealed, the son of perdition; Who opposeth and exalteth himself above all that is called God, or that is worshipped; so that he as God sitteth in the temple of God, shewing himself that he is God."*

Relentless in his demand for global worship, the Antichrist will partner with the false church in persecuting those who refuse to integrate their faith into this one-world religion.

Revelation 17:6 describes the persecuting false church as *"drunken with the blood of the saints, and with the blood of the martyrs of Jesus."* This clue helps us identify the predominant leaders of the false church as those who will come from a heritage of bloodshed.

The trail of blood spilt by Christian martyrs silently bears testimony to the cruelty of power-hungry religion. The Roman Catholic Inquisition is one of the more well-known examples of brutal church-initiated persecution. During this period in history, hundreds of thousands of men, women, and children were hanged, burned alive, drowned, imprisoned, and tortured because of their loyalty to Christ rather than the Catholic church.

Even in our own generation, we've seen harsh persecution as Christians in many parts of the world, particularly in areas where the state dictates religious beliefs, are tortured and murdered for their faith.

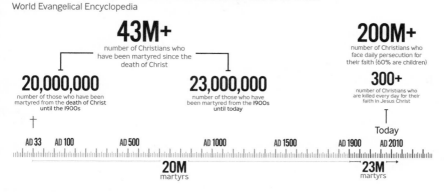

HISTORY OF THE RISE IN MODERN MARTYRS
World Evangelical Encyclopedia

43M+
number of Christians who have been martyred since the death of Christ

200M+
number of Christians who face daily persecution for their faith (60% are children)

20,000,000
number of those who have been martyred from the **death of Christ** until the 1900s

23,000,000
number of those who have been martyred from the 1900s until today

300+
number of Christians who are killed every day for their faith in Jesus Christ

AD 33   AD 100   AD 500   AD 1000   AD 1500   AD 1900   AD 2010
Today

20M martyrs   **23M** martyrs

The idolatrous church of the Tribulation will exponentially swell this "river of blood" as she determinedly annihilates those who refuse the mark of the beast and reject the worship of the Antichrist.

Integration politically

Discontented with mere religious supremacy, the false church will seek political power as well, and world leaders will find themselves intermixed with this religious body: *"With whom the kings of the earth have committed fornication, and the inhabitants of the earth have been made drunk with the wine of her fornication"* (Revelation 17:2).

The false church will push for a state church—on a global scale. The description we saw earlier of the church riding the Antichrist's government (Revelation 17:3) portrays a unique roundabout. The church will ride the state to gain power, and the state will carry the church to gain Antichrist worship. Both will have self-serving motives.

A state church of this size and influence is difficult to comprehend. There is already, however, a religious power that has an embassy with every major nation in the world—the Roman Catholic Church. The United States itself sends an ambassador to the Vatican. Although the political power held by the final days' church will far exceed that of today's Vatican, this model does provide an example of the political integration possible during the Tribulation.

Integration of theology

The unbiblical union of religion with a state church always results in gross theological compromise, for the simple truths of the Gospel do not lend themselves to the power advancements of men. Truth must be twisted and modified to meet the demands of a state church.

This false religion will blend faiths by insisting "No one religion can save by itself; let's all get together. We all believe in the same god!" This pluralistic mindset will be the foundation for a compromising world religion.

This philosophy of integration is already deeply engrafting itself into our culture. Pressure to become part of this pluralism increases regularly as the name of Christ is deliberately and systematically removed from the public sector.

In April 2010, the United States Pentagon rescinded the invitation previously extended to Evangelist Franklin Graham to lead prayer for a Pentagon National Day of Prayer service. Why was the invitation withdrawn? Because of Graham's beliefs of the Islamic faith and his stand on the exclusivity of the Gospel of Jesus Christ, as the following articles report.

> In an interview Tuesday with USA TODAY, Graham reiterated his belief that "Muslims do not worship the same 'God the Father' I worship." [Regarding Hinduism's

many manifestations of God he said:] "No elephant with 100 arms can do anything for me. None of their 9,000 gods is going to lead me to salvation.

"We are fooling ourselves if we think we can have some big kumbaya service and all hold hands and it's all going to get better in this world. It's not going to get better," Graham said.[7]

Graham called revoking his invitation to the prayer service "a slap at all evangelical Christians."

…"I'm being restricted from my religious rights, and from what I believe," Graham warned, as he complained of a growing "secularization" in the government.[8]

Oprah Winfrey clearly articulated the pluralism that denies the preeminence and exclusivity of Christ on one of her programs. When a guest on her show attempted to explain her belief that Jesus was the only way to Heaven, Oprah responded: "One of the mistakes human beings make is believing that there is only one way to live. [Referencing religious beliefs and the way of salvation.] And that we don't accept that there are diverse ways of being in the world….there are many paths to what you call God….*There couldn't possibly be just one way*"[9] [emphasis added].

Oprah expressed a belief common in today's world—"there couldn't possibly be just one way." People are already singing the tune of the one-world church—tolerance. Sadly, this is a tolerance that requires the sacrifice of truth. All religions cannot be true, for their teachings oppose each other. An attempt to make *all* of them true, essentially renders *none* of them true!

There cannot be many ways to Heaven, for Jesus Christ said, "*I am the way, the truth, and the life: no man cometh unto the Father, but by me*" (John 14:6). To attempt unity with all world religions necessitates a denial of Christ. As Charles Spurgeon so aptly explained, "You cannot have unity without compromising the truth, and to forsake truth for the sake of unity is to betray Jesus Christ."

Colossians 2:8–9 warns Christians to beware of following faulty human philosophies: *"Beware lest any man spoil you through philosophy and vain deceit, after the tradition of men, after the rudiments of the world, and not after Christ. For in him dwelleth all the fulness of the Godhead bodily."*

Scripture further instructs, *"Beloved, believe not every spirit, but try the spirits whether they are of God: because many false prophets are gone out into the world"* (1 John 4:1). The desire for unity sounds so laudable that undiscerning Christians are easily swept away from the truth.

Today people choose and change churches for all the wrong reasons. They make selections based on convenience, nursery facilities, music styles, family programming, entertainment value, and even décor! They choose a church based on what seems right and feels comfortable rather than choosing one that faithfully teaches biblical truths and proclaims Christ as the only way to Heaven.

The integration of faiths that will be required to facilitate a state church of global proportions can only come together with people who have allowed themselves to be blinded by Satan for the sake of unity. They will value political correctness and religious acceptance more than truth. Proverbs 14:12 warns of the end of such decisions: *"There is a way which seemeth right unto a man, but the end thereof are the ways of death."* (In chapter 9 we will see the tragic end of the Antichrist's government and the spiritually fornicating church's worship.)

As this book is going to press, a new book by the Dalai Lama has recently come off the press. Titled *Toward a True Kingship of Faiths: How the World's Religions Can Come Together*, the book promotes the kind of pluralism the Bible prophesies. In his chapter "The Problem of

Exclusivism," the Dalai Lama suggests that people can continue to accept their own religious beliefs as definitive truth while at the same time believe that opposing faiths are equally true.

> While allowing openness to interpretation in matters of practice and culture, which in any case pertain to guidelines for living within a society, even a religious pluralist can accept that the doctrines of his own scripture that primarily pertain to ultimate truth are definitive. In other words, one can be a religious pluralist yet maintain, for oneself, the doctrinal aspects of one's own tradition as representing definitive truth.[10]

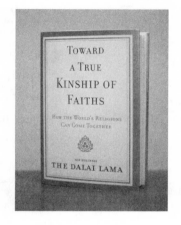

One might question if such extreme religious pluralism is truly possible in real life. Could diverse faiths really come together on a global scale? Is it even conceivable, for instance, that Buddhists, Muslims, and Catholics could set aside their differences to collectively push for a unified faith?

It is not only conceivable—it is already happening. The two largest religious groups in the world, Muslims and Catholics, are growing and are working toward unification.

Consider the following recent reports that show that the Muslim population is swelling quickly:

> The world's Muslim population stands at 1.57 billion, or 23 percent of the total population of 6.8 billion, a study released in Washington indicated.
>
> The Pew Research Center Forum on Religion & Public Life said its study was based on demographic data from 232

countries and territories. The study found Muslims inhabit all five continents but more than 60 percent of them are in Asia, and another 20 percent are in the Middle East and North Africa.

The Middle East-North Africa region has the highest percentage of Muslim-majority countries, with more than 20 countries and territories reporting a Muslim population of 95 percent or more.

About one-fifth the world's Muslim population, or more than 300 million, live in countries where Islam is not the majority religion.

India, which is predominantly Hindu, has the world's third-largest Muslim population. China has more Muslims than Syria, while Russia is home to more Muslims than Jordan and Libya combined, the study said.

Of the world's total Muslims, 10 percent to 13 percent are Shiites while 87 percent to 90 percent are Sunnis. Between 69 percent and 80 percent of all Shiites live in Iran, Pakistan, India and Iraq, the study found.[11]

Between the two most populous religions, the Roman Catholic Church and the Muslim faith, nearly two-thirds of the world's population is represented. If these two religions came together, the impact on and progress toward global religion would be phenomenal.

Actually, the lines of distinction between these diverse religions are already fading. Statements from the Catholic Church indicate these religions to be more compatible than one would assume.

But the plan of salvation also includes those who acknowledge the Creator, in the first place amongst whom are the Muslims: these profess to hold the faith of Abraham, and together with us they adore the one, merciful God, mankind's judge on the last day.... The Church has also a high regard for the Muslims. They worship God, who is one, living and subsistent, merciful and almighty, the Creator of heaven and earth, who has also spoken to men. They strive to submit themselves without reserve to the bidden decrees of God, just as Abraham submitted himself to God's plan, to whose faith Muslims eagerly link their own. Although not acknowledging him as God, they worship Jesus as a prophet, his virgin Mother they also honor, and even at times devoutly invoke.[12]

The above is an official church statement recognizing similarities in another religion and suggesting that the two are not really that different. Statements like these make an eventual one-world church much more plausible.

In June 2009, the pope visited Jordan and prayed with Muslim leaders. On a previous occasion, he prayed in the Blue Mosque of Istanbul. Concerning a November 4, 2008 meeting, a news article reported the following:

Catholics, Muslims Open Landmark Talks at Vatican

VATICAN CITY (Reuters)—**Senior Vatican and Islamic scholars launched their first Catholic-Muslim Forum on Tuesday to improve relations between the world's two largest faiths** by discussing what unites and divides them.

The meeting, including an audience with Pope Benedict, is the group's third conference with Christians after talks with United States Protestants in July and Anglicans last month.

Delegation leaders Cardinal Jean-Louis Tauran and Bosnian Grand Mufti Mustafa Ceric opened the session with a moment of silence so delegations, each comprising 28 members and advisers, could say their own prayers for its success.

"It was a very cordial atmosphere," one delegate said.

Delegates said the discussion that followed was friendly and respectful, not a clash of opinions. "We need to speak openly so we get to know each other," said one Muslim delegate.[13] [emphasis added]

The very inception of the Roman Catholic Church was the merging of Christianity and Greek and Roman paganistic rituals and practices. This poises the Catholic Church to be a catalyst that could merge Eastern thought with Western culture. Since the Roman Catholic Church has always been a religious movement that integrated local, cultural religious practices, it would provide a wide platform to draw all faiths into a one-world system under the Antichrist and the false prophet.

With the high value our culture places on tolerance and religious respect, some might question why Christians don't jump on the integration bandwagon. The following quote from Dr. Albert Mohler provides a helpful explanation of this Catholic/Muslim integration and why Bible-believing Christians reject it:

> While the Roman Catholic Church teaches that Islam is both erroneous and incomplete, it also holds that sincere Muslims can be included in Christ's salvation through their faithfulness to monotheism and Islam.
>
> Thus, when the Catholic Pope speaks of "respecting" Islam, he can do so in a way that evangelical Christians cannot. Within the context of official Catholic teaching, the Pope can create a fusion of diplomacy and doctrine.

While evangelical Christians face a different context to this question, the urgency is the same. We are not playing a diplomatic role as head of state, but we are called to be ambassadors for Christ and His Gospel.

...Thus, evangelical Christians may respect the sincerity with which Muslims hold their beliefs, but we cannot respect the beliefs themselves. We can respect Muslim people for their contributions to human welfare, scholarship, and culture. We can respect the brilliance of Muslim scholarship in the medieval era and the wonders of Islamic art and architecture. But we cannot respect a belief system that denies the truth of the gospel, insists that Jesus was not God's Son, and takes millions of souls captive.

This does not make for good diplomacy, but we are called to witness, not public relations.[14]

To best understand the significance of current events in relation to the false church, one must remember the relationship of the church to the state. We already see a political climate shaping to support the fusion of faiths that will introduce the one-world church. For example, in May 2009, the state legislature of Hawaii overwhelmingly approved a bill to celebrate an annual Islam Day.

HONOLULU—Hawaii's state Senate overwhelmingly approved a bill Wednesday to celebrate "Islam Day"—over the objections of a few lawmakers who said they didn't want to honor a religion connected to September 11, 2001.

"We are a state of tolerance...." said Sen. Will Espero, a Democrat.[15]

Political leverage is a strategic factor in the clamor for religious unity. The issues at stake are far broader than questions of faith.

As world religions and political forces are already beginning the rally cry for the false church, they unanimously claim that all roads lead to the same place. Under this presupposition, integration is the only reasonable course of action, and refusal to integrate is foolish. But, the question remains: *can* all faiths lead to salvation? Revelation 22 answers this question with an unparalleled invitation from the true Saviour.

THE INVITATION OF A TRUE SAVIOUR

I Jesus have sent mine angel to testify unto you these things in the churches. I am the root and the offspring of David, and the bright and morning star. And the Spirit and the bride say, Come. And let him that heareth say, Come. And let him that is athirst come. And whosoever will, let him take the water of life freely.
—REVELATION 22:16–17

The source of the invitation
In contrast to the spiritually deceptive church of the Antichrist, Christ is the only legitimate source to eternal life. None but God could extend the invitation given in Revelation 22:16–17.

Centuries before Christ came to earth, Old Testament prophets foretold that the Messiah would be of the lineage of David (Isaiah 9:6–7; 11:1–5; Psalm 132:11; Jeremiah 23:5; 33:14–16). When the angel announced Christ's conception to Mary, he also noted that, while Christ was conceived of the Holy Ghost, He was the earthly descendent of David: *"And, behold, thou shalt conceive in thy womb, and bring forth a son, and shalt call his name JESUS. He shall be great, and shall be called the Son of the Highest: and the Lord God shall give unto him the throne of his father David"* (Luke 1:31–32).

So when Christ proffers His invitation of Revelation 22, He points out His legitimizing lineage: *"I am the root and the offspring of David...."* I (or any other person) could *offer* eternal life, but we could never make good such a claim. Only Christ can rightfully extend such an invitation.

Not only is Christ a legitimate source for this invitation, He is the *only* source. In John 14:6, Christ declared, *"I am the way, the truth, and the life: no man cometh unto the Father, but by me."* Christ is the only way to know God and the only one who can grant the forgiveness of sins.

This message of "Christ alone" is in direct contradiction to the message of the false church. In a political and religious climate that is rapidly developing a global religion mindset, the exclusive claims of the Gospel are offensive.

Scripture plainly states, *"Neither is there salvation in any other: for there is none other name under heaven given among men, whereby we must be saved"* (Acts 4:12). Yet, in direct contradiction to God's Word, people are attempting to bring followers of every other name together for peace talks and religious forums. There's one problem—no other name can bring salvation; all other avenues to Heaven are futile.

With a straight and accurate beam, God's Word shines past the plethora of religious opinions and spiritual revelations to the only reliable source—Jesus Christ. First John 5:11 plainly tells us: *"And this* [God's Word] *is the record, that God hath given to us eternal life, and this life is in his Son."* Eternal life can never be found in the assortment of religions that will one day integrate and organize into the church of the Antichrist. This life is in Jesus Christ—alone.

Allowing no room for doubt, the next verse continues, *"He that hath the Son hath life; and he that hath not the Son of God hath not life."* It's that simple. Either you have Christ and eternal life, or you don't have Christ or eternal life.

Tragically, many religions have convinced their followers that salvation is a complicated matter of works and question marks. People try to do the best they can, but the final verdict for eternity, they say, cannot be known this side of the grave. God tells us plainly, *"These things have I written unto you that believe on the name of the Son of God; that ye may* **know** *that ye have eternal life, and that ye may believe on the name of the Son of God"* (1 John 5:13, emphasis added).

Notice the certainty of possessing eternal life has nothing to do with works; it comes by believing on the name of Christ. Ephesians 2:8–9 specifically rules out works as a component of salvation: *"For by grace are ye saved through faith; and that not of yourselves: it is the gift of God: Not of works, lest any man should boast."*

Jesus Christ is the only true source of an eternal salvation—not works, not religion, not spiritual leaders, and not good intentions.

The subjects of the invitation

The source of the invitation is exclusive. It is only available through Christ, but the subjects of the invitation are gloriously inclusive. Salvation is open to all who will come! *"And the Spirit and the bride say, Come. And let him that heareth say, Come. And let him that is athirst come. And whosoever will, let him take the water of life freely"* (Revelation 22:17).

With kingly generosity, Christ invites anyone who is thirsty to receive the gift of eternal life: *"Ho, every one that thirsteth, come ye to the waters, and he that hath no money; come ye, buy, and eat; yea, come, buy wine and milk without money and without price"* (Isaiah 55:1). No purchase necessary (or possible); this is a gift! You can't earn it, deserve it, or purchase it. You simply believe and receive Jesus Christ.

Christ's invitation is not limited to a select few. Nationality, color, background, location—none of these restrict the invitation of Christ.

With the widest open door possible, Christ calls out *"whosoever will, let him take…"* (Revelation 22:17). *Whosoever* means anyone, everyone you!

One of the most well-known verses in the entire Bible reiterates this invitation: *"For God so loved the world, that he gave his only begotten Son, that whosoever believeth in him should not perish, but have everlasting life"* (John 3:16). God's love behind this invitation is so great that He gave His only begotten Son to die in our place—to pay the penalty for our sin—that we might receive the gift of everlasting life. *"But God commendeth* [proved or demonstrated] *his love toward us, in that, while we were yet sinners, Christ died for us"* (Romans 5:8).

Three days later, Christ rose from the grave—the victor over death—and He offers salvation to anyone who will receive it: *"For whosoever shall call upon the name of the Lord shall be saved"* (Romans 10:13).

Salvation is not something we achieve; it is something we receive. Don't be deceived, some churches that use the name "Christian" and claim to follow Christ actually distort true salvation and make it a process of atonement—requiring that you do good works to pay for your own sin. This is not the Christianity of the Bible. A Christian doesn't pay for or atone for his own sin—Jesus atoned for all sin on the Cross. There's nothing left to pay. It's a gift to be received!

When a person believes that Jesus Christ paid for his sin in full and puts his faith in the finished work of Christ on the Cross, he receives salvation—at that very moment. No one is saved because he earns salvation through good works; that would be impossible. Salvation can only be received as a gift.

Have you received this gift? Have you accepted Christ's gracious invitation? He invites—actually implores—you to come: *"And the Spirit and the bride say, Come. And let him that heareth say, Come. And let him that is athirst come. And whosoever will, let him take the water of life freely"* (Revelation 22:17).

Several times in this text, I've asked you about your salvation—if you know Jesus Christ personally. After all that we've studied, I invite you again to consider the choice before you. We've seen that mankind, throughout all of time, has desired to resist the one living God. He is bent on denying Him. We've seen a God who has revealed Himself clearly—through His Word, through His dealings with Israel, through His Son, Jesus, and through His sovereignty throughout the ages.

In this chapter we've studied two basic forms of belief. The first is man-made and says, "All roads lead to the same place." It teaches that salvation is up to you—so long as you truly believe in the god of your own choosing. It lifts up mankind as the final authority, and it points to the ultimate coming together of the world religions into one mystical system of deception.

The second is all about Jesus Christ and is exclusive to Him. It heralds the Bible as the final authority, God as the only living God, and Jesus Christ as His perfect Son who came to earth to pay for our sins and offer us the gift of eternal life. This truth has been validated in a multitude of ways. A sincere and open heart cannot ignore the obvious hand of God in all that we've seen in these pages.

You must make a choice. Do you choose man-made religion? Or do you choose Jesus Christ? Are you ready to choose to be a follower of the God of the Bible—the one who is God alone? Are you ready to align yourself and your eternity with what you know is true? If so, now would be a great time to set this book down, open your heart in prayer, and call out to Christ to be your personal Saviour.

If you would like to receive God's free and gracious gift of salvation, I encourage you to pray something like this right now: *Dear God, I know that I cannot reach Heaven through my own works or merit. I confess that in my sin, I cannot save myself. I believe that Jesus Christ is Your Son, that He died for my sin and rose again. Right now, I trust Jesus Christ alone to be my Saviour. I ask You to save me from the penalty of my sin, and I trust You to give Your gift of eternal life to me—Amen.*

The prayer above is not a formula—it's merely one example of how you might pray to God to receive His free offer of eternal salvation. If you have just made that decision, please contact us at strivingtogether.com so we can help you begin to walk in your new relationship with Jesus Christ.[16]

There are really only two systems of religious beliefs. One system is currently divided, but it will come together as the false church during the Tribulation. This system emphasizes social good works and religion for salvation. It is represented today by every religion that denies that Christ is the Son of God and the only way to Heaven.

And then there's the way of grace—salvation through Jesus Christ alone. With an all-inclusive invitation, Christ offers an exclusive guarantee of eternal life.

The choice is individual. You must decide for yourself if you will place your credence in works-based religion or if you will trust the true Saviour and accept His invitation to eternal life.

Revelation 22:20 encourages us to make this choice today, for Christ has promised, *"Surely I come quickly."* For those who receive Christ as their true Saviour, the return of Christ will be a glorious event. We who know Christ look for His return with anticipation, and we can echo the words of the Apostle John, *"Even so, come, Lord Jesus"* (Revelation 22:20).

CHAPTER EIGHT

The Seven Years of Judgment

Everyone, Christian and non-Christian alike, demonstrates immense interest in the culminating of this age and the Earth as we know it. Even the early disciples were curious about the end of the world. In a passage commonly known as "the Olivet Discourse," Christ answered their questions with a description of the seven-year Tribulation.

> And as he sat upon the mount of Olives, the disciples came unto him privately, saying, Tell us, when shall these things be? and what shall be the sign of thy coming, and of the end of the world? And Jesus answered and said unto them, Take heed that no man deceive you. For many shall come in my name, saying, I am Christ; and shall deceive many. And ye shall hear of wars and

rumours of wars: see that ye be not troubled: for all these things must come to pass, but the end is not yet. For nation shall rise against nation, and kingdom against kingdom: and there shall be famines, and pestilences, and earthquakes, in divers places. All these are the beginning of sorrows. Then shall they deliver you up to be afflicted, and shall kill you: and ye shall be hated of all nations for my name's sake. And then shall many be offended, and shall betray one another, and shall hate one another. And many false prophets shall rise, and shall deceive many.
—MATTHEW 24:3–11

Because the end times provides fascinating subject matter, Hollywood borrows from the imagery of Scripture with movie titles such as *Apocalypse* and *Armageddon*. Satan craftily uses these media distortions to desensitize people to the reality of prophetic judgments. By presenting this material in a fashion similar to science fiction, the subject remains intriguing but lacks the weight of reality and distorts the severity of its facts.

Truly, the study of the end times is captivating, but the reality of experiencing the outpoured wrath of God during the Tribulation will be harrowing for all those who deny and defy Christ. The pages ahead will not be light reading. In fact, studying and writing of these events is difficult. I would much rather pretend that these portions of Scripture did not exist. It is difficult to comprehend mankind becoming so collectively defiant against God and desperate to defeat Him.

The Bible speaks of events that will transpire at the end of the Antichrist's kingdom. These events warn us of the judgment of God upon a planet and a race that would rather suffer destruction than repent and turn to Him. What we are about to study does not delight God. Frankly, it breaks His heart. But God is holy—He will not allow sin and rebellion to continue forever. God is just—He never unjustly pours out random wrath or unwarranted judgment. And God is love—even in judgment, He would save any who would call upon Him for salvation.

I write these pages with a heavy heart, for we will see in Scripture that in the future mankind grows irrevocably intolerant and defiant of God in total and outright rejection—even cursing His name to His very face. This extreme and ultimate rejection of the living God will result in the pouring out of a cataclysmic series of judgments that no sane person would choose to endure.

And so, with great respect to God's Word, let us venture forward and see what God says is yet to come. This is no science fiction movie or cleverly crafted script. It is the grave and sobering end of a humanity that has once and for all rejected a great God of love and mercy. It is the end of sin—which is a wonderful thing. But for those who choose sin instead of God, it will be their end as well. The rest of this chapter is very heavy, but rest assured, good news is still ahead!

In his book *Prophecy for Today,* Dwight Pentecost describes what the Bible calls a time of great tribulation:

> The Great Tribulation is a term that strikes terror into people's hearts, and the word *Armageddon* chills the spine. People everywhere dread God's wrath. Even those with little or no knowledge of the Bible have the conviction that God must judge the earth because of its wickedness.
>
> When we look at history, we see a continuous and unbroken record of rebellion against God. Civilization after civilization and nation after nation have walked in the way of godlessness and unrighteousness, and people anticipate God's wrath as a result. And yet few are clear about what the Bible teaches concerning the tribulation.[1]

Scripture itself provides many references to the Tribulation.[2] In *The Popular Bible Prophecy Workbook,* authors LaHaye and Hindson write: "The Tribulation is mentioned in more than 60 passages in the Bible. More space is allotted to it than any other subject except for salvation and the second coming of Christ."

Although Scripture does not provide a calendar date for the Tribulation, we know from Matthew 24 that these years will directly preface the Second Coming of Christ (see chapter 9). The cataclysmic events Jesus described to His disciples will bring the world to a point of readiness for Christ's return.

Through examining and cross-referencing the many prophecies of the Tribulation, we can trace its progression and understand its purpose.

THE PROPHECIES OF THE TRIBULATION

When Jesus described the Tribulation to His inquisitive disciples, He didn't mince words or attempt to moderate its horrors. He plainly said, *"For then shall be great tribulation, such as was not since the beginning of the world to this time, no, nor ever shall be"* (Matthew 24:21). Jesus described the last half of the period as characterized by unparalleled tribulation—great tribulation such as the world has never seen, nor ever will see.

The first prophecies of the Tribulation were delivered to Israel via her Old Testament prophets. These prophecies reveal that the Tribulation

---

[2] Scripture does not always refer to this time period as "the Tribulation," nor does every instance of the word *tribulation* in Scripture refer to this specific event. Dwight Pentecost explained it this way: "We must remember that the word tribulation is used in the Bible in both a technical and a non-technical sense. When used non-technically, it speaks of any trial or suffering through which an individual may go. When used in its technical sense, it refers to the seven-year period following the translation of the church, a time of unprecedented judgment and wrath from God upon the earth."

relates specifically and primarily to the nation of Israel. The prophecies given by three men in particular—Jeremiah, Daniel, and Zechariah—provide a good cross view into this seven-year segment of time.

Jeremiah revealed the purpose.

> Alas! for that day is great, so that none is like it: it is even the time of Jacob's trouble; but he shall be saved out of it. For it shall come to pass in that day, saith the LORD of hosts, that I will break his yoke from off thy neck, and will burst thy bonds, and strangers shall no more serve themselves of him: But they shall serve the LORD their God, and David their king, whom I will raise up unto them.—JEREMIAH 30:7–9

The *"time of Jacob's trouble"* is one of the phrases used to refer to the Tribulation in Scripture.[3] It speaks of a time when Israel will be ruled by Gentile nations as God judges His people for their ungodliness.

Yet even God's judgment during the Tribulation is a manifestation of His unquenchable grace, for all of the horrific events that will take place have a purpose: to turn Israel and the world back toward God in repentance.

Daniel revealed the plan.

> Seventy weeks are determined upon thy people and upon thy holy city, to finish the transgression, and to make an end of sins, and to make reconciliation for iniquity, and to bring in everlasting righteousness, and to seal up the vision and prophecy, and to anoint the most Holy. Know therefore and understand, that from

---

[3] Authors LaHaye and Hindson note that other references to the Tribulation include "the day of the Lord" (1 Thessalonians 5:2), the seventieth week of Daniel (Daniel 9:27), "a day of…desolation" (Zephaniah 1:15), "the wrath to come" (1 Thessalonians 1:10), "the hour of his judgment" (Revelation 14:7), and "the great tribulation" (Matthew 24:21).

the going forth of the commandment to restore and to build
Jerusalem unto the Messiah the Prince shall be seven weeks, and
threescore and two weeks: the street shall be built again, and the
wall, even in troublous times. And after threescore and two weeks
shall Messiah be cut off, but not for himself: and the people of the
prince that shall come shall destroy the city and the sanctuary;
and the end thereof shall be with a flood, and unto the end of
the war desolations are determined. And he shall confirm the
covenant with many for one week: and in the midst of the week
he shall cause the sacrifice and the oblation to cease, and for the
overspreading of abominations he shall make it desolate, even
until the consummation, and that determined shall be poured
upon the desolate.—DANIEL 9:24–27

As we saw in chapter 5, each of the prophetic weeks of which
Daniel spoke actually refers to a period of seven years. Both Daniel
and John prophesied that the Tribulation itself would last seven years
(Daniel 9:24–27; Revelation 11:2–3). This is the last "week" (seven year
period) of Daniel's prophecy. The complete prophecy, detailing God's
plan leading up to the Tribulation, can be detailed as follows:

1. Daniel's 70 weeks are 7 years each for a total of 490 years.
2. From the commandment to rebuild Jerusalem, there were 483
   years (69 weeks).
3. After the 483rd year, the Messiah was "cut off."
4. The remaining 7 years (70th week of the prophecy) is suspended
   for the "church age."
5. The Antichrist begins the 70th week with a peace covenant
   with Israel, which will resume the time clock of the 70 weeks
   prophecy to finish the final week.

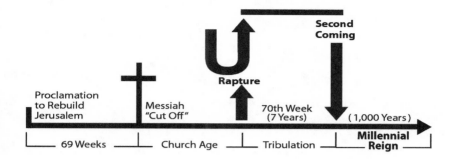

The final week of Daniel's prophecy, then, is what we know as the Tribulation. These seven years will be divided into two segments, each lasting three-and-a-half years. This week will begin with the Antichrist's covenant which takes place during a time of peace in Israel—the temple will have been rebuilt and temple worship resumed. (Please note, the rebuilding of the temple and Israel experiencing peace with her neighbors could take place before this covenant is established—it's the covenant that begins the Tribulation week.)

Daniel prophesies, however, that the Antichrist will break this covenant in the middle of the Tribulation and establish himself as the object of worship in the temple. Other Scriptures mention this midpoint of the Tribulation as well:

> *When ye therefore shall see the abomination of desolation, spoken of by Daniel the prophet, stand in the holy place, (whoso readeth, let him understand:) Then let them which be in Judaea flee into the mountains:*—MATTHEW 24:15–16

> *Let no man deceive you by any means: for that day shall not come, except there come a falling away first, and that man of sin be revealed, the son of perdition; Who opposeth and exalteth himself above all that is called God, or that is worshipped; so that he*

as God sitteth in the temple of God, shewing himself that he is God.—2 THESSALONIANS 2:3–4

Zechariah revealed the product.

And I will bring the third part through the fire, and will refine them as silver is refined, and will try them as gold is tried: they shall call on my name, and I will hear them: I will say, It is my people: and they shall say, The LORD is my God.
—ZECHARIAH 13:9

God will deliver Israel from this time of great tribulation, and when He does, Israel will cleave to Him in tender love and devoted loyalty. The product of God's judgment will be a great host of people, Jews and Gentiles alike, turning to God.

God will finally establish the New Covenant, promised in Jeremiah 31:31–34, with His people:

Behold, the days come, saith the LORD, that I will make a new covenant with the house of Israel, and with the house of Judah: Not according to the covenant that I made with their fathers in the day that I took them by the hand to bring them out of the land of Egypt; which my covenant they brake, although I was an husband unto them, saith the LORD: But this shall be the covenant that I will make with the house of Israel; After those days, saith the LORD, I will put my law in their inward parts, and write it in their hearts; and will be their God, and they shall be my people. And they shall teach no more every man his neighbour, and every man his brother, saying, Know the LORD: for they shall all know me, from the least of them unto the greatest of them, saith the

LORD: *for I will forgive their iniquity, and I will remember their* *sin no more.*

Once again, the Jews will be "God's people," belonging to Him through their own chosen devotion, and He will be their God, bound to them with cords of love.

THE PROGRESSION OF THE TRIBULATION

Daniel revealed the plan leading up to the Tribulation, but let's now examine the sequence of events *during* the Tribulation.

Authors LaHaye and Jenkins commented:

> No one wants to think of a future period—even a short one of seven years—that will be the greatest time of suffering and terror in all of human history. But the Bible is clear on the traumas of this period. …It is unrealistic to spiritualize away the devastations God is going to unleash on this world during the Tribulation. While that period may be short, the judgments will seem endless to those caught in them.[4]

Revelation 4–19 vividly describes the progression of the Tribulation. The first three chapters of Revelation are addressed to seven churches in Asia Minor. After John heard the call, *"Come up hither"* in Revelation 4:1, there is no more mention in Revelation of the church on Earth until the end of the Tribulation. This is one of the many indicators (others covered more thoroughly in chapter 4) that Christians will be raptured to Heaven and delivered from the outpouring of God's wrath (1 Thessalonians 1:10) before the Tribulation begins. This deliverance for God's children is also suggested in the biblical account of Lot, as God would not bring judgment on Sodom until He removed righteous Lot (Genesis 19:22).

The removal of the saints

In a moment, in the twinkling of an eye, at the last trump: for the trumpet shall sound, and the dead shall be raised incorruptible, and we shall be changed.—1 CORINTHIANS 15:52

The word *moment* in 1 Corinthians 15:52 is translated from the Greek word *atomos*. It is from this word that we get our English word *atom*, which means "indivisible" or "undivided." The Rapture will happen so quickly that no one will realize an incident transpired until they see the results.

And what results there will be! Millions will suddenly disappear, and graves will be left open, empty and void of their former bodily occupants. Pandemonium will reign as man-made disasters, caused by this sudden disappearance, devastate the world. Vehicles, planes, and machinery will suddenly be left unmanned, generating a tremendous toll of accidents.

Quite possibly, the chaos created by the Rapture will be instrumental in ushering the Antichrist into full power.

The rise of the Antichrist

Launching the Tribulation itself will be the covenant the Antichrist will arbitrate for peace. His diplomatic ability will so impress the world, that the ten ruling world powers will hand their scepters to this beast.

As we saw in chapter 7, when the Antichrist rises to power, his false church will ascend with him. Thanks to the work of the false prophet, people will believe that the Antichrist is their long-awaited answer to political and spiritual unity.

The spiritual vacuum left by the disappearance of millions of Christians will also enable the Antichrist to further his plan for a forced one-world religion. This pagan religion will unite all religions—with the lone exception of biblical

Christianity—into one. In the midst of all this, the Holy Spirit will work through the 144,000 evangelists and the two witnesses in Jerusalem to draw countless numbers of people to Christ during the Tribulation—despite the fact that such a choice will most likely result in martyrdom.[5]

For three-and-a-half years, the Antichrist will honor the treaty he instituted. At the midpoint of the Tribulation, however, he will lash out against Israel and defile her rebuilt temple, blasphemously insisting on being worshipped: *"And they worshipped the dragon which gave power unto the beast: and they worshipped the beast, saying, Who is like unto the beast? who is able to make war with him? And there was given unto him a mouth speaking great things and blasphemies; and power was given unto him to continue forty and two months. And he opened his mouth in blasphemy against God, to blaspheme his name, and his tabernacle, and them that dwell in heaven"* (Revelation 13:4–6).

Although heralded by a godless society, the rise of the Antichrist will in itself become a judgment of the Tribulation.

The revelation of Christ's witnesses

One of the most oft-asked questions concerning the Tribulation is whether or not people will be saved during this period. The answer is a resounding yes! Second Thessalonians 2:10–12, however, indicates that those who have previously made a deliberate choice to reject Christ will not only remain lost, but they will continue to harden their hearts toward God and have no desire to be saved: *"And with all deceivableness of unrighteousness in them that perish; because they received not the love of the truth, that they might be saved. And for this cause God shall send them strong delusion, that they should believe a lie: That they all might be damned who believed not the truth, but had pleasure in unrighteousness."*

The many thousands who will be saved during the Tribulation will be the fruit of the diligent efforts of faithful Jewish witnesses. Revelation 14:3–5 introduces us to the 144,000 witnesses preaching the Gospel of Jesus Christ: *"And they sung as it were a new song before the throne, and before the four beasts, and the elders: and no man could learn that song but the hundred and forty and four thousand, which were redeemed from the earth. These are they which were not defiled with women; for they are virgins. These are they which follow the Lamb whithersoever he goeth. These were redeemed from among men, being the firstfruits unto God and to the Lamb. And in their mouth was found no guile: for they are without fault before the throne of God."*

The Jehovah's Witnesses teach that inclusion in this 144,000 is granted through their organization and is based on one's performance as a witness. Somehow, the Jehovah's Witnesses have missed the qualifications Scripture gives for this group of Tribulation witnesses. According to the passage above, they are all male virgins. Revelation 7:4–8 further designates them as being of the twelve tribes of Israel. Because most people who are converted by the Jehovah's Witnesses are not male Jewish virgins, we must conclude that their ideas are confused and not founded on Scripture.

So who *are* the 144,000? These men are *"the firstfruits unto God and to the Lamb."* This indicates that they will be the first to be saved in the Tribulation. Considering the godless political and spiritual climate throughout the Tribulation, this will be no easy time to be a Christian. These firstfruits and their converts will be heavily persecuted by the state church of the Antichrist (see chapter 7). Yet even in the midst of such terror, these men will faithfully proclaim the Gospel to every nation.

After this I beheld, and, lo, a great multitude, which no man could number, of all nations, and kindreds, and people, and tongues, stood before the throne, and before the Lamb, clothed with white robes, and palms in their hands; And cried with a loud voice, saying, Salvation to our God which sitteth upon the throne, and unto the Lamb.…And one of the elders answered, saying unto me, What are these which are arrayed in white robes? and whence came they? And I said unto him, Sir, thou knowest. And he said to me, These are they which came out of great tribulation, and have washed their robes, and made them white in the blood of the Lamb.—REVELATION 7:9–10, 13–14

In addition to the 144,000 evangelists, God will place two witnesses on Earth whose ministry involves standing in opposition to the Antichrist: *"And I will give power unto my two witnesses, and they shall prophesy a thousand two hundred and threescore days, clothed in sackcloth"* (Revelation 11:3). During the last part of the Tribulation, these two witnesses will prophesy 1,260 days, or 3.5 years (based on the prophetic year of 360 days).

Many prophecy students believe these two men will be Moses and Elijah, by virtue of the miraculous works they will do through the power of God: *"These have power to shut heaven, that it rain not in the days of their prophecy: and have power over waters to turn them to blood, and to smite the earth with all plagues, as often as they will"* (Revelation 11:6).

Revelation 11:7–12 records the final days of these men of God:

And when they shall have finished their testimony, the beast that ascendeth out of the bottomless pit shall make war against them, and shall overcome them, and kill them. And their dead bodies shall lie in the street of the great city, which spiritually is called Sodom and Egypt, where also our Lord was crucified. And they of the people and kindreds and tongues and nations shall see their dead bodies three days and an half, and shall not suffer their dead bodies to be put in graves. And they that dwell upon the earth shall rejoice over them, and make merry, and shall send gifts one to another; because these two prophets tormented them that dwelt on the earth. And after three days and an half the Spirit of life from God entered into them, and they stood upon their feet; and great fear fell upon them which saw them. And they heard a great voice from heaven saying unto them, Come up hither. And they ascended up to heaven in a cloud; and their enemies beheld them.—REVELATION 11:7–12

When the two witnesses have finished their work, they will suffer martyrdom at the hands of the Antichrist, and the world will celebrate with sadistic delight. In its sin-twisted thinking, the world will actually believe that the faithful witness of these men "*tormented them.*" In actuality, the testimony of these witnesses and the missionary efforts of the 144,000 are a powerful demonstration of the grace of God; for, even as He pours out His wrath against sin, He offers people the opportunity to turn to Him and receive salvation.

The retribution of God's judgment

These seven years will witness judgments such as the world has never seen. Revelation presents these judgments as the focal point of the Tribulation.

Revelation divides the judgments into three categories: seven seals (Revelation 6), seven trumpets (Revelation 8–11), and seven vials (Revelation 16). All of these refer to the same period of time, and generally, they respectively divide into the following three categories:

1. LIFE-ENDING JUDGMENTS

Millions upon millions of people will lose their lives through the judgments unsealed in Revelation 6.

Although the Tribulation begins with a peace treaty finagled by the Antichrist, wars will claim many lives.

> *And I saw, and behold a white horse: and he that sat on him had a bow; and a crown was given unto him: and he went forth conquering, and to conquer. And when he had opened the second seal, I heard the second beast say, Come and see. And there went out another horse that was red: and power was given to him that sat thereon to take peace from the earth, and that they should kill one another: and there was given unto him a great sword.*
> —REVELATION 6:2–4 (see also Matthew 24:6–7A)

This would include, if not primarily refer to, the war of Ezekiel 38–39 that we studied in chapter 5.

Famine, perhaps as a result of war, will ravish the supplies of the Antichrist's new world order.

> *And when he had opened the third seal, I heard the third beast say, Come and see. And I beheld, and lo a black horse; and he that sat on him had a pair of balances in his hand. And I heard a voice in the midst of the four beasts say, A measure of wheat for a penny, and three measures of barley for a penny; and see thou hurt not the oil and the wine. And when he had opened the fourth seal, I heard the voice of the fourth beast say, Come and see.*—REVELATION 6:5–7

People will be forced to tightly ration even meager portions of food in an attempt to escape famine's deadly clutches. In his commentary on Revelation, Charles Ryrie explains: "The black horse forebodes death, and the pair of balances bespeaks a careful rationing of food. Normally, a 'penny' (a Roman denarius, a day's wages in Palestine in Jesus' day, Matthew 20:2) would buy eight measures of wheat or twenty-four of barley. Under these famine conditions the same wage will buy only one measure of wheat or three of barley."[6] This could mean that only one-eighth of the necessary food supply will be available.

The phrase *"and see thou hurt not the oil and the wine"* suggests a twist of irony. An abundance of luxury items will be available, but they will be too costly for famine-stricken people to purchase.

Increasing the death toll of the wars and famine will be pestilences. Disease and plagues often follow war as a result of contaminated water supplies, infection, and dead bodies not properly disposed of. Revelation 6:8 also speaks of the *"beasts of the earth"* in connection with the pestilence. This may indicate that some of these illnesses are results of bites from diseased animals or of insect attacks.

To understand the severity of this judgment, consider the devastating effects of epidemic plagues the world has already experienced or is enduring: At least one-third of the European population died during the Black Plague in the fourteenth century. Africa today is experiencing extreme loss of life through the AIDS virus. Other epidemics include the SARS outbreak several years ago and the H1N1 flu virus pandemic.

New super strains of antibiotic-resistant bacteria have been developing over the course of the last few decades. The epidemic diseases of the Tribulation will be impossible to substantially curb.

The life-ending judgments of the Tribulation will claim the lives of at least one-fourth of the world's population: *"…And power was given unto them over the fourth part of the earth, to kill with sword, and with hunger, and with death, and with the beasts of the earth"* (Revelation 6:8).

2. ENVIRONMENTALLY DEVASTATING JUDGMENTS

No amount of environmental awareness or conservation will save Earth from the judgments proclaimed by the trumpets of Revelation 8–11.

Earthquakes will be the first to thunder this series of judgments. Matthew 24:7–8 speaks of *"earthquakes in divers places"* and explains that *"these are the beginning of sorrows."*

A September 2009 news article prophesied increased seismic activity as a result of the 2004 Sumatran quake:

San Andreas Affected by 2004 Sumatran Quake; Largest Quakes Can Weaken Fault Zones Worldwide

U.S. seismologists have found evidence that the massive 2004 earthquake that triggered killer tsunamis throughout the Indian Ocean weakened at least a portion of California's famed San Andreas Fault. The results, which appear this week in the journal *Nature*, suggest that the Earth's largest earthquakes can weaken fault zones worldwide and may trigger periods of increased global seismic activity.

"An unusually high number of magnitude 8 earthquakes occurred worldwide in 2005 and 2006," said study co-author Fenglin Niu, associate professor of Earth science at Rice University. "There has been speculation that these were somehow triggered by the Sumatran-Andaman earthquake that occurred on Dec. 26, 2004, but this is the first direct evidence that the quake could change fault strength of a fault remotely."[7]

Since the writing of the above article, three more serious earthquakes have shaken the countries of Haiti, Chile, and Japan. Thankfully, the United States and others have been quick to respond to the needs of those whose lives have been turned upside down as a result. One wonders, however, if these frequent earthquakes are foreshocks of the winding down of time.

The rumblings of the Tribulation quakes are but a prediction of heavier judgment to follow. Fires will consume one-third of Earth's trees and plants (Revelation 8:7). This will inevitably interrupt the photosynthesis cycle and disturb Earth's oxygen balance. With lower oxygen and increased smoke, respiratory illnesses will abound. Those who worship the planet will be appalled by the devastation of these fires.

A giant meteorite will lend its weight to God's judgment (Revelation 8:8–9). Its landing in the Mediterranean Sea will destroy one-third of the aquatic life and will doubtless destroy numerous ships as well. The tidal wave created by this falling meteorite will render vast destruction of its own.

A December 30, 2009 article by the *Associated Press* reported Russia's concern that a large asteroid may impact Earth in several years.

> Russia is considering sending a spacecraft to a large asteroid to knock it off its path and prevent a possible collision with Earth, the head of the country's space agency said Wednesday....
>
> When the 270-meter (885-foot) asteroid was first discovered in 2004, astronomers estimated the chances of it smashing into Earth in its first flyby in 2029 were as high as 1-in-37, but have since lowered their estimate....
>
> In October, NASA lowered the odds that Apophis could hit Earth in 2036 from a 1-in-45,000 as earlier thought to a 1-in-250,000 chance after researchers recalculated the asteroid's path. It said another close encounter in 2068 will involve a 1-in-330,000 chance of impact....
>
> "People's lives are at stake. We should pay several hundred million dollars and build a system that would allow to prevent a collision, rather than sit and wait for it to happen and kill hundreds of thousands of people," Perminov said....

Hollywood action films "Deep Impact" and "Armageddon," have featured space missions scrambling to avoid catastrophic collisions. In both movies space crews use nuclear bombs in an attempt to prevent collisions.

Boris Shustov, the director of the Institute of Astronomy under the Russian Academy of Sciences, hailed Perminov's statement as a signal that officials had come to recognize the danger posed by asteroids.[8]

Although NASA considers this collision highly unlikely, this article demonstrates both the great concern attached to a meteorite strike as well as the mental association such a possibility has with Armageddon in people's minds. The meteorite of the Tribulation will likely be a different one than Apophis, and it may strike much sooner than 2036.

Another of the environmentally devastating judgments during the Tribulation will be water contamination, which will cause unprecedented pollution. The fresh water poisoning prophesied in Revelation 8:10–11 may be the direct work of an angelic creature, or it may be the result of a fallout from another cataclysmic event.

For an unspecified time duration, the loss of the sun's power will cast another dark judgment (Revelation 8:12). When the sun's power is diminished by one-third, not only will it rob Earth of her light, but it will concurrently diminish her heat as well.

3. RETALIATORY JUDGMENTS

This final category of judgments is primarily referred to as the "vial judgments" in Revelation 16. These supernatural judgments will essentially focus against the beast and his kingdom during the second half of the Tribulation. They will be God's specific response to the Antichrist's attack and persecution of Israel.

These vial judgments are referred to in Revelation 16:1 as *"the wrath of God."* Anytime someone goes against God's own people, as the Antichrist will do during the Tribulation, like a loving father would do, God hears the cries of His suffering people and pours out His retribution toward her enemies.

The first retaliatory judgment is actually a trumpet judgment, and it is described in Revelation 9:3–6:

> *And there came out of the smoke locusts upon the earth: and unto them was given power, as the scorpions of the earth have power. And it was commanded them that they should not hurt the grass of the earth, neither any green thing, neither any tree; but only those men which have not the seal of God in their foreheads. And to them it was given that they should not kill them, but that they should be tormented five months: and their torment was as the torment of a scorpion, when he striketh a man. And in those days shall men seek death, and shall not find it; and shall desire to die, and death shall flee from them.*

Locusts from Hell will begin the torment of the beast's followers. For five months, those who have rejected Christ and the testimony of His witnesses will endure heinous agony. The tremendous pain inflicted by these locusts will be like the sting of a scorpion, inducing its sufferers to unsuccessfully seek an evading death. Thus, God will revenge the persecutors of His people with His own persecution.

Moving to the vial judgments, agonizing sores will develop on those who take the mark of the beast. Some commentators speculate that this *"noisome and grievous sore upon the men which had the mark of the beast, and upon them which worshipped his image"* (Revelation 16:2) is an infection caused by the chip they allowed to be implanted in their bodies. In whatever way the sore develops, it will directly judge men for identifying with the beast.

In retribution for the blood of the martyrs, both the Mediterranean Sea and fresh water supplies will be turned to literal blood (Revelation 16:3–6). When this judgment takes place, an angel proclaims God's justice: *"For they have shed the blood of saints and prophets, and thou hast given them blood to drink; for they are worthy"* (Revelation 16:6).

Torments by the sun in two extremes will follow: unrelenting heat and permeating darkness.

> And the fourth angel poured out his vial upon the sun; and power was given unto him to scorch men with fire. And men were scorched with great heat, and blasphemed the name of God, which hath power over these plagues: and they repented not to give him glory. And the fifth angel poured out his vial upon the seat of the beast; and his kingdom was full of darkness; and they gnawed their tongues for pain, And blasphemed the God of heaven because of their pains and their sores, and repented not of their deeds.—REVELATION 16:8–11

As staggering as the Tribulation judgments are, even more amazing is man's refusal to repent. Even as sin-hardened men literally gnaw their tongues in pain, they will shake their fists toward Heaven. Rather than acknowledging their guilt and accepting God's salvation, they will curse and blaspheme Him for His righteous judgment.

THE PURPOSE OF THE TRIBULATION

We must remember that the Tribulation has a purpose. Each phase of the Tribulation is God giving men yet another opportunity to repent before they are destroyed. At any moment, they could turn to Christ, but instead they choose to endure the Tribulation judgments. Through gritted teeth, they say, in effect, "I choose my sin; I defy You, God!"

When God pours out His wrath, He does not merely "vent"; He brings men to a point of decision. Yet over and over, men willfully choose not to repent.

> And the rest of the men which were not killed by these plagues **yet repented not** of the works of their hands, that they should not worship devils, and idols of gold, and silver, and brass, and stone, and of wood: which neither can see, nor hear, nor walk:
> —REVELATION 9:20

> And men were scorched with great heat, and blasphemed the name of God, which hath power over these plagues: **and they repented not** to give him glory.—REVELATION 16:9

> And the fifth angel poured out his vial upon the seat of the beast; and his kingdom was full of darkness; and they gnawed their tongues for pain, And blasphemed the God of heaven because of their pains and their sores, **and repented not** of their deeds.
> —REVELATION 16:10–11 [emphasis added]

God cannot allow the unrepentant sin of man to go unchecked for eternity. His justice requires judgment, and yet, in His grace, He has both provided a sin payment through the blood of Christ for all who will trust Him, and He has withheld His judgment for millennia, giving man more opportunities to trust Christ. In spite of all of this, many will still spurn God's gracious patience: *"And I gave her space to repent of her fornication; and she repented not"* (Revelation 2:21).

The Tribulation marks the beginning of the end of this space for repentance. Through the Tribulation judgments, God validates His goodness and vindicates His justice. In His goodness, He still allows men to turn from their sin and trust Christ; and in His justice, He metes out judgment to those who defy Him and blaspheme His holiness.

Even as God uses the Tribulation judgments to accomplish these purposes, He deals very specifically and individually with two groups of people: Israel and the Gentile nations.

The purpose as it relates to Israel

Christians tend to view modern Israel in her biblical context, assuming most residents are devout, practicing Jews. In reality, the nation is secular, and most Israelis today are agnostics. Israel as a whole turned from her God centuries ago. Paul described the coldness of the Jews' heart toward God in 1 Thessalonians 2:15: *"Who both killed the Lord Jesus, and their own prophets, and have persecuted us; and they please not God, and are contrary to all men."* Thus, one purpose for the supernatural judgments of the Tribulation is to reprove Israel for her unbelief.

God's hand of judgment is not intended to merely reprove, but also to bring glorious restoration. As we saw from Jeremiah 30 earlier in this chapter, God will release the Gentile's hold on Israel and restore her to Himself. As a result of the Tribulation, Israel will return to her God and receive her Messiah.

The purpose as it relates to the Gentile nations

For all the Gentile nations, God has a two-fold purpose in the Tribulation. Authors LaHaye and Jenkins expressed it well:

> We believe with all our hearts that the Tribulation judgments of God serve a dual purpose: to punish hardened sinners *and* to move others to repentance and faith. The Tribulation will be God's ultimate illustration of the truth found in Romans 11:22: "Behold [consider] therefore the goodness

and severity of God." It is true that the Tribulation will demonstrate God's severity, but is equally true that it will showcase His goodness.[9]

First, these judgments are His direct retribution for their rebellion— especially their cooperation with the Antichrist and their antagonism against Israel. The climax of God's retribution will take place at the Battle of Armageddon (which we will address in chapter 9) when all the nations of the world join to fight God Himself.

> *Why do the heathen rage, and the people imagine a vain thing?*
> *The kings of the earth set themselves, and the rulers take counsel*
> *together, against the LORD, and against his anointed, saying, Let*
> *us break their bands asunder, and cast away their cords from us.*
> *He that sitteth in the heavens shall laugh: the Lord shall have*
> *them in derision. Then shall he speak unto them in his wrath,*
> *and vex them in his sore displeasure....Ask of me, and I shall*
> *give thee the heathen for thine inheritance, and the uttermost*
> *parts of the earth for thy possession. Thou shalt break them with*
> *a rod of iron; thou shalt dash them in pieces like a potter's vessel.*
> —PSALM 2:1–5, 8–9

The majority of world leaders are already set against Christ and are intolerant of Christianity. There seems, in fact, to be tolerance for every religion *except* Christianity. Through the judgments of the Tribulation, God will set the record straight.

Yet, even in judgment, God extends His grace. Far more than retribution, God desires the repentance of the nations. To quote again from LaHaye and Jenkins:

> ...while this period is primarily a time of wrath and
> judgment, it also features a very strong note of mercy and

grace—a note that too often gets overlooked. Sometimes we think God gets a "bad rap" when people focus exclusively on the judgments and terrors to come. They see the Lord as some kind of angry monster, heaping up catastrophes and pouring them on the heads of defenseless, innocent men and women...But this is all wrong! First, those who suffer the judgments of God in the Tribulation are *not* "innocent men and women." As we will see...the rebels alive at that time will not only reject God and His offer of salvation but will run greedily toward every vile sin known to man, including blasphemy of a kind beyond description. And second, despite their gross sin, God intends that these Tribulation judgments *might lead even these wicked sinners to faith in His Son, Jesus Christ.*[10]

Even before the final outpouring of wrath at Armageddon, God gives men the seven years of the Tribulation to repent, and He provides 144,000 witnesses to encourage them to do so. Unfortunately, few will. Their hardened, truth-resistant hearts will actually believe the lie that they can fight God and win (Revelation 16:12–16).

At the pinnacle of his pride, the Antichrist will gather a one-world army and set himself against Christ in battle. This battle—and Christ's victory—is the subject of our next chapter.

CHAPTER NINE

The Second Coming of Christ

In the early summer of 2009, my oldest daughter and son-in-law made an announcement that thrilled our entire family—they were expecting a little one, our first grandchild! As our grandson's arrival drew nearer, anyone could see that Danielle was with child. Eventually, we could even feel his kicks by placing our hand over Danielle's womb. These changes were accompanied with great anticipation because we all understood that they were the prelude to a far more exciting event—Camden Matthew's birth.

Even so, the global changes we've studied in previous chapters, including the horrific judgments of the Tribulation, are the precursor to one glorious event—Christ's Second Coming. The grand climax of the Tribulation comes at the end of that seven-year period when the King of kings and Lord of lords battles and defeats the armies of the Antichrist.

As Christ left Earth at the close of His first advent, an angel promised His astonished disciples a second advent: *"And while they looked stedfastly toward heaven as he went up, behold, two men stood by them in white apparel; Which also said, Ye men of Galilee, why stand ye gazing up into heaven? this same Jesus, which is taken up from you into heaven, shall so come in like manner as ye have seen him go into heaven"* (Acts 1:10–11). In the same physical, literal way that Jesus ascended, He will come again.

Bible scholars have counted in the Bible more than 1,480 references to the Second Coming of Christ. Old Testament prophets foretold this event. Zechariah 14:4 even pinpoints the location where He will return: *"And his feet shall stand in that day upon the mount of Olives, which is before Jerusalem on the east, and the mount of Olives shall cleave in the midst thereof toward the east and toward the west, and there shall be a very great valley; and half of the mountain shall remove toward the north, and half of it toward the south."*

Jesus Himself prophesied His Second Coming. When He described the Tribulation to His disciples, He did not omit this grand finale: *"Immediately after the tribulation of those days shall the sun be darkened, and the moon shall not give her light, and the stars shall fall from heaven, and the powers of the heavens shall be shaken: And then shall appear the sign of the Son of man in heaven: and then shall all the tribes of the earth mourn, and they shall see the Son of man coming in the clouds of heaven with power and great glory"* (Matthew 24:29–30).

Students of prophecy sometimes grapple with the specific timing of the Rapture or individual events of the Tribulation. No Bible-believing Christian, however, questions the Second Coming. Scripture provides overwhelming details regarding Christ's return:

1. He will return personally. Jesus promised He will return in person (Matthew 24:30).

2. He will appear as the Son of Man. Since Pentecost, Christ has ministered through the Holy Spirit (John 14:16–23; 16:7–20). But when He returns, He will appear as the Son of Man in His glorified human form (Matthew 24:30; 26:64; Daniel 7:13–14).

3. He will return literally and visibly (Acts 1:11; Revelation 1:7). Nowhere in Scripture is there a suggestion that Christ's Second Coming in power and great glory will be anything but visible and physical. He will come suddenly and dramatically (1 Thessalonians 5:2; Matthew 24:27).

4. He will come in the clouds of Heaven (Matthew 24:30; Daniel 7:13; Luke 21:27; Revelation 1:7).

5. He will come in a display of glory (Matthew 16:27; 24:30).

6. He will come with all His angels (Matthew 24:31; Matthew 13:41).

7. He will come with His bride, the church. That of course is the entire point of Revelation 19 (Colossians 3:4; Zechariah 14:5).

8. He will return to the Mount of Olives (Zechariah 14:4). Where the glory of God ascended into Heaven, it will return (Ezekiel 11:23). Where Jesus ascended into Heaven, He will return (Acts 1:9–11).

9. He will return in triumph and victory (Zechariah 14:9; Revelation 19:16). He will triumph over the Antichrist, the false prophet, and Satan (Revelation 19:19–21).[1]

Scripture is replete with promises of this glorious day when Jesus will come in fiery judgment and establish His kingdom on Earth.

THE APPEARANCE OF CHRIST

And I saw heaven opened, and behold a white horse; and he that
sat upon him was called Faithful and True, and in righteousness
he doth judge and make war. His eyes were as a flame of fire,
and on his head were many crowns; and he had a name written,
that no man knew, but he himself. And he was clothed with a
vesture dipped in blood: and his name is called The Word of God.
—Revelation 19:11–13

The description of Christ's appearance

Still breathing out blasphemies against God for the judgments of the
Tribulation, armies have assembled for battle on the plains of Megiddo.
But when God Almighty rolls back the heavens and the rebels catch a
glimpse of Christ triumphantly riding on a white horse with an army of
saints in His train, their rage will turn to sheer terror:

> *And the heaven departed as a scroll when it is rolled together; and*
> *every mountain and island were moved out of their places. And*
> *the kings of the earth, and the great men, and the rich men, and*
> *the chief captains, and the mighty men, and every bondman, and*
> *every free man, hid themselves in the dens and in the rocks of the*
> *mountains; And said to the mountains and rocks, Fall on us, and*
> *hide us from the face of him that sitteth on the throne, and from*
> *the wrath of the Lamb: For the great day of his wrath is come;*
> *and who shall be able to stand?*—Revelation 6:14–17

When the curtains of Heaven are opened, He who is called *"Faithful
and True"* will appear, prepared for battle as the only faithful and true
Witness and Judge. Jesus Christ is the embodiment of faithfulness.
His Word is faithful, His execution of God's plan is faithful, and His

appearance at Armageddon will be the faithful fulfillment of His promise to return and reign over Israel and the world.

In contrast to the false Christ—the Antichrist—who has deceived the world during the Tribulation, Revelation 19:11 identifies Jesus as *True*. In John 14:6, Christ proclaimed, *"I am the way, the truth, and the life: no man cometh unto the Father, but by me."* When He appears in the heavens, no one will question this claim, although millions will wish they had believed it sooner.

The flaming fire of Christ's eyes refers to His omniscience. His gaze will pierce through the fearful countenances and stony hearts to the very depths of men's souls and will easily discern the very thoughts and intents of the heart. As the righteous judge, Jesus will know everything.

Revelation 6:2 pictures the Antichrist during the Tribulation as crowned and seated on a white horse. In glorious contrast, when Christ appears, He will be wearing *many* crowns, for He alone is the King of kings!

An interesting side note here comes from the Greek words used for the crown of the Antichrist and the many crowns of Christ. The Antichrist's crown of Revelation 6:2 is *stephanos*—the victor's crown. The word for Christ's crowns, however, is translated from *diadhma*—a kingly crown. It refers to the blue band marked with white used by the Persian kings as a kingly ornament for their turbans or tiaras. The Antichrist may be the victor for a season, but Christ is the ultimate and eternal king!

Psalm 2 identified one who would rule as King over all kings and kingdoms and prophesied that He will wield a *"rod of iron"* (Psalm 2:9). When Christ returns at His Second Coming, He will hold this iron septor, identifying Him as the King of kings: *"...and he shall rule them with a rod of iron: and he treadeth the winepress of the fierceness and wrath of Almighty God"* (Revelation 19:15).

The story is told of Queen Victoria worshipping at St. George's Chapel in Windsor Castle. After she heard a message on the Second Coming of Christ, she approached the chaplain, Dean Farrar, and exclaimed, "Oh, how I wish that the Lord would come during my lifetime."

"Why does Your Majesty feel this very earnest desire?" he questioned.

"Because," the Queen answered, "I should so love to lay *my* crown at His feet."

Those who rule on Earth when Christ returns will have a markedly contrasting response than to that of Queen Victoria, for they will have already presented their crowns to the Antichrist. It will be with horror that they behold the faithful and true King already wearing many crowns.

To avoid any possible question about the identity of this King, John records His exclusive name: *"The Word of God."* John's Gospel opens with the words, *"In the beginning was the Word, and the Word was with God, and the Word was God"* (John 1:1). Clearly, the King seated on the white horse is Jesus Himself.

Scripture provides other names for Jesus as well. He is the Timeless One, for He is eternal in His nature (John 1:1). He is the Triune One, for He is equal with the Father and the Holy Spirit (Colossians 2:9). He is the Triumphant One, for, although His name has been cursed and denied, He will triumph over those who have mocked Him (Revelation 19:13). The blood-dyed garment Jesus will be wearing when He returns signifies He is coming to bring judgment on those who have so long denied Him.

The description of Christ's appearance is ominous for those who have rejected Him and taken the mark of His arch enemy—the Antichrist. But His appearance will be awesome for those who have trusted Christ as their Saviour and rejoice to see His victory. This description should awaken our senses to the holiness of our God.

The declaration of the Son

> And the armies which were in heaven followed him upon white
> horses, clothed in fine linen, white and clean. And out of his mouth
> goeth a sharp sword, that with it he should smite the nations:
> and he shall rule them with a rod of iron: and he treadeth the
> winepress of the fierceness and wrath of Almighty God. And he
> hath on his vesture and on his thigh a name written, KING OF
> KINGS, AND LORD OF LORDS.—REVELATION 19:14–16

President Theodore Roosevelt often quoted the African proverb:
"Speak softly and carry a big stick." Indeed, many leaders have found that
the presence of a strong military often deters enemy attacks.

The train of saints following Christ on horseback makes a similar
statement—it is a declaration of the strength of their Leader. Every rider
in this heavenly army was redeemed from Satan's clutches by the grace
of God and the blood of the Lamb. Their very position behind Christ at
Armageddon is a statement of His victory and His great love and grace.
Each and every life represented in that "army" is an affirming testimony
of God's compassion and mercy.

Who are these saints who comprise the heavenly army? Lehman
Strauss suggests, "It is quite possible that they include the Old Testament
saints, the Church, and the saints of the Tribulation."[2] When Zechariah
prophesied of this event, he proclaimed, *"and the LORD my God shall
come, **and all the saints with thee"*** (Zechariah 14:5, emphasis added).
This indicates that the redeemed of all ages will come with the Lord Jesus
to Armageddon.

If you have trusted Christ as your Saviour—you too are in that army
that John saw behind the Lord.

The *"fine linen, white and clean"* in which the heavenly army is
clothed reminds us that the saints in this army are also described as the

spotless Bride of Christ in Revelation 19:7–8: *"Let us be glad and rejoice, and give honour to him: for the marriage of the Lamb is come, and his wife hath made herself ready. And to her was granted that she should be arrayed in fine linen, clean and white: for the fine linen is the righteousness of saints."*

The pure robes reveal the righteousness of Christ which is freely given to every person who calls on Him for salvation. This righteousness is not earned through personal merit; it is imputed through the shed blood of Jesus Christ. It is through *Christ's* righteousness that His bride, the church, will be presented *"a glorious church, not having spot, or wrinkle, or any such thing; but that it should be holy and without blemish"* (Ephesians 5:27).

An even more significant declaration of Christ's power than this dazzlingly pure heavenly army will be the sharp sword by which He will smite the nations. The sword is none other than the very Word of God (Ephesians 6:17). Thus, Christ's weapon at Armageddon will be far more powerful than nuclear bombs or earthly weaponry. *"For the word of God is quick, and powerful, and sharper than any twoedged sword, piercing even to the dividing asunder of soul and spirit, and of the joints and marrow, and is a discerner of the thoughts and intents of the heart"* (Hebrews 4:12).

Some six thousand years ago, Christ spoke, and the universe was established. At Armageddon, Christ will speak, and fiery judgment will destroy those who have mocked His name. There will be no battle. It will be over in an instant when Jesus simply speaks the word. Second Thessalonians 2:8 says of this moment: *"And then shall that Wicked* [the Antichrist] *be revealed, whom the Lord shall consume with the spirit of his mouth, and shall destroy with the brightness of his coming."*

Imagine the shock of the average soldier who has marched to Armageddon to defy the sovereignty of God. He's a member of the one-world church and is wearing the mark of the beast. He has rejected and blasphemed the name of Christ, and he is eager to prove, once and for all, the superiority of his leader—the Antichrist.

Suddenly, the heavens open, and before Christ even descends, the soldier realizes his defeat. Gripped with terror, he views the Christ he denied, whom he now realizes is the King of kings and Lord of lords. His eyes are as a flame of fire; on His head are many crowns; His vesture is dipped in blood and carries His name "KING OF KINGS, AND LORD OF LORDS"; out of His mouth proceeds a sharp sword—the judgment of God.

Perhaps at that moment the soldier participates in fulfilling the prophecy of Philippians 2:10–11: *"That at the name of Jesus every knee should bow, of things in heaven, and things in earth, and things under the earth; And that every tongue should confess that Jesus Christ is Lord, to the glory of God the Father."*

The very appearance of this Conqueror of Armageddon will spell victory.

THE ADVANCEMENT OF THE HEAVENLY ARMY

During the eight years former President Ronald Reagan served in the White House, he kept a daily diary. In his May 15, 1981 entry, the president expressed his frustration and perplexity of the seemingly irresolvable tension between tiny Israel and the surrounding Arab nations. He recorded, "Sometimes I wonder if we are destined to witness Armageddon."[3]

Considerable changes have taken place in the past three decades, but the desire for Israel to be demolished still thrives. With all the peace initiatives and treaties, arbitrators and summits, there is yet seething hatred toward Israel. Even after the lull that will be created by the Antichrist's peace treaty, Armageddon is indeed bound to take place.

The prelude to the attack

> And I saw an angel standing in the sun; and he cried with a loud
> voice, saying to all the fowls that fly in the midst of heaven, Come
> and gather yourselves together unto the supper of the great God;
> That ye may eat the flesh of kings, and the flesh of captains, and
> the flesh of mighty men, and the flesh of horses, and of them that
> sit on them, and the flesh of all men, both free and bond, both
> small and great. And I saw the beast, and the kings of the earth,
> and their armies, gathered together to make war against him that
> sat on the horse, and against his army.—REVELATION 19:17–19

The invitation extended to the birds of prey will sound as God's declaration of the coming carnage of the battle. God beckons the fowls to prepare for the feast of their lives—the destroyed armies of the world.

As if answering the call for the birds, the Antichrist and the kings of Earth will gather with their armies for the battle of their destruction. God will even dry up the mighty Euphrates to make a way for the armies of the east to make their way to the scene: *"And the sixth angel poured out his vial upon the great river Euphrates; and the water thereof was dried up, that the way of the kings of the east might be prepared"* (Revelation 16:12).

To ensure massive military strength, the devilish trio—Satan, the Antichrist, and the false prophet—will send demonic messengers to convince the leaders of every army in the world to join the battle: *"And I saw three unclean spirits like frogs come out of the mouth of the dragon, and out of the mouth of the beast, and out of the mouth of the false prophet. For they are the spirits of devils, working miracles, which go forth unto the kings of the earth and of the whole world, to gather them to the battle of that great day of God Almighty"* (Revelation 16:13–14).

Where does this great battle take place? Revelation 16:16 provides the answer: *"And he gathered them together into a place called in the Hebrew tongue Armageddon.*" The Hebrew word *harmageddon* (or *Armageddon*) literally means "the mount of slaughter."

It is on the plains of Megiddo, in Israel, that the armies of every nation will gather in livid hatred to stage a point of attack against Christ. And it is here that Christ, the faithful and true Judge, will win the war.

The powerful advance

Several stages will unfold as Christ makes His advance on the scene of battle. Just before His coming, an earthquake eclipsing any the world has ever seen will launch a sequence of judgments: *"And I beheld when he had opened the sixth seal, and, lo, there was a great earthquake; and the sun became black as sackcloth of hair, and the moon became as blood"* (Revelation 6:12).

A giant hailstorm will rend the sky and devastate the Earth: *"And there fell upon men a great hail out of heaven, every stone about the weight of a talent: and men blasphemed God because of the plague of the hail; for the plague thereof was exceeding great"* (Revelation 16:21).

The Hebrew measurement of weight for a *talent* was about ninety-three pounds, twelve ounces. In New Testament times, this weight was about one hundred pounds. Hail of this size will produce serious damage and claim countless lives.

Many believe this hailstorm will directly follow the parting of the heavens. Man will see the throne of God and Christ descending, or preparing to descend, with His army of saints. The entire world will be struck with fear and awe at His coming.

All the armies of the world, gathered for war against Christ, will discover they are really gathered for judgment and destruction: *"For I will gather all nations against Jerusalem to battle; and the city shall be taken, and the houses rifled, and the women ravished; and half of the city shall go forth into captivity, and the residue of the people shall not be cut off from the city. Then shall the* LORD *go forth, and fight against those nations, as when he fought in the day of battle"* (Zechariah 14:2–3).

THE ALLOCATION OF JUDGMENT

And the beast was taken, and with him the false prophet that wrought miracles before him, with which he deceived them that had received the mark of the beast, and them that worshipped his image. These both were cast alive into a lake of fire burning with brimstone. And the remnant were slain with the sword of him that sat upon the horse, which sword proceeded out of his mouth: and all the fowls were filled with their flesh.
—REVELATION 19:20–21

When Christ returns, judgment day will finally arrive: *"And the nations were angry, and thy wrath is come, and the time of the dead, that they should be judged, and that thou shouldest give reward unto thy servants the prophets, and to the saints, and them that fear thy name, small and great; and shouldest destroy them which destroy the earth"* (Revelation 11:18).

Dr. David Jeremiah suggests a three-fold purpose for which Christ will mete out judgment at His appearing:

- To finish His judgment upon Israel (Joel 3:7–9)
- To finalize His judgment upon the nations that have persecuted Israel (Joel 3:2)
- To formally judge all the nations that have rejected Him (Revelation 16:9)[4]

The judgment Christ metes will accomplish all of these purposes with complete justice. Tim LaHaye wrote of this day, "When Christ consumes all before Him through the earthquakes, lightning, and the sword that proceeds out of His mouth, not only will the Holy Land be destroyed but the entire country will be literally bathed in blood of the unregenerate, God-hating, Christ-opposing men."[5]

The fate of the Antichrist

Having spearheaded the rejection of Christ throughout the Tribulation, the Antichrist will finally receive his just judgment. Second Thessalonians 2:9 describes the crafty deception for which he will be judged: *"Even him, whose coming is after the working of Satan with all power and signs and lying wonders."*

Together with the false prophet, the Antichrist will dupe the world into worshipping him. This delusion will not last, however, when his followers see him cast into a lake of fire. *"And the beast was taken, and with him the false prophet that wrought miracles before him, with which he deceived them that had received the mark of the beast, and them that worshipped his image. These both were cast alive into a lake of fire burning with brimstone"* (Revelation 19:20).

Many today reject the literal lake of fire that Scripture describes, and some churches have stopped proclaiming this biblical reality. An article published by *US News and World Report* gave the following statistics: 78% of Americans believe in Heaven, 60% believe in Hell, but only 4% think they will go to Hell.

The article quoted Reverend Mary Kraus to explain that people simply don't like to hear about Hell.

> "My congregation would be stunned to hear a sermon on hell." Her parishioners, she says, are "upper middle class, well-educated critical thinkers" who view God as "compassionate and loving, not someone who's going to push them into eternal damnation."[6]

Undoubtedly, the denial of Hell that is taking place across our land today is the result of Satan's deception. Our view of God, however, is only clear when seen through the lens of His Word. Scripture is quite clear about the fate of the beast (Antichrist) and the false prophet: they will both be *"cast alive into a lake of fire burning with brimstone"* (Revelation 19:20). Satan doesn't want people to embrace these truths, and when churches accommodate their theology for others' comfort, they become part of Satan's deception.

How convenient it would be to dismiss all of the Bible's teaching on Hell. But remember, our goal is truth, not convenience. It is not ours to tamper with God's Word. Admittedly, Hell is an inconvenient truth—but it is God's truth. Jesus often affirmed the reality of Hell, and therefore we cannot deny its reality either.

The fate of the Antichrist's army

The Antichrist's army has rejected the truth and will likewise receive judgment. Revelation 19:21 describes their fate: *"And the remnant were slain with the sword of him that sat upon the horse, which sword proceeded out of his mouth: and all the fowls were filled with their flesh."* The fowls summoned just before Christ's appearance can finally converge on their feast.

In his commentary *The Revelation of Jesus Christ*, John Walvoord described the judgment of the Antichrist's armies:

> In bringing to conclusion the battle of the great day of God Almighty, those not killed in the first stage of the conflict and in the capture of the beast and false prophet are now put to death. The evidence seems to be that the entire army of the wicked are killed.[7]

As noted a moment ago, it has become culturally unacceptable to believe in God's right to bring judgment. Satan attempts to cast doubt on the integrity of God by making Him appear unjust and harsh in meting out judgment. In reality, it is man who has blatantly spurned God's grace. Romans 1:18–32 points out man's vicious rejection of God's mercy and truth as he turns from the true and living God to his own devices—sin and vile affections. These vices lead him to lifestyles so contrary to God that he becomes reprobate.

John Walvoord pointed out the truth that puts God's judgment into perspective.

> The Word of God makes plain that God so loved the world that He gave His Son, and that all who avail themselves of the grace of God are immeasurably blessed in time and eternity. On the other hand, the same Word of God states plainly that those who spurn God's mercy must experience His judgment without mercy. How foolish it is to rest in the portions of the Word of God that speak of the love of God and reject the portions that deal with His righteous judgment.[8]

Those who have put their faith in the merciful sacrifice of Christ for their sins (see chapter 7), have no need to fear His judgment on the Antichrist's army, for they will be in Christ's army when He returns and plants His feet on the Mount of Olives (Zechariah 14:4).

Not only does Christ's victory at Armageddon end the reign of the Antichrist, but it will also begin the literal thousand year reign of Christ on Earth. Opposite in every way from the Antichrist's regime, Christ's kingdom will be the first and only kingdom of perfect peace. When the curse of sin is lifted, even the animal kingdom will know perfect peace. Isaiah prophesied that the wolf and the lamb will feed together

(Isaiah 65:25), and children will be able to safely play by the hole of the asp (Isaiah 11:8).

Everything that was destroyed through the Tribulation will blossom once again under Christ. The Earth will have come full circle—from paradise lost to paradise gained. Where sin, vileness, and blasphemy was rampant, there will be peace, tranquility, holiness, righteousness, justice, and true love. It will be everything many always wanted but could never achieve without God.

With His first advent, Christ altogether fulfilled the initial prophecy of Isaiah 9:6: *"For unto us a child is born, unto us a son is given...."* He will fulfill the remainder of the verse at His Second Coming: *"...and the government shall be upon his shoulder: and his name shall be called Wonderful, Counsellor, The mighty God, The everlasting Father, The Prince of Peace."*

As victor of the Battle of Armageddon, Christ will establish His eternal kingdom, and those who have trusted Christ as Saviour will live in the peace of Almighty God forever. Let's examine God's promise of this eternal kingdom more closely, for it's the "happily ever after" that is the common thread of every childhood story and the deepest longing of every human soul.

CHAPTER TEN

The One Eternal Kingdom

A Christian doctor was attending his dying patient. "Can you tell me, sir, what is on the other side of death's door?" the patient asked. The doctor knew his patient was a Christian and, therefore, had Heaven to look forward to, yet the doctor groped for words to answer the question. In the moments of silence, the two men heard a scratching at the door.

"Do you hear that?" the doctor queried. "That is my little dog. I left him downstairs when I arrived, but hearing my voice up here made him impatient to be with me. He has no idea what is on the other side of this door, but he knows that I am here, and so he wants to come in as well.

"Isn't it the same with you?" the doctor continued. "You don't know exactly what lies beyond death's door, but you know that your Saviour is on the other side."[1]

The knowledge that Jesus is on the other side of the door of eternity should result in the Christian's desiring to go there as well. Christ's presence should be the key focal point in the Christian's view of eternity. The eternal kingdom will have glorious features, and the details God gives us in His Word increase our anticipation for His return. Ultimately, however, the greatest draw for the Christian is the promise of living in the physical presence of Jesus Christ for all eternity.

In our last chapter we saw that Jesus will return to the Mount of Olives, conquer the Antichrist, and reign over a literal kingdom on Earth. Scripture prophesies the marvelous peace of this kingdom:

> *And he shall judge among the nations, and shall rebuke many people: and they shall beat their swords into plowshares, and their spears into pruninghooks: nation shall not lift up sword against nation, neither shall they learn war any more.*—ISAIAH 2:4

> *But with righteousness shall he judge the poor, and reprove with equity for the meek of the earth: and he shall smite the earth with the rod of his mouth, and with the breath of his lips shall he slay the wicked. And righteousness shall be the girdle of his loins, and faithfulness the girdle of his reins. The wolf also shall dwell with the lamb, and the leopard shall lie down with the kid; and the calf and the young lion and the fatling together; and a little child shall lead them. And the cow and the bear shall feed; their young ones shall lie down together: and the lion shall eat straw like the ox. And the sucking child shall play on the hole of the asp, and the weaned child shall put his hand on the cockatrice' den.*
> —ISAIAH 11:4–8

No peace negotiated through the United Nations can be as complete and thorough as the peace Jesus Christ will bring when He establishes His kingdom.

THE ESTABLISHMENT OF THE KINGDOM

Through every age of history, empires, kingdoms, and nations have risen and fallen; but after the victory of Armageddon, Christ will establish a final kingdom. This kingdom will far surpass the most remote dreams of any earthly ruler. Peace will reign when the Prince of Peace rules.

The banishing of Satan

> And I saw an angel come down from heaven, having the key of the bottomless pit and a great chain in his hand. And he laid hold on the dragon, that old serpent, which is the Devil, and Satan, and bound him a thousand years, And cast him into the bottomless pit, and shut him up, and set a seal upon him, that he should deceive the nations no more, till the thousand years should be fulfilled: and after that he must be loosed a little season.
> —REVELATION 20:1–3

Christ's first step in establishing a kingdom of peace will be to banish the enemy of peace. Evicted from Earth and bound in the bottomless pit for one thousand years, Satan will be disallowed from his deceiving work of the ages during Christ's millennial reign.

God determined Satan's doom when, as the angel Lucifer, Satan first exalted himself in pride:

> How art thou fallen from heaven, O Lucifer, son of the morning! how art thou cut down to the ground, which didst weaken the

nations! For thou hast said in thine heart, I will ascend into heaven, I will exalt my throne above the stars of God: I will sit also upon the mount of the congregation, in the sides of the north: I will ascend above the heights of the clouds; I will be like the most High. Yet thou shalt be brought down to hell, to the sides of the pit.—ISAIAH 14:12–15

Ever since this unsuccessful rebellion, Satan and his band of fallen angels have targeted God's people with their demonic oppression and opposition. The ruined lives, wrecked marriages, and wounded hearts around us today serve as a sad testimony to Satan's work of destruction. What a freeing day it will be for the world when Satan is bound in the bottomless pit!

The word translated *bottomless pit* is the Greek word *abyssos*, from which we get the English word *abyss*. This pit of unbounded, immeasurable depth has sides but no top or bottom: *"Yet thou shalt be brought down to hell, to the sides of the pit"* (Isaiah 14:15).

The only place such a pit could exist on Earth is inside the Earth's core. Here, gravity would always pull from every angle to the center, so one would be in the state of falling at all times.

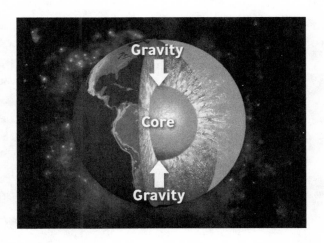

This bottomless pit will be the temporary holding place for Satan during Christ's millennial kingdom. As we'll soon see, he will then be released for a brief season and finally sentenced and banished to Hell forever.

The beginning of service

And I saw thrones, and they sat upon them, and judgment was given unto them: and I saw the souls of them that were beheaded for the witness of Jesus, and for the word of God, and which had not worshipped the beast, neither his image, neither had received his mark upon their foreheads, or in their hands; and they lived and reigned with Christ a thousand years.—REVELATION 20:4

Rid of Satan, Christ will establish the judicial aspect of His kingdom by rewarding His faithful servants with positions of authority.

The thrones that John saw are judicial seats of regal authority. They are not displayed for mere empty show. ...Once God's saints were judged and persecuted by the world, and are so treated even now, but the day will come when "the saints will judge the world."[2]

Those who have paid an earthly price to be true to Christ, some through persecution and even martyrdom, will then receive the heavenly reward of reigning with Him. They will joyfully serve as judges and rulers for the one they love most dearly.

Revelation 20 is not the first mention of the saints' service in Christ's kingdom. Daniel spoke of it no less than three times in Daniel 7:

But the saints of the most High shall take the kingdom, and possess the kingdom for ever, even for ever and ever.—DANIEL 7:18

Until the Ancient of days [Jesus Christ] came, and judgment was given to the saints of the most High; and the time came that the saints possessed the kingdom.—DANIEL 7:22

And the kingdom and dominion, and the greatness of the kingdom under the whole heaven, shall be given to the people of the saints of the most High, whose kingdom is an everlasting kingdom, and all dominions shall serve and obey him.—DANIEL 7:27

Paul, too, spoke of the day when God's people will be judging rulers in Christ's kingdom:

Do ye not know that the saints shall judge the world? and if the world shall be judged by you, are ye unworthy to judge the smallest matters? Know ye not that we shall judge angels? how much more things that pertain to this life?—1 CORINTHIANS 6:2–3

What a privilege Christ will give His servants to allow them to serve with Him in His glorious kingdom from which Satan has been banished!

The blessing of salvation

But the rest of the dead lived not again until the thousand years were finished. This is the first resurrection. Blessed and holy is he that hath part in the first resurrection: on such the second death hath no power, but they shall be priests of God and of Christ, and shall reign with him a thousand years.—REVELATION 20:5–6

Among the many blessings of knowing Christ as our personal Saviour is that we will be participants in the first of two resurrections. The *"rest of the dead"* spoken of in Revelation 20:5 who *"lived not again until the thousand years were finished"* are the unsaved. These will not be a part of the first resurrection but will be resurrected and judged at the end of the Millennium (see chart on page 157).

By the time Christ establishes His kingdom, the first resurrection will have already taken place. This is obvious because 1 Thessalonians 3:13 prophesies that when Christ returns at Armageddon, He will come *"with all his saints." All* saints would include saints from the Old Testament, saints of the church age, and those saved during the Tribulation.

So when does the first resurrection occur? Actually, this takes place in three phases. As we've seen in previous chapters, Christ's return has two phases—the Rapture and Armageddon; so the first resurrection has phases as well.

1. THE RESURRECTION OF THE OLD TESTAMENT SAINTS

As Christ gave His life on the Cross, Old Testament saints were resurrected: *"Jesus, when he had cried again with a loud voice, yielded up the ghost. And, behold, the veil of the temple was rent in twain from the top to the bottom; and the earth did quake, and the rocks rent; And the graves were opened; and many bodies of the saints which slept arose, And came out of the graves after his resurrection, and went into the holy city, and appeared unto many"* (Matthew 27:50–53).

Some believe the resurrection spoken of in Matthew 27 was only a partial resurrection of the Old Testament saints, and their full resurrection will take place at the end of the Tribulation. This view cites Daniel 12:1–2 which describes the Tribulation and concludes with, *"And many of them that sleep in the dust of the earth shall awake, some to everlasting life, and some to shame and everlasting contempt."*

Whatever the case, whether resurrected at the time of Calvary or at the end of the Tribulation, we know the Old Testament saints will be raised prior to Christ's Second Coming.

2. THE RESURRECTION OF THE CHURCH AGE SAINTS

The second phase of the first resurrection will take place when *"…the Lord himself shall descend from heaven with a shout, with the voice of the archangel, and with the trump of God: and the dead in Christ shall rise first: Then we which are alive and remain shall be caught up together with them in the clouds, to meet the Lord in the air: and so shall we ever be with the Lord"* (1 Thessalonians 4:16–17).

As we learned in chapter 4, all the church age saints (those saved since Christ's death and resurrection) will be raptured to meet the Lord in the air. This is the blessed hope of all those who trust Christ as their personal Saviour.

3. THE RESURRECTION OF THE TRIBULATION SAINTS

What of those who trust Christ during the seven year Tribulation? We are not given the exact timing of their phase of the first resurrection, but we know they have already been resurrected before Christ's coming at Armageddon, as Revelation 20:4 shows them already seated with Christ: *"And I saw thrones, and they sat upon them, and judgment was given unto them: and I saw the souls of them that were beheaded for the witness of Jesus, and for the word of God, and which had not worshipped the beast, neither his image, neither had received his mark upon their foreheads, or in their hands; and they lived and reigned with Christ a thousand years."*

These are those who, as testimony to their faith in Christ, have refused the mark of the beast and have willingly suffered martyrdom. Because we see here their ruling with Christ, we conclude that they will be resurrected at the end of the Tribulation and then return with Christ at His Second Coming.

All those who have part of the first resurrection, at any of the three phases, are referred to as *"blessed and holy"* (Revelation 20:6). These have received the imputed righteousness of Christ and are cleansed of their sin. They will have the privilege of reigning with Christ for a thousand years in His millennial kingdom.

THE EXECUTION OF FINAL JUDGMENT

For one thousand years, Christ, as the faithful and true Judge, will execute perfect judgment in His kingdom. Righteousness will reign, and peace will prosper.

At the close of the Millennium, Christ will execute His final judgment.

The judgment of Satan

> And when the thousand years are expired, Satan shall be loosed out of his prison, And shall go out to deceive the nations which are in the four quarters of the earth, Gog and Magog, to gather them together to battle: the number of whom is as the sand of the sea. And they went up on the breadth of the earth, and compassed the camp of the saints about, and the beloved city: and fire came down from God out of heaven, and devoured them. And the devil that deceived them was cast into the lake of fire and brimstone, where the beast and the false prophet are, and shall be tormented day and night for ever and ever.—REVELATION 20:7–10

Since the earliest moments of history, Satan has vehemently fought God and every work of God on Earth. He resisted Christ from the manger to the Cross. Christ's resurrection, however, proved Him to be the real Conqueror. Yet even as a defeated foe, Satan has persisted in persecuting the church and the spread of the Gospel.

Always working behind the scenes, and sometimes in the limelight, Satan has attacked from every front to exalt himself over God. Politically, he has assaulted Israel. Socially, he has attacked righteousness and legalized wickedness. Religiously, he has created a false system of worship. Economically, he will make all nations dependent on his one-world puppet, the Antichrist, and his government. For thousands of years, Satan has attempted every means possible to overthrow Christ and Christianity.

But when Christ reigns on Earth and banishes Satan, this world will finally know what it is to live in peace, free from Satan's dark presence and bathed in the light of pure worship of Christ. While Satan is bound in the bottomless pit, Israel will experience safety, and Christ Himself will sit on the throne of David.

At the end of these years of bliss, just before Christ executes His final judgment, Satan will be released for a brief season. Like a felon who has not recovered or a convict who has never changed, Satan will immediately return to his old dirty deeds. He will deceive men, raise an army and, with the ease of an expert, lead the nations into defying Christ one final time.

The nations specifically mentioned in Revelation 20, *"Gog and Magog,"* may refer back to the nation of Russia directly (see chapter 5), or they may refer to Russia's position as an enemy of God's people in her earlier battle (Ezekiel 38–39). Either way, this army gathered by Satan is massive, *"the number of whom is as the sand of the sea"* (Revelation 20:8).

The size of this army is incredible. How could people who have enjoyed living in the only kingdom with the perfect Ruler agree to join Satan's army? This is a testimony to the depravity of man's heart. People who know the peace of perfection will still choose an army of deception.

Of course, those who entered Christ's kingdom directly after the Battle of Armageddon were all redeemed and part of Christ's army. But in one thousand years, many generations will have been born, each individual with a choice to receive or reject Christ. Undoubtedly, many will choose to trust Him as Saviour, but others will harden their hearts in pride. These will jump at the opportunity to join Satan's army.

Having amassed his army, Satan will encompass the city of Jerusalem. Much like the Battle of Armageddon (see chapter 9), Christ will easily strike a defeating blow. Satan simply cannot match the omnipotence of Christ. Fire will fall from Heaven, and Satan will be cast into the lake of fire where he will join the Antichrist and the false prophet in eternal torment. This evil trio will finally and eternally be done away with.

The judgment of the unbelievers

*And I saw a great white throne, and him that sat on it, from whose face the earth and the heaven fled away; and there was found no place for them. And I saw the dead, small and great, stand before God; and the books were opened: and another book was opened, which is the book of life: and the dead were judged out of those things which were written in the books, according to their works. And the sea gave up the dead which were in it; and death and hell delivered up the dead which were in them: and they were judged every man according to their works. And death and hell were cast into the lake of fire. This is the second death. And whosoever was not found written in the book of life was cast into the lake of fire.—*Revelation 20:11–15

Revelation now draws our attention to the great white throne and its Judge. John Phillips described the scene as "bright, dazzling to the eye, reflecting as a purity so intense that before it the very Seraphim shrink."[3]

One glimpse of this austere judgment seat creates an intense feeling of soberness and finality. As one commentator wrote, "These verses are among the most solemn in the Bible. They tell us of that dread and final assize called the *great white throne* judgment. The judicial benches of this world pale into insignificance when placed alongside the staggering scene of this throne and the judgment which issues from it."[4]

It is the presence of the Judge—Christ Himself—that grips men with terror. For ages they have rejected, scorned, and mocked Him; but now, their eternity lies in His hands. At this throne of righteousness, they know the inevitable verdict of the just Judge.

It is important to remember that the Great White Throne judgment is only for the unsaved. Their very presence before this throne indicates their sentence, for this is the second resurrection. The first resurrection, delineated earlier in this chapter, is for those who at any stage of history trusted Christ, and it was followed with eternal blessings. This second resurrection, however, is followed by the second death—the lake of fire.

At this judgment, there will be no respect of persons, no appeal of God's impeccable records, and no hope of escape from punishment. Small and great will stand before Christ and be sentenced to eternal judgment.

If one pulled the verses about the Great White Throne judgment out of the context of the rest of Revelation or the whole of the Bible, the judgment passed here might appear unreasonable. We must remember that the Judge who passes the sentence is the God who offered salvation. He humbled Himself to take on flesh and suffer on Calvary for these who have rejected Him. He rose triumphant over death and freely extended salvation to all who would believe. He even delayed His return for judgment, *"not willing that any should perish, but that all should come to repentance"* (2 Peter 3:9).

These who now stand before Him had been given the choice of eternal life, but they refused to trust Christ; and therefore, their names were not recorded in the Book of Life. Now the book is opened, and their fate is sealed. This scene is grievous to say the least. But it is just, and no one present at that judgment will be arguing the rightness of the sentence.

THE ENTRANCE INTO THE ETERNAL AGES

The millennial kingdom only represents the first thousand years of Christ's reign, and the end of this kingdom, consummated with the final judgment of Satan and the Great White Throne judgment, will be just the beginning of the eternal kingdom replete with eternal joys.

Isaiah 9:7 explains that during the Millennium, Christ will order and establish His eternal kingdom. After the final overthrow of Satan and the Great White Throne judgment, the millennial kingdom will transition into the eternal kingdom with the new heavens and new earth and the New Jerusalem.

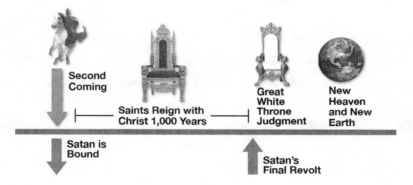

The eternal heavens

And I saw a new heaven and a new earth: for the first heaven and the first earth were passed away; and there was no more sea. And I John saw the holy city, new Jerusalem, coming down from God out of heaven, prepared as a bride adorned for her husband. And I heard a great voice out of heaven saying, Behold, the tabernacle of God is with men, and he will dwell with them, and they shall be his people, and God himself shall be with them, and be their God.—REVELATION 21:1–3

The first heaven and earth, corrupted through sin, will pass away, but the new heaven and earth will last in glorious perfection for all eternity. The prophet Isaiah foretold this new creation: *"For, behold, I create new heavens and a new earth: and the former shall not be remembered, nor come into mind"* (Isaiah 65:17). Its glory will be so great that even the finest aspects of the first creation will fade and be completely forgotten.

The stunning glory of Heaven will be its capital city—New Jerusalem—unparalleled in her beauty and perfection. This focal location of the eternal kingdom is the city God promised to prepare for His people: *"In my Father's house are many mansions: if it were not so, I would have told you. I go to prepare a place for you. And if I go and prepare a place for you, I will come again, and receive you unto myself; that where I am, there ye may be also"* (John 14:2–3).

The New Jerusalem is Heaven's preeminent location, because it is where God's throne will reside. Here we will sit at the feet of Jesus and bask in His presence for all eternity. Oh, what a wonderful place!

The eternal state

And God shall wipe away all tears from their eyes; and there shall be no more death, neither sorrow, nor crying, neither shall there be any more pain: for the former things are passed away. And he that sat upon the throne said, Behold, I make all things new. And he said unto me, Write: for these words are true and faithful.
—REVELATION 21:4–5

The King of the eternal kingdom will be the restorer of perfect joy and a perfect world. Death, sorrow, crying, and pain will all vanish when God Himself wipes all tears from our eyes. Our entrance into Heaven will be our exit from "the former things"—all suffering and sorrow ever experienced in the history of mankind. Anything sinful or hurtful will be forever banished. What a wonderful place—a place of perfect joy!

With a security no earthly entity could provide, Heaven will be free of even the threat of danger. Satan, who has harassed and maimed Christians for centuries, will have no port of entrance from the lake of fire. Living in the direct presence of God, we will know perfect security and a total absence of fear.

The scenery of Heaven will be breathtaking beyond description. A paradise of beauty and glory, the streets of pure gold will reflect the landscape of perfection. Every corner will glisten with the light of Christ's presence.

In times of suffering here on Earth, Heaven shines as a dawn of hope and a beacon of anticipation. A great preacher of yesteryear, Dr. W.A. Criswell, once found himself seated on a plane next to a well-known theologian. As they talked, the theologian related that he and his wife had just buried their five-year-old son after a short, but very violent form of meningitis.

On the afternoon the boy died, the father kept vigil over his son. "Daddy," the boy asked, his brain and vision becoming clouded from the disease, "it's getting dark, isn't it?"

"Yes, Son, it's time for you to sleep," the father answered, and he helped his son make his pillow more comfortable.

"Good night, Daddy," the little boy murmured, "I'll see you in the morning." Moments later, he was in the presence of Jesus.

The theologian turned toward the window to regain his composure. "Dr. Criswell," he finally said with tears streaming down his cheeks, "I can hardly wait till the morning."

Heaven will be the eternal dawn of an eternal day, for Jesus is the Bright and Morning Star of Heaven. Pain will be gone forever, and in its place will be a joy exponentially increased by living in the direct presence of Christ. Martin Luther wrote, "I would not give one moment of Heaven for all the joy and riches of the world, even if it lasted for thousands and thousands of years."

Charles Spurgeon said, "Time is short. Eternity is long. It is only reasonable that this short life be lived in the light of eternity."

Christians of the past looked forward to Heaven with great anticipation. They spoke of it, sang about it, and lived with its reality in view. In today's world of materialism, however, we tend to find our joy in the immediate rather than the future, in the temporal rather than the eternal. Colossians 3:2 instructs us, *"Set your affection on things above, not on things on the earth."*

The material advancements of today cannot last forever. They are but insignificant grains in the sands of changing time. When we live with eternity in view, however, we will invest our lives and our resources in that which will last forever. This was the perspective of the heroes of faith written of in Hebrews 11:16: *"But now they desire a better country, that is, an heavenly: wherefore God is not ashamed to be called their God: for he hath prepared for them a city."* This final kingdom of glory is the never-ending climax of joy for those who know Christ as their Saviour.

The promise of living forever in the presence of Christ is the perfect destination for our journey through Bible prophecy. It is a rock of hope in the midst of changing times.

The biblical prophecies we have studied in these chapters provide an accurate lens through which to view the present times. Studying these events provides hope and strength for the believer. But beyond that, these truths compel us and challenge us. In our next chapter, we will make our last stop on this journey and examine how we should live in light of Christ's coming and the truth of Bible prophecy.

CHAPTER ELEVEN ____

Challenges in Light of His Coming

Throughout this book we've traveled a far-reaching trail of prophecy. From the ancient empires of Daniel's vision (chapter 2) to the final kingdom of Christ (chapter 10), we've covered detailed descriptions of how present changing times fit into the larger landscape of God's plan for the ages.

We've seen how current events are paving the way for a globalism that will affect the monetary and political world and lead to a one-world ruler—the Antichrist. We've observed the mounting hatred that nations harbor toward Israel, and, through the lens of Scripture, we've foreseen where the final explosion of current terrorism will lead.

Strengthening us in our journey, we've learned of the hope of the Rapture. We looked with horror on the Tribulation judgments but rejoiced in the Second Coming of Jesus Christ, the King of kings and Lord of lords. We've covered a lot of ground!

But we stand in the present. Today. Now.

Sprawling behind us are the already fulfilled prophesies of the past (as historic as the ancient empires and as recent as the modern state of Israel), and stretching before us are the yet unfulfilled events of tomorrow (the Rapture, Tribulation, and Second Coming).

Now as we peer down the trail ahead to the final destination of Christ's eternal kingdom, we are faced with a compelling question: What does it all mean for right now? How should what we've studied change the way we live? How does what we believe about the future impact our reality today?

In other words, what should we do with the information we have garnered on our journey? Should it only shape our belief regarding future events and sharpen our perception of current news? Should it draw us into endless speculation, conspiracy theories, and the frivolous attempt to unravel the nuances of the future that God has not placed within our grasp?

Too many Bible-believing Christians get sidetracked by this information. They step off of the road of engaged obedience and mire themselves in the stalled quest for details that God has not called us to understand at this point. Acts 1:7 gives us a clear warning to avoid becoming enmeshed in attempting to decipher what only God truly knows, *"And he said unto them, It is not for you to know the times or the seasons, which the Father hath put in his own power."* God does not intend for these truths to lead us into unhealthy obsessions and unanswerable questions. He intends this information to lead us in a different direction.

What should be the practical side of a study of Bible prophecy? Peter addressed this two thousand years ago:

*Seeing then that all these things shall be dissolved, **what manner
of persons ought ye to be** in all holy conversation and godliness,
Looking for and hasting unto the coming of the day of God, wherein
the heavens being on fire shall be dissolved, and the elements
shall melt with fervent heat? Nevertheless we, according to his
promise, look for new heavens and a new earth, wherein dwelleth
righteousness. Wherefore, beloved, seeing that ye look for such
things, be diligent that ye may be found of him in peace, without
spot, and blameless.*—2 PETER 3:11–14 [emphasis added]

God did not relate the prophecies of Scripture simply to provide
material for intellectual study or personal intrigue. Rather, He gives us
prophetic truths to motivate us to live with eternal values. These truths
should seep into the very depths of our being and stimulate our everyday
behavior and responses. They should compel us to active duty—full
engagement in the mission of Jesus Christ. James 5:8 reminds us, *"the
coming of the Lord draweth nigh."* Studying past and future events is only
helpful as we allow these truths to motivate us to live today in the light
of Christ's coming.

As we conclude this book, I believe God's reasons for giving us
prophetic information can be summarized in two challenges for living.
Of all that we've seen in Scripture, this is the practical "take away"—so
follow carefully.

A CHALLENGE TO STEADFASTNESS

In a world where values and norms are constantly shifting, we must remain
steadfast in our faith. Rather than changing with our surroundings, we
must remain anchored to the Rock, the Lord Jesus Christ. Scripture gives

us four areas specifically related to Christ's return in which we must remain steadfast.

Steadfast to assemble

And let us consider one another to provoke unto love and to good works: Not forsaking the assembling of ourselves together, as the manner of some is; but exhorting one another: and so much the more, as ye see the day approaching,—HEBREWS 10:24–25

Faithfulness to the local church is directly linked in Scripture to the return of Christ. In fact, the writer of Hebrews actually admonishes us to *increase* our church attendance and participation as the day of Christ's return draws nearer.

We are living in an era when more and more people are jumping ship and claiming that the New Testament local church is either non-essential or irrelevant. I believe this is part of Satan's plan to undermine the local church as he works to establish the false church we studied in chapter 7. Jude spoke of these who, in the last days, would separate themselves from, and even mock, the assembly of the local church and the truth for which it stands:

How that they told you there should be mockers in the last time, who should walk after their own ungodly lusts. These be they who separate themselves, sensual, having not the Spirit. But ye, beloved, building up yourselves on your most holy faith, praying in the Holy Ghost, Keep yourselves in the love of God, looking for the mercy of our Lord Jesus Christ unto eternal life.—JUDE 18–21

Christ designed the church to be the *"pillar and ground of the truth"* (1 Timothy 3:15). Obeying the command of Hebrews 10:24–25 to be steadfast in church attendance helps us keep the moorings of our hearts firmly tied to God's truth, *"building up yourselves on your most holy faith."*

I heard of a father who was prodding his son to get ready for Sunday school. "Dad," the little boy asked, "did you go to Sunday school when you were my age?"

"Yes, I did."

"Well," the little guy commented as he continued getting ready, "it probably won't do me a lot of good either."

The truth is that faithful attendance in a Bible-preaching church coupled with a sincere and obedient heart towards God's Word *will* change our lives. And that is precisely why God commands us to assemble together. The teaching and preaching of God's Word challenges us to prepare our lives for Christ's Second Coming.

As a pastor, I've observed many families over the years who have helped their children build a solid foundation for life by bringing them to church from the time they were very young. As these parents have been faithful to church and consistent in their homes, biblical principles and convictions form in their children's hearts.

In addition to biblical preaching and teaching, the local church provides another form of help as Christians *"consider one another to provoke unto love and to good works...exhorting one another"* (Hebrews 10:24–25). Each member of the church is to encourage others to love and serve. The word *provoke* means "incitement; irritation." We normally think of this word in a negative aspect, such as being provoked to anger, but in Hebrews 10:24 it is a positive and encouraging trait. We are to incite other Christians to be faithful in their service for Christ.

I thank the Lord for godly Christians I have known who have been obedient to this command to assemble faithfully. Their steadfast example of being in church at every service is a testimony to their love for Christ and commitment to His Word. And their dedicated service in church ministry encourages others in steadfast service to the Lord.

Steadfast to preach

Shortly before Paul's death as a martyr for the faith, he wrote the epistle of 2 Timothy. From the dungeon of the Mamertine Prison in Rome, Paul challenged the young preacher Timothy to be steadfast to preach God's Word—especially in light of the Second Coming of Christ.

> *I charge thee therefore before God, and the Lord Jesus Christ, who shall judge the quick and the dead at his appearing and his kingdom; Preach the word; be instant in season, out of season; reprove, rebuke, exhort with all longsuffering and doctrine. For the time will come when they will not endure sound doctrine; but after their own lusts shall they heap to themselves teachers, having itching ears;*—2 TIMOTHY 4:1–3

As Paul pointed out to Timothy, preaching should include more than exhortation and encouragement. A pastor must also reprove, rebuke, and teach doctrine. Many today want to only hear preaching that makes them feel good, but a commitment to biblical preaching requires great steadfastness on the part of the preacher.

Almost two thousand years ago Paul said *"the time will come"* when people no longer accept or seek sound doctrine. It seems that this time has indeed come. A trend that is gaining more and more momentum is to adjust preaching to an accommodating style of theology—to drop convictions and tell people any lifestyle is acceptable so long as it is adopted with sincerity. Unfortunately, this is exactly the kind of preaching that will find prominence in the Antichrist's false church.

Occasionally someone will comment to me after I preach, "Pastor, you stepped on my toes this morning." I usually reply, "I'm sorry. I wasn't aiming for your *toes*; I was aiming for your *heart!*" Preaching that has the comfort of the listener as its main goal will never challenge us to change our lives to be ready for Christ's Second Coming.

Paul's admonition to Timothy serves as a warning to preachers and laypeople alike. As a layperson, let this admonition remind you that not all churches are equal. Join yourself to a Bible-preaching church that is true to the doctrines of God's Word and teaches you to live according to its principles. As part of such a church, encourage your pastor as he takes a stand for truth. While others criticize or become offended, let God's truth change your heart.

If you are a preacher, do not dilute or compromise the truths of God's Word to gain acceptance. When Christ returns, only His approval will matter as you give an account for your care of the flock (Hebrews 13:17). People *need* to hear the truth. Howard Hendricks said, "In the midst of a generation screaming for answers, Christians are stuttering." Yes, some will scoff the truth, but others will hear and heed it if you will be steadfast to preach it.

Someone once asked the evangelist D.L. Moody to share the secret to his success as a preacher. "For many years," Moody replied, "I have never given an address without being conscious that the Lord may come before I have finished." Preachers who remember their accountability to Christ at His imminent return will be more bold to preach the truths of God's Word rather than the current philosophies of society. Especially, they will be faithful to preach the Gospel and urge the lost to turn to Christ.

Steadfast to witness

There is nothing the knowledge of Christ's return should compel us to do more than to tell others of salvation. The last command Christ gave before He ascended to Heaven was, *"Go ye into all the world, and preach the gospel to every creature"* (Mark 16:15). This should be our highest priority.

If we believe that Jesus is coming again and that He invites anyone who will to trust Him as Saviour and spend eternity in Heaven, we ought to do everything we can to tell others, especially our loved ones.

Conversely, if we believe that those who do not know Christ as Saviour will experience the horrors of the Tribulation judgments and stand before the Great White Throne before being cast into a lake of fire for all eternity, we ought to do all we can to warn them of the danger and implore them to trust Christ.

As Jude 21–23 suggests, when the reality of Christ's return grips our hearts, we will give of ourselves in every way possible to communicate the message of the Gospel to every person: *"Keep yourselves in the love of God, looking for the mercy of our Lord Jesus Christ unto eternal life. And of some have compassion, making a difference: And others save with fear, pulling them out of the fire; hating even the garment spotted by the flesh."*

Paul wrote about the abounding joy he experienced knowing he had led others to Christ and would see them in His presence for all eternity: *"For what is our hope, or joy, or crown of rejoicing? Are not even ye in the presence of our Lord Jesus Christ at his coming? For ye are our glory and joy"* (1 Thessalonians 2:19–20).

Imagine the joy that will be ours when we return with the Lord at His Second Coming and see people who were saved because we faithfully supported missions and witnessed to our friends and neighbors. There is already tremendous joy in leading a soul to Christ, but think of the joy we will experience then! Any sacrifice we make now to be steadfast in our witness will pale in significance to the eternal rewards we will receive for our labor.

Steadfast to remember

The night before Jesus gave His life for us on the Cross, He met with His disciples in an upper room. There He instituted the Lord's Table—a way for us to remember.

And when he had given thanks, he brake it, and said, Take, eat: this is my body, which is broken for you: this do in remembrance of me. After the same manner also he took the cup, when he had supped, saying, this cup is the new testament in my blood: this do ye, as oft as ye drink it, in remembrance of me. For as often as ye eat this bread, and drink this cup, ye do shew the Lord's death till he come.—1 CORINTHIANS 11:24–26

Each time a church family partakes of the Lord's Table, they commemorate the sacrifice of Christ. He gave His body to be broken and shed His blood for us, and He wants us to remember His great love.

The Lord's Table is also meant to remind us of Christ's soon return, for we are to observe this ordinance "…*till he come.*" Even in the upper room, Christ promised His disciples He would return after His ascension to Heaven: "*In my Father's house are many mansions: if it were not so, I would have told you. I go to prepare a place for you. And if I go and prepare a place for you, I will come again, and receive you unto myself; that where I am, there ye may be also*" (John 14:2–3).

As we search and purify our hearts before partaking of the Lord's Table (1 Corinthians 11:27–28), we prepare ourselves to be ready for Christ's return. The Lord's Table is meant to be a frequent motivation to our next challenge—the challenge to godly living in an ungodly world.

A CHALLENGE TO SANCTIFICATION

The salvation that Christ so freely offers is really just the entryway to a life of growth, joy, and blessing. As we look down the path of Bible prophecy to the end of our journey—eternity in the presence of Christ—it becomes apparent that between salvation and eternity God wants to do a work of grace in our hearts to conform us to the image of Christ. This process is called sanctification.

There are actually two aspects to the doctrine of sanctification. The first is one's positional standing. When you trusted Christ as your Saviour, you were immediately made a child of God (John 1:12) and included in His family. God forgave your sin, and the Holy Spirit now indwells you (Ephesians 1:13). Your position in Christ is absolutely secure.

The second aspect of sanctification is one's practical standing. This relates to your daily walk and your moment by moment relationship with Christ. Just as a person can belong to a family but have no interaction with the rest of the family, so a Christian can be a member of the family of God (positional sanctification) and yet ignore his relationship with the Father (practical sanctification). The challenge of practical sanctification is that our daily lifestyle would honor the Lord, and our lives proclaim to others that we are Christians who love Christ supremely. Our lifestyle should be one of biblical distinction.

The modern church cares little for sanctification and holiness, and some churches even mock the very doctrine. Yet Paul's earnest desire and fervent prayer for the church of Thessalonica was sanctification: *"And the very God of peace sanctify you wholly; and I pray God your whole spirit and soul and body be preserved blameless unto the coming of our Lord Jesus Christ"* (1 Thessalonians 5:23).

The word *sanctification* literally means "set apart." God desires that we would be set apart to be His exclusively in every area of life. Notice two areas in which He calls us to separate:

Sanctified from this world's system

As we have seen in previous chapters, the many changes taking place around us are part of a larger plan, preparing the world for the reign of the Antichrist. Paul wrote of this escalating development and challenged us, in light of Christ's return, to remain separated from this system:

Now we beseech you, brethren, by the coming of our Lord Jesus Christ, and by our gathering together unto him, That ye be not soon shaken in mind, or be troubled, neither by spirit, nor by word, nor by letter as from us, as that the day of Christ is at hand. Let no man deceive you by any means: for that day shall not come, except there come a falling away first, and that man of sin be revealed, the son of perdition; Who opposeth and exalteth himself above all that is called God, or that is worshipped; so that he as God sitteth in the temple of God, shewing himself that he is God.—2 THESSALONIANS 2:1–4

Two significant events are mentioned in this text. First, there is the falling away from truth. The ultimate end of this departure from truth will be the Antichrist's state church we studied in Chapter 7. Even now we see compromise and pragmatism rising in an attempt to trample the truth.

The Greek word translated *falling away* in this passage is *apostasia*, from which we get the word *apostasy*. The apostasy already taking place today is rampant. Churches that once believed and preached salvation by grace alone have changed their stance and now teach that all religions lead to the same place. This type of pluralism is paving the way for the Antichrist's religion during the Tribulation.

God expressly forbids us to have any association with or affinity for a system that shuns Christ: "*Love not the world, neither the things that are in the world. If any man love the world, the love of the Father is not in him. For all that is in the world, the lust of the flesh, and the lust of the eyes, and the pride of life, is not of the Father, but is of the world*" (1 John 2:15–16). He commands us to "*come out from among them, and be ye separate, saith the Lord, and touch not the unclean thing; and I will receive you"* (2 Corinthians 6:17). Remembering Christ's return gives us the courage to separate from the world's system and stand for Jesus as a faithful soldier of His Cross.

Sanctified from this world's sin

Since Louis Pasteur's breakthrough research and experiments that proved germs cause disease, we have become a germ-conscious society. And I am no exception. My wife smiles when she remembers that before I allowed people to see our first baby in our apartment, I made them don a gown, gloves, and a mask lest they pass along germs. Our grandson was born during the H1N1 virus scare, and I was careful to remind our family to regularly wash their hands and be very careful what germs they might inadvertently pass along to him.

Something that has always puzzled me, however, is our culture's greater concern over germ pollution than sin pollution. In reality, sickness of the soul is a much greater danger than sickness of the body. The one destroys our physical health and the other our spiritual. So why is it that we will do all we can to avoid germs that cause sickness, but we don't guard ourselves from the sin that will destroy our lives? Why is it that parents will be cautious and protective of their children's physical health but allow the home to be infiltrated with media that pollutes their hearts and minds?

In light of Christ's soon return, we should avoid sin and *"abide in him; that, when he shall appear, we may have confidence, and not be ashamed before him at his coming"* (1 John 2:28).

First Peter 5:8 informs us, *"your adversary the devil, as a roaring lion, walketh about, seeking whom he may devour."* Because Satan, as the enemy of God, has appointed himself the enemy of every Christian as well, we must be watchful and wary. Peter and James both instruct us, in light of

Christ's return, to be spiritually alert and diligently persistent in the fight against sin. *"But the end of all things is at hand: be ye therefore sober, and watch unto prayer"* (1 Peter 4:7). *"Be ye also patient; stablish your hearts: for the coming of the Lord draweth nigh"* (James 5:8).

Separation from sin frees us to live set apart for God. Titus 2:11–13 tells us that the grace that brought us salvation also motivates us to live godly lives in view of Christ's return: *"For the grace of God that bringeth salvation hath appeared to all men, Teaching us that, denying ungodliness and worldly lusts, we should live soberly, righteously, and godly, in this present world; Looking for that blessed hope, and the glorious appearing of the great God and our Saviour Jesus Christ."*

While some use the grace of God as a license to indulge in sin and ungodly lifestyles, those who live with the awareness of Christ's return see the grace of God as the power to honor and glorify Him through godliness and purity. Romans 13:12 admonishes: *"The night is far spent, the day is at hand: let us therefore cast off the works of darkness, and let us put on the armour of light."* In other words, because Christ is coming soon, sanctify yourself from sin and engage in the spiritual battle on the side of Christ.

The very hope of Christ's return is a challenge to sanctification: *"Beloved, now are we the sons of God, and it doth not yet appear what we shall be: but we know that, when he shall appear, we shall be like him; for we shall see him as he is. And every man that hath this hope in him purifieth himself, even as he is pure"* (1 John 3:2–3).

I have been told that when a silversmith refines silver in a furnace, freeing it of its impurities and preparing it for use, he has a simple test to know when the refining process is complete—when he can see his reflection in the metal. Even so, the goal of the sanctification process for us is that Christ's image would be reflected in us.

One of the most clearly seen qualities of Christ in our lives should be His love. First Thessalonians 3:12–13 instructs us to grow in both purity and love: *"And the Lord make you to increase and abound in love one toward another, and toward all men, even as we do toward you: To the end he may stablish your hearts unblameable in holiness before God, even our Father, at the coming of our Lord Jesus Christ with all his saints."* Not only does God command us to abstain from sin, but He also instructs us to grow in love and godliness. This brings us back to the challenge to be steadfast in our witness. We free ourselves from sin that we might more effectively share Christ's love with others.

Although times are changing, we know through Scripture where these changes will lead—the ultimate victory of Christ. For those of us who know Christ as Saviour, Christ's return is both a glorious hope and a stirring challenge. Our knowledge of Bible prophecy should compel us to steadfastness and sanctification. It should motivate us to witness, live, and serve as if Christ may come today.

After studying Bible prophecy, there are several potential responses. You could become *alarmed* and begin seeing a new conspiracy behind every election and every news story. You could become *distracted* by venturing into pointless speculation. You should become *focused* in living out God's plan in steadfast, sanctified obedience until He comes!

C O N C L U S I O N _____

I n the very beginning of Revelation, before disclosing the details surrounding the events we have studied in this book, God delivers a unique promise: *"Blessed is he that readeth, and they that hear the words of this prophecy, and keep those things which are written therein: for the time is at hand"* (Revelation 1:3). At the end of Revelation, God repeats this promise, emphasizing the last portion of it: *"Behold, I come quickly: blessed is he that keepeth the sayings of the prophecy of this book"* (Revelation 22:7).

As we've seen in our study, God has a sovereign plan for the ages, and He has revealed much of this plan through Bible prophecy. He encourages us to study prophetic truth, but more than just hearing or reading about the end times, God desires that we would *keep* the truth. He wants it to transform our lives today.

Many have studied prophecy for the sake of knowledge alone, but few live with its eternal truths in mind. Understanding the past and knowing the future is profitable, but we each have to live today. My challenge to you: before you put down this book, purpose to live with the end in view.

History yet to happen—it's a fascinating study. It truly makes me deeply grateful that I am a child of God—that I have chosen to be a follower of the living God. I pray these pages have had the same impact upon you.

Knowing these truths gives confidence and hope in uncertainty. Studying them enriches our lives. But we must remember, there is still a great work to do today. God has given us our marching orders.

Be sure, He is sovereign in the shifting sands of time. The hourglass is emptying, and time is running out. Let us be about our Father's business. He has placed us in this moment for such a time as this. Determine that you will live courageously and biblically until He comes. Live as the Apostle Paul who said in Romans 1:16, *"I am not ashamed…."*

Christ has commanded us, *"Go ye into all the world, and preach the gospel to every creature"* (Mark 16:15). Like a servant hurrying to finish the task before his master's return, may we fully give ourselves to the assignment with which Christ has left us. When He returns in glory, may we joyfully enter His presence and hear the words, *"Well done, thou good and faithful servant"* (Matthew 25:21), thankful that we lived with the end in view.

NOTES

CHAPTER ONE

1. Cathy Lynn Grossman, "Pope calls for 'God-centered' global economy," *USA Today*, July 7, 2009, Faith and Reason section, http://www.usatoday.com/news/religion/2009-07-07-pope-encyclical_N.htm.

2. FOX News, "Ahmadinejad: Israels's Destruction Getting Close," FOX News, June 3, 2001, World section, http://www.foxnews.com/story/0,2933,277448,00.html.

3. Dr. David Jeremiah, *What in the World Is Going On?* (Nashville, Tennessee: Thomas Nelson, 2008), 174.

4. Aaron Klein, *The Late Great State of Israel* (Los Angeles, California: WorldNetDaily, 2009), 71.

5. Jamal Halaby, "Jordan King: Israel must accept Palestinian state,"
    Associated Press, May 14, 2009, Business section, http://www.
    haaretz.com/news/jordan-king-to-netanyahu-israel-must-accept-
    palestinian-state-1.276020.

6. *IRNA*, "Full text of President Ahmadinejad's Speech," *Islamic
    Republic News Agency*, September 17, 2005, http://www.globalsecurity.
    org/wmd/library/news/iran/2005/iran-050918-irnao2.htm.

7. CQ Transcripts Wire, "President Ahmadinejad Delivers Remarks at
    Columbia University," *Washington Post*, September 24, 2007, http://
    www.washingtonpost.com/wp-dyn/content/article/2007/09/24/
    AR2007092401042.html.

8. Lehman Strauss, *The Book of Revelation* (Loizeaux Brothers:
    Neptune, NJ 1964), 17.

9. Tim LaHaye and Ed Hindson, *The Popular Bible Prophecy Workbook*
    (Eugene, Oregon: Harvest House Publishers, 2006), 19–20.

10. Ibid., 18.

11. Ibid., 10–11.

12. Ibid., 12.

13. Ibid., 12–13.

CHAPTER TWO

1. Tim LaHaye and Ed Hindson, *The Popular Bible Prophecy Workbook*
    (Eugene, Oregon: Harvest House Publishers, 2006), 52.

2. Warren Wiersbe, *Wiersbe's Expository Outlines: Old Testament* (Victor
    Books/SP Publications, Inc., 1993), 557–58.

3. Dwight Garner, "What Obama Is Reading," *New York Times*, May 21,
    2008, http://papercuts.blogs.nytimes.com/2008/05/21/what-obama-
    is-reading.

4. FOX News, "Biden Says Brussels Could Be 'Capital of the Free World,'" FOX News, May 25, 2010, http://www.foxnews.com/politics/2010/05/25/biden-says-brussels-capital-free-world.

5. David L. Larsen, *Telling the Old, Old Story: The Art of Narrative Preaching* (Grand Rapids, Michigan: Kregel, 1995), 214.

6. William R. Clark, *Petrodollar Warfare: Oil, Iraq and the future of the Dollar* (Gabrioila Island, British Columbia, 2005), 198.

7. *Jerusalem Post*, "EU will soon agree on offer to Syria for closer ties," *Jerusalem Post*, September 4, 2009, http://wwwtmporigin.jpost.com/servlet/Satellite?cid=1251804493320&pagename=JPost%2FJPArticle%2FshowFull.

8. Michael Logan, "Gorbachev calls on EU & Russia to unite as a US counterbalance," *Budapest Times*, December 3, 2007, http://www.budapesttimes.hu/content/view/2813/26.

9. Michael Scherer/Strasbourg, "Barack Obama's New World Order," *TIME Magazine*, April 3, 2009, http://www.time.com/time/world/article/0,8599,1889512,00.html.

10. David Barboza, "China Urges New Money Reserve to Replace Dollar," *New York Times*, March 23, 2009, http://www.nytimes.com/2009/03/24/world/asia/24china.html.

11. Ambrose Evans-Pritchard, "US Backing for World Currency Stuns Markets," *London Telegraph*, March 25, 2009, http://www.telegraph.co.uk/finance/economics/5050407/US-backing-for-world-currency-stuns-markets.html.

12. John F. Walvoord, *Daniel: The Key to Prophetic Revelation* (Chicago: Moody Press, 1971), 72–3.

CHAPTER THREE

1. Aaron Klein, *The Late Great State of Israel* (Los Angeles, California: WorldNetDaily, 2009), 61.

2. Nina Burleigh/Efrat, "Two Views of the Land," *TIME Magazine*, July 27, 2009, http://www.time.com/time/magazine/article/0,9171,1910975,00.html.

3. Ethan Bronner, "As Biden Visits, Israel Unveils Plan for New Settlements," *New York Times*, March 9, 2010, http://www.nytimes.com/2010/03/10/world/middleeast/10biden.html.

4. *Jerusalem Post*, "Rivlin: J'lem will not be built by destroying Hebron," *Jerusalem Post*, September 7, 2009, http://www.jpost.com/servlet/Satellite?cid=1251804512380&pagename=Jpost%2FJPArticle%2FShowFull.

5. Jamal Halaby, "Jordan King: Israel Must Accept Palestinian State," *Associated Press*, May 14, 2009, http://www.haaretz.com/news/jordan-king-to-netanyahu-israel-must-accept-palestinian-state-1.276020.

6. Dan Ephron and Michael Hirsh, "The Peace Maker: Rahm Emanuel's Mideast Mission," *Newsweek*, May 23, 2009, http://www.newsweek.com/id/199146.

7. CBS News, "Time Running Out for a Two-State Solution," *60 Minutes*, January 25, 2009, http://www.cbsnews.com/stories/2009/01/23/60minutes/main4749723.shtml.

8. Jewish Virtual Library, "The Balfour Declaration," Jewish Virtual Library, November 2, 1917, http://www.jewishvirtuallibrary.org/jsource/History/balfour.html.

9. Dr. Motti Friedman, "The Department for Jewish Zionist Education," The Pedagogic Center, (Jewish Agency for Israel: 1997).

10. Clark Clifford, *Counsel to the President: A Memoir* (Pennsylvania: Anchor Books, 1992).

11. Arthur W. Kac, *The Rebirth of the State of Israel: Is It of God or of Men?* (Kessinger Publishing, LLC, 2009), 43.

12. Tim LaHaye, *Revelation: Illustrated and Made Plain* (Zondervan, 1975), 95.

CHAPTER FOUR

1. Alfred Tennyson, *In Memoriam A.H.H.* (California: Bankside Press, 1900), 137.

2. Kevin Phillips, *American Theocracy: The Peril and Politics of Radical Religion, Oil, and Borrowed Money in the 21st Century* (Penguin Books, 2007), VII.

3. Joel C. Rosenberg, *Epicenter: Why the Current Rumblings in the Middle East Will Change Your Future* (Tyndale House Publishers, Inc., 2008), 655–57.

4. Dr. George Sweeting, "Today in the Word," *Moody Bible Institute*, December 1989, 40.

CHAPTER FIVE

1. Joel C. Rosenberg, *Epicenter: Why the Current Rumblings in the Middle East Will Change Your Future* (Tyndale House Publishers, Inc., 2008), 79.

2. In this book, and particularly in this chapter, where I point out the danger to Israel and other nations through Islamic terrorism, I recognize an important distinction between the religion of Islam (which denies the deity of Jesus Christ and many doctrines of the Christian faith) and a Muslim person (who needs to hear the Gospel of Jesus Christ). Jesus loves and died for all people, and

He teaches us to love all people. I rejoice in reports of Muslims trusting Christ here in the United States and in Islamic countries around the world. I look forward to the day when I stand with people out of every "kindred, and tongue, and people, and nation" and together we sing praises to Christ who redeemed us all by His blood (Revelation 5:9).

3. Dr. Don Richardson, *Secrets of the Koran* (Regal Books, 2003), 69.

4. Dr. David Jeremiah, *What in the World Is Going On?* (Nashville, Tennessee: Thomas Nelson, 2008), 81.

5. Aaron Klein, *The Late Great State of Israel* (Los Angeles, California:WorldNetDaily, 2009), 126.

6. *Associated Press*, "UN Iran," *Associated Press*, September 23, 2009, http://www.aparchive.com/OneUp.aspx?st=k&showact=results&sort=relevance&xslt=1&sh=1180&kwstyle=and&adte=1272751175&dah=20.

7. Meet the Press, "Transcript for April 2," NBC News, April 2, 2006, http://www.msnbc.msn.com/id/12067487/ns/meet_the_press.

8. Edmund Morris, *Dutch: A Memoir of Ronald Reagan* (Modern Library, 2000), 835.

9. Judson Berger and Greg Palkot, "Iran Nuclear Site Could Pose Test to U.S., Israel Ties," FOX News, http://www.foxnews.com/politics/2009/09/25/iran-site-disclosure-pose-test-israel-ties.

10. *Webster's 1828 Dictionary of the English Language*, 3rd ed., s.v. "week."

11. John F. Walvoord, *The Nations in Prophecy* (Zondervan, 1972), 107.

12. *Imperial Dictionary*, 1st ed., s.v. "Togarmah."

13. Klein, 157.

14. FOX News, "Putin: Russia Will Not Support Force, Sanctions on Iran," FOX News, September 11, 2009, http://www.foxnews.com/world/2009/09/11/putin-russia-support-force-sanctions-iran/?test=latestnews.

15. Rosenberg, 13.

16. Joseph Federman, "Netanyahu Mystery Trip Sets off Flap in Israel," *Associated Press*, September 10, 2009, http://abcnews.go.com/International/wireStory?id=8541152.

17. Nazila Fathi, "Iran's President Says 'Israel Must Be Wiped Off the Map,'" *New York Times*, October 26, 2005, http://www.nytimes.com/2005/10/26/international/middleeast/26cnd-iran.

18. Klein, 166.

19. Ibid., 149.

20. Jeremiah, 169.

21. Ibid., 166.

22. *Associated Press*, "Gadhafi Calls U.N. Security Council a 'Terror Council,'" *Associated Press*, September 23, 2009, http://www.chicagotribune.com/topic/ktla-gadhafi,0,7604184.story.

23. Jeremiah, 172.

24. M. Fattah Hassan, "Putin Visits Qatar for Talks on Natural Gas and Trade," *New York Times*, February 13, 2007, http://www.nytimes.com/2007/02/13/world/middleeast/13putin.html.

25. Klein, 178.

26. Rosenberg, 243–44.

27. *Haaretz Newspaper*, "Israeli company discovers oil at drilling site near the Dead Sea," *Haaretz Newspaper*, May 10, 2006, http://www.haaretz.com/hasen/spages/770888.html.

28. Jad Mouawad, "Oil Industry Sets a Brisk Pace of New Discoveries," *New York Times*, September 24, 2009, http://www.nytimes.com/2009/09/24/business/energy-environment/24oil.html.

29. *Jerusalem Post*, "EU warns Netanyahu on hawkish government," *Jerusalem Post*, March 16, 2009, http://www.jpost.com/Home/Article.aspx?id=136061.

30. Dan Ephron and Michael Hirsh, "The Peace Maker: Rahm Emanuel's Mideast Mission," *Newsweek*, May 23, 2009, http://www.newsweek.com/id/199146.

31. Hillel Fendel, "Signs of Obama-Clinton Pressure on Israel," *Arutz Sheva: Israel National News*, March 9, 2010, http://www.israelnationalnews.com/SendMail.aspx?print=print&type=0&item=130429.

32. FOX News, "Obama and Netanyahu Hold Closed-Door Talks," FOX News, March 24, 2010, http://www.foxnews.com/politics/2010/03/23/netanyahu-faces-warmer-treatment-house-lawmakers.

33. Matthew Lee, "Clinton Slams Israel's Settlement Plans: 'Deeply Negative Signal,'" *Huffington Post*, June 4, 2010, http://www.huffingtonpost.com/2010/03/12/clinton-delivers-strong-m_n_497052.html.

34. FOX News, "Obama: U.S. Does Not Recognize 'Legitimacy of Continued Israeli Settlements,'" FOX News, September 23, 2009, http://www.foxnews.com/politics/2009/09/23/obama-world-dont-expectamerica-fix.

35. *Times*, "Binyamin Netanyahu humiliated after Barack Obama 'dumped him for dinner,'" *Times*, March 26, 2010, http://www.timesonline.co.uk/tol/news/world/us_and_americas/article7076431.ece.

36. FOX News, "Koch Outraged By Obama's Treatment of Israel Over Housing Construction," FOX News, April 1, 2010, http://www.foxnews.com/politics/2010/04/01/koch-outraged-obamas-treatment-israel-housing-construction.

37. Brian Hutchinson, "United Church puts anti-Israel resolutions on hold," *National Post*, August 14, 2009, http://network.nationalpost.

com/np/blogs/holy-post/archive/2009/08/14/united-church-puts-anti-israel-resolutions-on-hold.aspx.

CHAPTER SIX

1. Kenneth L. Woodward, "The Way the World Ends," *Newsweek*, November 1, 1999, http://www.newsweek.com/id/90049.
2. Cathy Lynn Grossman, "Pope calls for 'God-centered' global economy," *USA Today*, July 7, 2009, http://www.usatoday.com/news/religion/2009-07-07-pope-encyclical_N.htm.
3. Ben Feller, "G-20 Taking on Permanent Coordinating Role," *Associated Press*, September 24, 2009, http://abcnews.go.com/Politics/wireStory?id=8668262.
4. American Humanist Association, *Humanist Manifesto II*, (The American Humanist Association: 1973).
5. Tim LaHaye and Ed Hindson, *The Popular Bible Prophecy Workbook* (Eugene, Oregon: Harvest House Publishers, 2006), 52.
6. Henry Morris, *The Revelation Record: A Scientific and Devotional Commentary on the Prophetic Book of the End of Times* (Tyndale House Publishers, Inc., 1983), 234.
7. From the context of Daniel 9, we know this treaty is specific to Israel. Verse 24 makes it clear that the entire seventy-week prophecy was a prediction of the future for the Jewish people.
8. Shawn Pogatchni, "EU Treaty Back on Track After Decisive Irish Vote," *Associated Press*, October 5, 2009, http://www.cnsnews.com/news/article/54993.
9. Dr. David Jeremiah, *Escape the Coming Night* (Nashville, Tennessee: Thomas Nelson Incorporated, 1990), 177.

10. Yehudah Lev Kay, "Temple Institute to Build Sacrificial Altar onTisha B'av," *Arutz Sheva: Israel National News*, July 29, 2009, http://www.israelnationalnews.com/News/News.aspx/132630.

11. Aaron Klein, *The Late Great State of Israel* (Los Angeles, California: WorldNetDaily, 2009), 77.

12. Klein, 85.

13. U.S. Department of Homeland Security, "Rightwing Extremism: Current Economic and Political Climate Fueling Resurgance in Radicalization and Recruitment," April 7, 2009, 6–7.

14. Joseph Abrams, "Obama's Science Czar Considered Forced Abortions, Sterilization as Population Growth Solutions," FOX News, July 21, 2009, http://www.foxnews.com/politics/2009/07/21/obamas-science-czar-considered-forced-abortions-sterilization-population-growth/.

CHAPTER SEVEN

1. Lehman Strauss, *The Book of Revelation* (Neptune, New Jersey: Loizeaux Brothers, 1977), 291.

2. John Phillips, *Exploring Revelation* (Chicago: Moody Press, 1987), 202.

3. Donald Barnhouse, *Revelation: An Expository Commentary* (Grand Rapids, Michigan: Zondervan, 1971), 324.

4. The word integration is often used to refer to bringing cultures or races together. In this sense, the true church should be integrated—every person should be welcome in the church. In this chapter, however, integration refers to bringing all faiths together. This cannot be done without compromising Bible truth.

5. Dr. H.A. Ironside, *Lectures on the Book of Revelation* (Neptune, New Jersey: Loizeaux Brothers, 1976), 287–88.

6.   A masterpiece on the subject of Babylonian influence in world religion is *The Two Babylons*, a book written in 1858 by Alexander Hyslop (available at amazon.com).

7.   Cathy Lynn Grossman, "Franklin Graham wants Obama to step in on Prayer Day slight," *USA Today*, May 4, 2010, Faith and Reason section, http://www.usatoday.com/news/religion/2010-05-05-graham05_ST_N.htm.

8.   David A. Patten, "Franklin Graham: Obama 'Giving Islam a Pass,' Warns of Persecution," *News Max*, May 3, 2010, http://www.newsmax.com/Headline/franklin-graham-islam-obama/2010/05/03/id/357711.

9.   Oprah Winfrey, Oprah Show, From YouTube, Oprah Winfrey Believes Many Paths to Heaven, http://www.youtube.com/watch?v=F-HNNAqJrxw.

10. Dalai Lama, *Toward a True Kinship of Faiths* (The Doubleday Religious Publishing Group, 2010), 157.

11. *UPI*, "Study: World Muslim Population in 1.57B," *United Press International*, October 8, 2009, http://www.upi.com/Top_News/2009/10/08/Study-World-Muslim-population-is-157B/UPI-43531254982349.

12. Pope Paul VI, "Lumen Gentium," *Vatican II*, November 21, 1964.

13. Tom Heneghan, "Catholics, Muslims Open Landmark Talks at Vatican," November 4, 2008, http://www.reuters.com/article/topNews/idUSTRE49T54420081104.

14. Dr. Albert Mohler, "R-E-S-P-E-C-T: Should Christians 'Respect' Other Religions?" May 14, 2009, http://www.albertmohler.com/2009/05/14/r-e-s-p-e-c-t-should-christians-respect-other-religions/.

15. *Associated Press*, "Hawaii Lawmakers Pass Bill to Create 'Islam Day,'" *Associated Press*, May 6, 2009, http://www.foxnews.com/politics/2009/05/06/hawaii-lawmakers-pass-create-islam-day.

16. If you have made the decision to trust Christ as your personal Saviour, or if you would like more information about that decision, please contact us at 800.688.6329, or visit lancasterbaptist.org.

CHAPTER EIGHT

1. J. Dwight Pentecost, *Prophecy for Today: God's Purpose and Plan for Our Future* (Discovery House Publishers, 1989), 36.

2. Scripture does not always refer to this time period as "the Tribulation," nor does every instance of the word *tribulation* in Scripture refer to this specific event. Dwight Pentecost explained it this way: "We must remember that the word tribulation is used in the Bible in both a technical and a non-technical sense. When used non-technically, it speaks of any trial or suffering through which an individual may go. When used in its technical sense, it refers to the seven-year period following the translation of the church, a time of unprecedented judgment and wrath from God upon the earth."

3. Authors LaHaye and Hindson note that other references to the Tribulation include "the day of the Lord" (1 Thessalonians 5:2), the seventieth week of Daniel (Daniel 9:27), "a day of...desolation" (Zephaniah 1:15), "the wrath to come" (1 Thessalonians 1:10), "the hour of his judgment" (Revelation 14:7), and "the great tribulation" (Matthew 24:21). From *The Popular Bible Prophecy Workbook* (Eugene, Oregon: Harvest House Publishers, 2006), 69.

4. Tim LaHaye and Jerry Jenkins, *Are We Living in the End Times?* (Tyndale House Publishers, Inc., 1999), 149.

5. Tim LaHaye and Ed Hindson, *The Popular Bible Prophecy Workbook* (Eugene, Oregon: Harvest House Publishers, 2006), 73.

6. Charles C. Ryrie, *Revelation: Everyman's Bible Commentary* (Moody Press, 1968).

7. *ScienceDaily*, "San Andreas Affected by 2004 Sumatran Quake; Largest Quakes Can Weaken Fault Zones Worldwide," *ScienceDaily*, September 30, 2009, http://www.sciencedaily.com/releases/2009/09/090930132700.htm.

8. Vladimir Isachenkov, "Russia May Send Spacecraft to Deflect Incoming Asteroid" *Associated Press*, December 30, 2009, http://news.discovery.com/space/incoming-asteroid-spacecraft-russia.html.

9. LaHaye and Jenkins, 156.

10. Ibid., 155–56.

CHAPTER NINE

1. Tim LaHaye and Ed Hindson, *The Popular Bible Prophecy Workbook* (Eugene, Oregon: Harvest House Publishers, 2006), 82–3.

2. Lehman Strauss, *The Book of the Revelation* (Loizeaux Brothers, 1970), 324.

3. Douglas Brinkley, ed., *The Reagan Diaries* (New York: HarperCollins, 2007), 19.

4. Dr. David Jeremiah, *What in the World Is Going On?* (Nashville, Tennessee: Thomas Nelson, 2008), 197–98.

5. Tim LaHaye, *Revelation: Illustrated and Made Plain* (Zondervan, 1975), 271.

6. *US News and World Report*, March 25, 1991.

7. John Walvoord, *The Revelation of Jesus Christ* (Moody Publishers, 1989), 280–81.

8. Ibid., 281.

CHAPTER TEN

1. A.M. Hunter, "Sermon Illustrations," http://www.sermonillustrations.com/a-z/h/heaven.htm.

2. Lehman Strauss, *The Book of Revelation* (Neptune, New Jersey: Loizeaux Brothers, 1977), 334.

3. John Phillips, *Exploring Revelation* (Kregel Academic & Professional, 2001), 242.

4. Strauss, 340.

BIBLIOGRAPHY _____

Abrams, Joseph. "Obama's Science Czar Considered Forced Abortions, Sterilization as Population Growth Solutions." FOX News, July 21, 2009, http://www.foxnews.com/politics/2009/07/21/obamassience-czar-considered-forced-abortions-sterilization-populationgrowth (accessed October 2009).

AFP. "Russia scraps Libya's debts as Putin visits Tripoli." *Agence Frace-Presse,* April 2008, http://findarticles.com/p/articles/mi_kmafp/is_200804/ai_n25344293 (accessed September 2009).

AFP. "UN boss alarmed by Hezbollah's threat against Israel." *Agence France-Presse,* March 3, 2008, http://findarticles.com/p/articls/mi_kmafp/is_200803/ai_n24365391 (accessed September 2009).

American Humanist Association. *Humanist Manifesto II.* AmericanHumanist.org, 1973.

Associated Press. "Gadhafi Calls U.N. Security Council a 'Terror Council.'" *Associated Press,* September 23, 2009, http://www.chicagotribune. com/topic/ktla-gadhafi,0,7604184.story (accessed May 2010).

Associated Press. "Hawaii Lawmakers Pass Bill to Create 'Islam Day.'" FOX News, May 6, 2009, http://www.foxnews.com/politics/2009/05/06/ hawaii-lawmakers-pass-create-islam-day (accessed October 2009).

Associated Press. "UN Iran." *Associated Press,* September 23, 2009, http:// www.aparchive.com/OneUp.aspx?st=k&showact=results&sort=re levance&xslt=1&sh=1180&kwstyle=and&adte=1272751175&dah=20 (accessed September 2009).

Barboza, David. "China Urges New Money Reserve to Replace Dollar." *New York Times,* March 23, 2009, http://www.nytimes.com/2009/03/24/ world/asia/24china.html (accessed September 2009).

Barnhouse, Donald. *Revelation: An Expository Commentary.* Grand Rapids: Zondervan, 1971.

Berger, Judson and Greg Palkot. "Iran Nuclear Site Could Pose Test to U.S., Israel Ties." FOX News, September 25, 2009, http://www.foxnews. com/politics/2009/09/25/iran-site-disclosure-pose-test-israel-ties (accessed September 2009).

Biederwolf, William. *The Second Coming Bible Commentary.* Baker Book House, 1985.

Brinkley, Douglas, ed., *The Reagan Diaries.* New York: HarperCollins, 2007.

Brisco, Thomas C. *Holman Bible Atlas.* Nashville, Tennessee: Broadman & Holman Publishers, 1998.

Bronner, Ethan. "As Biden Visits, Israel Unveils Plan for New Settlements." *New York Times,* March 9, 2010, http://www.nytimes.com/2010/03/10/ world/middleeast/10biden.html (accessed March, 2010).

Burleigh/Efrat, Nina. "Two Views of the Land." *Time Magazine,* July 27, 2009, http://www.time.com/time/magazine/article/0,9171,1910975,00. html (accessed September 2009).

CBS News. "Time Running Out for a Two-State Solution." *60 Minutes,* January 25, 2009, http://www.cbsnews.com/

stories/2009/01/23/60minutes/main4749723.shtml (accessed
September 2009).

Clark, William R. *Petrodollar Warfare: Oil, Iraq, and the Future of the Dollar.* New Society Publishers, 2005.

Clifford, Clark. *Counsel to the President: A Memoir.* Pennsylvania: Anchor Books, 1992.

CQ Transcripts Wire. "President Ahmadinejad Delivers Remarks at Columbia University." *Washington Post,* September 24, 2007, http://www.washingtonpost.com/wp-dyn/content/article/2007/09/24/AR2007092401042.html (accessed September 2009).

Dalai Lama. *Toward a True Kinship of Faiths.* The Doubleday Religious Publishing Group, 2010.

Ephron, Dan and Michael Hirsh. "The Peace Maker: Rahm Emanuel's Mideast Mission." *Newsweek,* May 23, 2009, http://www.newsweek.com/id/199146 (accessed September 2009).

Evans-Pritchard, Ambrose. "US Backing for World Currency Stuns Markets." *London Telegraph,* March 25, 2009, http://www.telegraph.co.uk/finance/economics/5050407/US-backing-for-world-currency-stuns-markets.html (accessed September 2009).

Fathi, Nazila. "Iran's President Says 'Israel Must Be Wiped Off the Map.'" *New York Times,* October 26, 2005, http://www.nytimes.com/2005/10/26/international/middleeast/26cnd-iran (accessed September 2009).

Federman, Joseph. "Netanyahu Mystery Trip Sets off Flap in Israel." *Associated Press,* September 10, 2009, http://abcnews.go.com/International/wireStory?id=8541152 (accessed September 2009).

Feinberg, Charles L. *Millennialism: The Two Major Views* Winona Lake, Indiana: BMH Books, 1985.

Feller, Ben. "G-20 Taking on Permanent Coordinating Role." *Associated Press,* September 24, 2009, http://abcnews.go.com/Politics/wireStory?id=8668262 (accessed September 2009).

Fendel, Hillel. "Signs of Obama-Clinton Pressure on Israel." *Arutz Sheva: Israel National News*, March 9, 2010, http://www.israelnationalnews.com/SendMail.aspx?print=print&type=0&item=130429 (accessed June 2010).

FOX News. "Ahmadinejad: Israels's Destruction Getting Close." FOX News, June 3, 2001, http://www.foxnews.com/story/0,2933,277448,00.html (accessed August 2009).

FOX News. "Biden Says Brussels Could Be 'Capital of the Free World,'" FOX News, May 25, 2010, http://www.foxnews.com/politics/2010/05/25/biden-says-brussels-capital-free-world (accessed May 2010).

FOX News. "Koch Outraged By Obama's Treatment of Israel Over Housing Construction." FOX News, April 1, 2010, http://www.foxnews.com/politics/2010/04/01/koch-outraged-obamas-treatment-israel-housing-construction (accessed September 2009).

FOX News. "Obama: U.S. Does Not Recognize 'Legitimacy of Continued Israel Settlements.'" FOX News, September 23, 2009, http://www.foxnews.com/politics/2009/09/23/obama-world-dont-expectamerica-fix (accessed September 2009).

FOX News. "Obama and Netanyahu Hold Closed-Door Talks." FOX News, March 24,2010, http://www.foxnews.com/politics/2010/03/23/netanyahu-faces-warmer-treatment-house-lawmakers (accessed June 2010).

FOX News. "Putin: Russia Will Not Support Force, Sanctions on Iran." FOX News, September 11, 2009, http://www.foxnews.com/world/2009/09/11/putin-russia-support-force-sanctions-iran/?test=latestnews (accessed September 2009).

Friedman, Dr. Motti. "The Department for Jewish Zionist Education." The Pedagogic Center. Jewish Agency for Israel: 1997.

Garner, Dwight. "What Obama is Reading." *New York Times*, May 21, 2008, http://papercuts.blogs.nytimes.com/2008/05/21/what-obama-is-reading (accessed September 2009).

Grossman, Cathy Lynn. "Franklin Graham wants Obama to step in on Prayer Day slight." *USA Today,* May 4, 2010, Faith and Reason section, http://www.usatoday.com/news/religion/2010-05-05-graham05_ST_N.htm (accessed May 2010).

Grossman, Cathy Lynn. "Pope calls for 'God-centered' global economy." *USA Today,* July 7, 2009, Faith and Reason section, http://www.usatoday.com/news/religion/2009-07-07-pope-encyclical_N.htm (accessed August 2009).

Haaretz Newspaper. "Israeli company discovers oil at drilling site near the Dead Sea." *Haaretz Newspaper,* May 10, 2006, http://www.haaretz.com/hasen/spages/770888.html (accessed September 2009).

Halaby, Jamal. "Jordan King: Israel must accept Palestinian state." *Associated Press,* May 14, 2009, http://www.haaretz.com/news/jordan-king-to-netanyahu-israel-must-accept-palestinian-state-1.276020 (accessed September 2009).

Hassan, M. Fattah. "Putin Visits Qatar for Talks on Natural Gas and Trade." *New York Times,* February 13, 2007, http://www.nytimes.com/2007/02/13/world/middleeast/13putin.html (accessed September 2009).

Heneghan, Tom. "Catholics, Muslims Open Landmark Talks at Vatican." Reuters.com, November 4, 2008, http://www.reuters.com/article/topNews/idUSTRE49T54420081104 (accessed October 2009).

Hunt, Dave. *A Woman Rides the Beast.* Eugene, Oregon: Harvest House Publishers, 1994.

Hunt, Dave. *How Close Are We?* Eugene, Oregon: Harvest House Publishers, 1993.

Hunt, Dave. *Whatever Happened to Heaven?* Eugene, Oregon: Harvest House Publishers, 1988.

Hunt, Dave and T.A. McMahon. *The Seduction of Christianity.* Eugene, Oregon: Harvest House Publishers, 1985.

Hunter, A.M. "Sermon Illustrations." http://www.sermonillustrations.com/a-z/h/heaven.htm (accessed October 2009).

IRNA. "Full text of President Ahmadinejad's Speech." *Islamic Republic News Agency*, September 17, 2005, http://www.globalsecurity.org/wmd/library/news/iran/2005/iran-050918-irna02.htm (accessed August 2009).

Ironside, Dr. H.A. *Lectures on the Book of Revelation.* Neptune, New Jersey: Loizeaux Brothers, 1976.

Isachenkov, Vladimir. "Russia May Send Spacecraft to Deflect Incoming Asteroid." *Associated Press*, December 30, 2009, http://news.discovery.com/space/incoming-asteroid-spacecraft-russia.html (accessed October 2009).

Jeremiah, Dr. David. *What in the World Is Going On?* Nashville, Tennessee: Thomas Nelson, 2008.

Jeremiah, Dr. David. *Escape the Coming Night.* Nashville, Tennessee: Thomas Nelson, 2001.

Jerusalem Post. "EU will soon agree on offer to Syria for closer ties." *Jerusalem Post*, September 4, 2009, http://wwwtmporigin.jpost.com/servlet/Satellite?cid=1251804493320&pagename=JPost%2FJPArticle%2FshowFull (accessed September 2009).

Jerusalem Post. "Rivlin: J'lem will not be built by destroying Hebron." *Jerusalem Post*, September 7, 2009, http://www.jpost.com/servlet/Satellite?cid=1251804512380&pagename=JPost%2FJPArticle%2FshowFull (accessed September 2009).

Jerusalem Post. "EU warns Netanyahu on hawkish government." *Jerusalem Post*, March 16, 2009, http://www.jpost.com/Home/Article.aspx?id=136061 (accessed September 2009).

Jewish Virtual Library. "The Balfour Declaration." Jewish Virtual Library, November 2, 1917, http://www.jewishvirtuallibrary.org/jsource/History/balfour.html (accessed September 2009).

Kac, Arthur W. *The Rebirth of the State of Israel: Is It of God or of Men?* Whitefish, Montana: Kessinger Publishing, LLC, 2009.

Kay, Yehudah Lev. "Temple Institute to Build Sacrificial Altar onTisha B'av." *Arutz Sheva: Israel National News*, July 29, 2009, http://

www.israelnationalnews.com/News/News.aspx/132630 (accessed September 2009).

Klein, Aaron. *The Late Great State of Israel*. Los Angeles, California: WorldNetDaily, 2009.

LaHaye, Tim. *Revelation: Illustrated and Made Plain*. Zondervan, 1975.

LaHaye, Tim and Ed Hindson. *The Popular Bible Prophecy Workbook*. Eugene, Oregon: Harvest House Publishers, 2006.

LaHaye, Tim and Ed Hindson. *The Popular Encyclopedia of Bible Prophecy*. Eugene, Oregon: Harvest House Publishers, 2004.

LaHaye, Tim and Jerry Jenkins. *Are We Living in the End Times?* Tyndale House Publishers, Inc., 1999.

LaHaye, Tim and Thomas Ice. *Charting the End Times*. Eugene, Oregon: Harvest House Publishers, 2001.

Larsen, David L. *Telling the Old, Old Story: The Art of Narrative Preaching*. Grand Rapids, Michigan: Kregel, 1995.

Larkin, Clarence. *The Greatest Book on "Dispensational Truth" in the World*. Philadelphia, Pennsylvania: Rev. Clarence Larkin Est., 1918.

Lee, Matthew. "Clinton Slams Israel's Settlement Plans: 'Deeply Negative Signal.'" *Huffington Post*, June 4, 2010, http://www.huffingtonpost. com/2010/03/12/clinton-delivers-strong-m_n_497052.html (accessed June 2010).

Logan, Michael. "Gorbachev calls on EU & Russia to unite as a US counterbalance." *Budapest Times*, December 3, 2007, http://www.budapesttimes.hu/content/view/2813/26 (accessed September 2009).

Meet the Press. "Transcript for April 2." NBC News, April 2, 2006, http:// www.msnbc.msn.com/id/12067487/ns/meet_the_press (accessed September 2009).

Mohler, Dr. Albert. "R-E-S-P-E-C-T: Should Christians 'Respect' Other Religions?" AlbertMohler.com, May 14, 2009, http://www. albertmohler.com/?cat=Blog&cid=3799 (accessed October 2009).

Morris, Edmund. *Dutch: A Memoir of Ronald Reagan.* Modern Library, 2000.

Morris, Henry. *The Revelation Record: A Scientific and Devotional Commentary on the Prophetic Book of the End of Times.* Tyndale House Publishers, Inc., 1983.

Mouawad, Jad. "Oil Industry Sets a Brisk Pace of New Discoveries." *New York Times,* September 24, 2009, http://www.nytimes. com/2009/09/24/business/energy-environment/24oil.html (accessed September 2009).

Nurwisah, Ron. "Israel question hangs over the air at United Church meeting."*National Post,* August 12, 2009, http://network. nationalpost.com/np/blogs/holy-post/archive/2009/08/12/ israelquestion-hangs-over-the-air-at-united-church-meeting.aspx (accessed September 2009).

Patten, David A. "Franklin Graham: Obama 'Giving Islam a Pass,' Warns of Persecution," *News Max,* May 3, 2010, http://www.newsmax. com/Headline/franklin-graham-islam-obama/2010/05/03/ id/357711 (accessed May 2010).

Pentecost, J. Dwight. *Prophecy for Today.* Discovery House Publishers, 1989.

Pentecost, J. Dwight. *Things to Come.* Grand Rapids, Michigan: Zondervan Publishing House, 1958.

Phillips, John. *Exploring Revelation.* Chicago: Moody Press, 1987.

Phillips, Kevin. *American Theocracy: The Peril and Politics of Radical Religion, Oil, and Borrowed Money in the 21st Century.* Penguin Books, 2007.

Pogatchni, Shawn. "EU Treaty Back on Track After Decisive Irish Vote." *Associated Press,* October 5, 2009, http://www.cnsnews.com/news/ article/54993 (accessed October 2009).

Pope Paul VI. "Lumen Gentium." *Vatican II.* November 21, 1964.

Rasmussen, Roland. *The Post-Trib, Pre-Wrath Rapture.* Canoga Park, California: The Post-Trib Research Center, 1996.

Richardson, Dr. Don. *Secrets of the Koran.* Regal Books, 2003.

Rosenberg, Joel C. *Epicenter: Why the Current Rumblings in the Middle East Will Change Your Future.* Tyndale House Publishers, Inc., 2008.

Ryrie, Charles C. *Revelation: Everyman's Bible Commentary.* Moody Press, 1968.

Scherer/Strasbourg, Michael. "Barack Obama's New World Order." *Time Magazine,* April 3, 2009, http://www.time.com/time/world/article/0,8599,1889512,00.html (accessed September 2009).

ScienceDaily. "San Andreas Affected By 2004 Sumatran Quake; Largest Quakes Can Weaken Fault Zones Worldwide." *ScienceDaily,* September 30, 2009, http://www.sciencedaily.com/releases/2009/09/090930132700.htm (accessed October 2009).

Strauss, Lehman. *The Book of Revelation.* Neptune, New Jersey: Loizeaux Brothers, 1964.

Strauss, Lehman. *The Prophecies of Daniel.* Winona Lake, Indiana: BMH Books, 1969.

Sweeting, Dr. George. "Today in the Word." *Moody Bible Institute,* December 1989.

Tennyson, Alfred. *In Memoriam A.H.H.* California: Bankside Press, 1900.

Times. "Binyamin Netanyahu humiliated after Barack Obama 'dumped him for dinner.'" *Times,* March 26, 2010, http://www.timesonline.co.uk/tol/news/world/us_and_americas/article7076431.ece (accessed September 2009).

U.S. Department of Homeland Security. "Rightwing Extremism: Current Economix and Political Climate Fueling Resurgance in Radicalization and Recruitment." April 7, 2009.

UPI. "Study: World Muslim Population in 1.57B." *United Press International,* October 8, 2009, http://www.upi.com/Top_News/2009/10/08/Study-World-Muslim-population-is-157B/UPI-43531254982349 (accessed October 2009).

Walvoord, John F. *The Blessed Hope and the Tribulation.* Grand Rapids, Michigan: The Zondervan Corporation, 1976.

Walvoord, John F. *Daniel: The Key to Prophetic Revelation.* Chicago: Moody Press, 1971.

Walvoord, John F. *Every Prophecy of the Bible.* Colorado Springs, Colorado: Chariot Victory Publishing, 1999 (Formerly called *The Prophecy Knowledge Handbook*).

Walvoord, John F. *Israel in Prophecy.* Grand Rapids, Michigan: Zondervan Publishing House, 1977.

Walvoord, John F. *The Nations in Prophecy.* Zondervan, 1972.

Walvoord, John. *The Revelation of Jesus Christ.* Moody Publishers, 1989.

Walvrood, John. *Armageddon Oil and the Middle East Crisis: What the Bible Says About the Future of the Middle East and the End of Western Civilization.* Zondervan; February 1991.

Wiersbe, Warren. *Wiersbe's Expository Outlines: Old Testament.* Victor Books/SP Publications, Inc., 1993.

Winfrey, Oprah. Oprah Show; 2 min., 35 sec. From YouTube, Oprah Winfrey Believes Many Paths to Heaven. http://www.youtube.com/watch?v=F-HNNAqJrxw (accessed February 2010).

Woodward, Kenneth L. "The Way the World Ends." *Newsweek,* November 1, 1999, http://www.newsweek.com/id/90049 (accessed October 2009).

Visit us online

strivingtogether.com

wcbc.edu

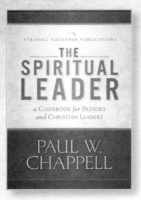
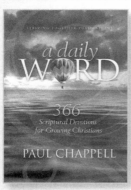
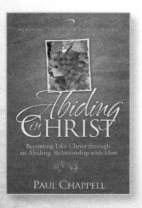

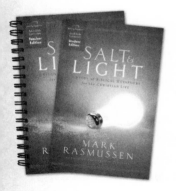